Passive smoking and children

A report by the Tobacco Advisory Group of the Royal College of Physicians

March 2010

Supported by the Royal College of Paediatrics and Child Health

With funding from

Acknowledgements

The members of the Tobacco Advisory Group acknowledge with thanks Nicholas Ridgman and Joanna Reid of the RCP Publications Department for the editing and production of this report.

This report was made possible by funding from Cancer Research UK, which enabled the systematic reviews, original analyses of primary care databases, and further analysis of data from the Health Survey for England to be carried out. Much of the content of the report was produced by staff and students at the UK Centre for Tobacco Control Studies (www.ukctcs.org), which is supported by core funding from the British Heart Foundation, Cancer Research UK, Economic and Social Research Council, Medical Research Council, and the Department of Health, under the auspices of the UK Clinical Research Collaboration. Health Survey for England data were available from a study funded by the Department of Health (England).

The Royal College of Physicians

The Royal College of Physicians is a registered charity that aims to ensure high quality care for patients by promoting the highest standards of medical practice. It provides and sets standards in clinical practice and education and training, conducts assessments and examinations, quality assures external audit programmes, supports doctors in their practice of medicine, and advises the Government, public and the profession on healthcare issues.

Citation for this report: Royal College of Physicians. *Passive smoking and children.* A report by the Tobacco Advisory Group. London: RCP, 2010.

ISBN 978-1-86016-375-3

Royal College of Physicians
11 St Andrews Place, London NW1 4LE

www.rcplondon.ac.uk

Registered Charity No 210508

Cover photograph: Image Source/SuperStock

Typeset by Danset Graphics, Telford, Shropshire
Printed in Great Britain by Cambrian Printers Ltd, Aberystwyth

Contents

Contributors

Deborah Arnott *Chief executive, Action on Smoking and Health, London*

Richard Ashcroft *Professor of bioethics, Queen Mary, University of London*

Fatima Bhayat *Research fellow, University of Nottingham*

John Britton *Professor of epidemiology; director, UK Centre for Tobacco Control Studies, University of Nottingham*

Hannah Burke *Foundation year doctor, Nottingham University Hospitals*

Yilu Chen *Lecturer in medical statistics, University of Nottingham*

Tim Coleman *Reader in primary care, University of Nottingham*

Derek Cook *Professor of epidemiology, St George's University of London*

Martin Dockrell *Director of research and policy, Action on Smoking and Health, London*

Richard Edwards *Professor of public health, University of Otago*

Anna Gilmore *Reader in public health, University of Bath; senior lecturer, London School of Hygiene and Tropical Medicine*

Christine Godfrey *Professor of health economics, University of York*

Ian Gray *Principal policy officer, Chartered Institute of Environmental Health, London*

Allan Hackshaw *Deputy director, Cancer Research UK and University College London Cancer Trials Centre*

Ahmed Hashim *Data analyst, University of Nottingham*

Amal Hassanien *Masters student, University of Nottingham*

Sally Haw *Senior scientific adviser, Scottish Collaboration for Public Health Research and Policy, Edinburgh*

Yue Huang *UK Centre for Tobacco Control Studies Data Analyst, University of Nottingham*

Richard Hubbard *British Lung Foundation professor of respiratory epidemiology, University of Nottingham*

Martin Jarvis *Professor emeritus of health psychology, University College London*

Mirriam Lisa Jere *Masters student, University of Nottingham*

Laura Jones *UK Centre for Tobacco Control Studies research fellow, University of Nottingham*

Shona Kelly *Lecturer in social epidemiology, University of Nottingham*

Jo Leonardi-Bee *Lecturer in medical statistics, University of Nottingham*

Tricia McKeever *Associate professor of medical statistics, University of Nottingham*

Ann McNeill *Professor of health policy and promotion; deputy director, UK Centre for Tobacco Control Studies, University of Nottingham*

Steve Parrott *Research fellow, Department of Health Sciences, University of York*

Michelle Sims *Research officer, University of Bath*

Lisa Szatkowski *UK Centre for Tobacco Control Studies postgraduate research student, University of Nottingham*

Laila Tata *Lecturer in epidemiology, University of Nottingham*

Andrea Venn *Associate professor of epidemiology, University of Nottingham*

Foreword

I welcome this report from the Royal College of Physicians.

The report quantifies the effects of second-hand smoke on children's health, and the related costs, and identifies ways in which smoke-free legislation could be improved to afford greater protection to children. Most importantly, it calls for a radical rethink of the acceptability of smoking anywhere in the presence of children.

One of the biggest impacts of smoking around children is that adult smokers can be seen as role models, increasing the likelihood that the child will, in due course, also become a regular smoker. Preventing this means that adults take responsibility to stop smoking in front of their children at home, or in places where children may see them smoke.

Success will demand far more radical approaches to tobacco prevention, particularly in terms of price, mass media campaigns, and the consideration of generic packaging, and wider smoke-free public policy covering cars, entrances to public buildings, parks, and other outdoor places frequented by children.

Protecting children is a health priority. Adult smoking behaviour must radically change to achieve that. This report identifies the reasons why, and what should be done to achieve it.

The Government continues to implement strong measures and policies to protect children from second-hand smoke, as featured in the new tobacco control strategy for England, *A smokefree future,** published earlier this year.

In my 2002 annual report,† I highlighted children's special vulnerability to second-hand smoke, owing to their smaller lungs and underdeveloped immune systems, making them more susceptible to respiratory and ear infections triggered by passive smoking. It was in this report that I first called for a smoking ban in all enclosed public places, which became law in 2007, and we must ensure we keep up the momentum, especially where children are exposed, to continue to reduce the harm of tobacco use in our communities, and create a truly smoke-free future.

March 2010

Sir Liam Donaldson
Chief Medical Officer

---

*Department of Health. *A smokefree future: a comprehensive tobacco control strategy for England.* London: DH, 2010.

†Department of Health. *Annual report of the Chief Medical Officer 2002.* London: DH, 2003.

Members of the Tobacco Advisory Group of the Royal College of Physicians

John Britton (Chair)

Deborah Arnott

Richard Ashcroft

Paul Belcher

Tim Coleman

Linda Cuthbertson

Anna Gilmore

Christine Godfrey

Allan Hackshaw

Zoe Horwich

Martin Jarvis

Jean King

Ann McNeill

Jennifer Percival

Huw Thomas

Mike Ward

Preface

In 2003, over 11,000 people in the UK are estimated to have died as a result of passive smoking.* Although regarded for many years as little more than a nuisance, exposure to ambient tobacco smoke released directly by burning tobacco and indirectly by exhalation of smoke by smokers (also variously referred to as environmental tobacco smoke, second-hand smoke, or tobacco smoke pollution) is now a recognised cause of significant short- and long-term harm to others. Many of those adverse health effects were summarised, particularly in relation to adult exposure, in an earlier Royal College of Physicians report.†

Increasing awareness of these health risks has led the UK and several other countries to introduce legislation restricting or prohibiting smoking in enclosed public places. This legislation has typically been justified by the legal and moral obligation to ensure safe working environments and, in the UK, to prevent the 600 or so deaths previously estimated to be caused each year by passive smoking at work.* However, these are the minority of deaths caused by passive smoking, the bulk of which (an estimated 10,700 deaths in adults in 2003)* arise from exposure to tobacco smoke in the home.

Passive smoking in the home is also a major hazard to the health of the millions of children in the UK who live with smokers, and the extent of this health problem has not, to date, been accurately quantified. In this report, we therefore use established literature and additional analysis to estimate the prevalence, determinants and trends in passive smoking exposure, present new systematic reviews and meta-analyses of the magnitude of the effects of passive smoking on the main recognised health consequences in children, and estimate the numbers of cases of illness and death arising from these effects. We also quantify the effect of exposure to smoking behaviour on the risk of children starting to smoke, and estimate the number of children who do take up smoking as a consequence. We then consider the financial cost of the disease burden for the NHS and wider society arising from all of these exposures. The report also explores ethical issues relating to passive smoking and children, and public opinion on measures to prevent passive smoking, concluding with policy options

---

*Jamrozik K. Estimate of deaths attributable to passive smoking among UK adults: database analysis. *BMJ* 2005;330:812–17.

†Royal College of Physicians. *Going smoke-free: the medical case for clean air in the home, at work and in public places.* A report by the Tobacco Advisory Group. London: RCP, 2005.

that would reduce exposure of children to this significant health hazard and negative behavioural model.

Governments, and societies, have a duty to ensure that children grow up in a safe environment, and are protected from explicit or implicit encouragement to take up hazardous behaviours such as smoking. This report provides some of the background and policy measures necessary to ensure that that duty is discharged.

I am personally very grateful to John Britton and the other members of the RCP's Tobacco Advisory Group, and the many contributors to this report who have continued the excellent tradition of the RCP in this important area.

March 2010

Professor Ian Gilmore
President, Royal College of Physicians

1 Smoke-free legislation in the UK

1.1 Background

For much of the 20th century, lighting up a cigarette in public or at work was regarded as entirely normal and acceptable behaviour. For many years, ashtrays were a routine component of office and domestic furniture, and offering a cigarette to a visitor or guest was common social practice. During the 1950s, and probably for some time afterwards, health ministers smoked at their desks. Most men in the UK smoked.

In the later years of the 20th century, however, things began to change. It became common for visitors to a range of public places in the UK, including cinemas, theatres, doctors' surgeries and places of worship, to be asked to refrain from smoking. After the fire that killed 31 people at Kings Cross Underground Station in London in 1987, smoking was prohibited throughout the London Underground. These and many other restrictions on smoking in public places gained rapid and widespread acceptance and compliance from the public, and hence established that smoke-free policies in public places were workable. By the end of the 20th century, nearly half of the UK population were working in smoke-free environments, and over 80% supported restrictions on smoking at work and in other public places.[1]

In 1998, the White Paper, *Smoking kills*, was published.[2] *Smoking kills* set out a UK-wide strategy to reduce smoking prevalence and also included measures intended to reduce exposure to passive smoke in public places. However, these measures were voluntary, comprising a proposed code of practice to limit smoking in enclosed workplaces, and a 'Public places charter' for pubs, restaurants and other hospitality venues.[2] The code of practice was drafted, but never implemented. The Public Places Charter was introduced in many hospitality venues, but was largely ineffective. After a public consultation in England in 2004, the Government therefore committed to use legislation, in the form of a Health Bill, to reduce exposure to passive smoke in the workplace. Since health is a devolved power in the UK, this allowed the administrations of Scotland, Wales and Northern Ireland to develop their own legislation and dates of implementation.

1.2 Implementation of smoke-free legislation in the UK

Smoke-free legislation was introduced in the UK first in Scotland in March 2006, then in Wales and Northern Ireland in April 2007, and in England in July 2007. The island Crown Dependencies of Guernsey and Jersey became smoke-free in 2006 and 2007, and the Isle of Man in March 2008. Although the legislation differs in detail between jurisdictions (see Table 1.1, page 5), the principal measures are the same throughout, making virtually all enclosed premises where people work and/or where the public has access, including public transport and work vehicles, smoke-free. The legislation does not extend into private dwellings, or into private rooms in residential accommodation. Detailed guidance on the application of the legislation has been published by the Local Authorities Coordinators of Regulatory Services (LACORS).[3]

1.3 Scope of the legislation

Under the legislation, any person who smokes in premises or vehicles included in the legislation commits an offence. It is also an offence for persons who control or manage such smoke-free premises or vehicles to permit others to smoke in them, or to fail to display official 'no smoking' signs at every entrance to smoke-free premises, or within each compartment of a smoke-free vehicle. Details of some of the definitions and other aspects of the legislation are summarised in Box 1.1, page 10.

1.4 Exemptions

Exemptions permitted by the smoke-free legislation are broadly limited to the following five categories.

1.4.1 Private dwellings

Private dwellings are exempt, except in rooms which are used solely as places of work, for example where a room is reserved for childminding or music lessons. Where work is undertaken solely to provide personal care for a person living in the dwelling, to assist with domestic work, or to maintain the building or other services in the dwelling, the private dwelling is not considered to be a workplace and is exempt from the smoke-free legislation. In England and some other administrations, common entrance areas (passageways, stairways and lifts) to private dwellings in multiple-occupation buildings, such as blocks of flats or halls of residence that are places of work for more than one person, are required to be smoke-free.

1.4.2 Residential institutions

These include places where people have their home, or live either permanently or temporarily, such as hotels, guest houses, inns, hostels and members' clubs, care homes, hospices, and adult prisons. The law allows the person in control of the premises to designate specific rooms for smoking, provided that defined conditions on construction and ventilation are met. In the cases of hotels, guest houses, inns, hostels and members' clubs, this applies only to bedrooms; in care homes and hospices, rooms used only for smoking can also be designated in addition to or as an alternative to bedrooms. Exemptions for designated areas or rooms in residential mental health units apply in some administrations, but temporary exemptions in England and Northern Ireland have expired. At the time of writing, the Scottish Government is consulting on removing the exemption. Adult prisons in the UK currently have an exemption allowing smoking in cells in which all occupants are smokers. The exemption for prisons was not applied to a new facility which was being built at the time the legislation came into force. Isle of Man Prison is therefore smoke-free.

1.4.3 Specified workplaces

These include enclosed workplaces where the smoke-free requirements are impracticable, or where smoking is held to be an essential activity, such as:

- offshore installations, where smoking in the open air is potentially more hazardous than in a designated room
- in live performances, if appropriate to the artistic integrity of a performance (applies in England and the State of Jersey only)

- specialist tobacconists, to allow sampling of cigars or pipe tobacco (applies in England and Northern Ireland only)
- facilities for researching and testing of tobacco products.

1.4.4 Crown bodies and Crown property

These are exempt, though in practice all central government departments, NHS buildings, and Ministry of Defence and Armed Services enclosed workplaces and vehicles in England, Wales, Northern Ireland and overseas were required to be smoke-free before legislation was introduced. Both Houses of Parliament have agreed to implement smoke-free policies consistent with the legislation. Royal Navy surface warships, ships of the Royal Fleet Auxiliary and HM submarines are smoke-free below decks.

1.4.5 Recognised diplomatic premises

These are inviolable, meaning that government officials cannot enter them without permission of the head of mission (such as the ambassador or high commissioner). Diplomats also enjoy immunity from criminal jurisdiction. In practice, therefore, smoke-free legislation cannot be enforced in diplomatic premises.

1.5 Extensions beyond legislative requirements

Many workplaces in the UK, including all of the NHS, had already introduced smoke-free policies consistent with the legislation before it was implemented. Others before and since have applied smoke-free policies that go beyond the requirements of the legislation. In those UK administrations covered by the Association of Train Operating Companies and Network Rail, comprehensive smoke-free policies, enforced by by-laws, apply to all railway facilities, meaning that smoking is prohibited on platforms, footbridges and other areas whether or not enclosed as defined by the smoke-free legislation. The Football League made all of its grounds smoke-free from August 2007. Some individual cricket and athletics stadia are also smoke-free. In hospitals and many other NHS facilities, smoke-free policies extend to their grounds as well as enclosed areas, although compliance has been inconsistent. School grounds are not required to be smoke-free under the legislation, but the majority in England now are, as a condition of achieving National Healthy Schools Status. Rampton high security psychiatric hospital prohibited smoking throughout its grounds and buildings from March 2007. This policy was upheld in 2009 after a challenge by inmates brought under Article 8 of the European Convention on Human Rights.

Table 1.1 Coverage of smoke-free legislation in UK jurisdictions and Crown dependencies.

	Scotland	States of Guernsey	States of Jersey	Wales	Northern Ireland	England	Isle of Man
Demographic information							
Population (thousands)	5,169	62	91	2,990	1,775	51,460	77
Area (km^2)	78,742	78	116	20,761	14,120	130,357	572
Date of general implementation	26 March 2006	2 July 2006	2 January 2007	2 April 2007	30 April 2007	1 July 2007	30 March 2008
Coverage of smoke-free legislation							
All enclosed and substantially enclosed workplaces and public places, including pubs, bars, restaurants and clubs	Yes	Yes	Yes	Yes	Yes	Yes	Yes
Public transport and shared vehicles used for work	Yes	Yes	Yes	Yes	Yes	Yes	Yes
Exemptions							
Private residential accommodation	Yes	Yes	Yes	Yes	Yes	Yes	Yes
Private motor vehicles	Yes	Yes	Yes	Yes	Yes	Yes	Yes
Hotels, guest houses, inns, hostels and members' clubs	Yes in designated bedrooms	Yes in designated bedrooms	Yes in designated bedrooms	Yes in designated bedrooms	Yes in designated bedrooms	Yes in designated bedrooms	Yes in designated bedrooms

continued over

Table 1.1 Coverage of smoke-free legislation in UK jurisdictions and Crown dependencies – *continued.*

	Scotland	States of Guernsey	States of Jersey	Wales	Northern Ireland	England	Isle of Man	
Exemptions – *continued*								
Residential care homes and nursing homes	Yes in designated rooms	Yes in designated areas	Yes in designated areas	Yes in designated rooms	Yes in designated rooms and bedrooms	Yes in designated rooms and bedrooms	Yes in designated rooms	
Hospices	Yes	Yes in designated areas	Yes in designated areas	Yes in designated rooms	Yes in designated rooms and bedrooms	Yes in designated rooms and bedrooms	Yes in designated rooms	
Mental health units	Yes in designated rooms	Yes in designated areas	Yes in designated areas	Yes in designated rooms	No (Yes in designated rooms and bedrooms until 30 April 2008)	No (Yes in designated rooms and bedrooms until 1 July 2008)	Yes in designated rooms	
Workplace used for charitable purposes	No	No	Yes in designated areas		No	No	No	No

continued

Table 1.1 Coverage of smoke-free legislation in UK jurisdictions and Crown dependencies – *continued.*

	Scotland	States of Guernsey	States of Jersey	Wales	Northern Ireland	England	Isle of Man
Exemptions – *continued*							
Staff sleeping accommodation in workplace	No	No	Yes in designated bedrooms for single occupancy	No	No	No	No
Police stations	Yes in detention and interview rooms (includes Revenue and Customs)	No	Yes in detention and interview rooms	No	No (Permitted in detention and inter-view rooms and exercise areas until 30 April 2008)	No	Yes in designated detention and interview rooms
Young offenders institutions	Yes	No	No	No	Yes, except for areas specified in legislation	No	No

continued over

Table 1.1 Coverage of smoke-free legislation in UK jurisdictions and Crown dependencies – *continued.*

	Scotland	States of Guernsey	States of Jersey	Wales	Northern Ireland	England	Isle of Man
Exemptions – *continued*							
Prisons	Yes, but smoking limited to cells under Prisons Scotland Act	Yes in all cells	Yes in designated cells	Yes in designated cells	Yes, except for areas specified in legislation	Yes in designated cells	No
Specialist tobacconists	No	No	No	No	Yes, in shop premises used for sampling cigars and pipe tobacco	Yes, in shop premises used for sampling cigars and pipe tobacco	No
Theatrical performance and public entertainment	No	No	Yes if integral part of play or production	No	No	Yes if artistic integrity makes it appropriate	No
Ships	See Note 1	Yes in fishing vessels solely operated by one master	See Note 1	See Note 1	See Note 1	See Note 1	No

continued

Table 1.1 Coverage of smoke-free legislation in UK jurisdictions and Crown dependencies – ***continued.***

Exemptions – ***continued***	**Scotland**	**States of Guernsey**	**States of Jersey**	**Wales**	**Northern Ireland**	**England**	**Isle of Man**
Aircraft	See Note 2	No	See Note 2	See Note 2	See Note 2	See Note 2	See Note 2
Offshore installations	Yes in designated rooms	No	No	Not applicable	No	Yes in designated rooms	Yes in designated rooms
Laboratories and research facilities	Yes in designated rooms	No	Yes in designated rooms	Yes in designated rooms	Yes in designated rooms	Yes in designated rooms	No

Note 1 UK-wide consultation on proposed regulations closed on 9 October 2009.
Note 2 Covered by existing legislation.

Box 1.1 Synopsis of UK smoke-free legislation terms and definitions

Smoking: smoking tobacco, or anything which contains tobacco, or other substance; including cigarettes, cigars, herbal cigarettes, pipes and waterpipes. Smoking includes being in possession of lit smoking materials, even if not actually being smoked at the time.

Workplaces: Workplaces covered by smoke-free legislation are places of work for more than one person, even if not simultaneously, or if used only by one person if members of the public enter the premises for any purpose. Work includes voluntary and unpaid work.

Public places: Public places subject to smoke-free legislation are premises open to the public, and include anywhere to which the public, or a section of the public, has access, including access restricted by invitation such as membership, or by payment such as an entrance fee.

Enclosed and substantially enclosed: Workplaces and public places are subject to smoke-free legislation only if they are 'enclosed' or 'substantially enclosed'.

- *Enclosed premises* have a ceiling or roof and, except for doors, windows or passageways which can be opened or shut, are wholly enclosed by walls, permanently or temporarily.
- *Substantially enclosed premises* have a ceiling or roof and permanent openings in walls which cannot be opened or shut, and which constitute less than 50% of the total wall area.

Temporary structures: Temporary structures, such as tents and marquees, are deemed to be enclosed premises if they can be enclosed, even if at times they are not, for example if they have side panels that can be removed and replaced.

Vehicles: A vehicle is subject to smoke-free legislation if it is used by members of the public or a section of the public, whether or not for reward or hire, in the course of paid or voluntary work. Public transport vehicles, including taxis and minicabs, and all vehicles used for work by more than one person at any time, must be smoke-free at all times, even when not in use. Vehicles are exempt if the vehicle roof has been removed or stowed such that it does not cover any part of a compartment in which persons may travel.

Aircraft: Smoking on aircraft is prohibited under the 2005 Air Navigation Order, which predated smoke-free legislation.

Ships: Proposals are currently out to consultation to prohibit smoking, under Section 85 of the Merchant Shipping Act 1995, on ships carrying at least one employee or passenger within the 12 mile UK territorial waters unless the vessel is in transit and will not be calling at a UK port. The proposals allow the Master of a ship to designate smoking areas, which may include decks and cabins.

Enforcement agencies and authorised officers: Local councils and port health authorities are the enforcement agencies for smoke-free legislation, and they authorise appropriate regulatory officers to carry out duties to secure compliance, including carrying out enforcement measures.

1.6 Evaluation of smoke-free legislation

Scotland, the first UK jurisdiction to go smoke-free, was also the first to develop a comprehensive strategy for the evaluation of the smoke-free policy and is thus the main source of evidence on the effect of the UK smoke-free legislation.[4] The Scottish evaluation focused on eight key outcome areas: compliance with the legislation, levels of passive smoke exposure, smoking prevalence and tobacco consumption, tobacco-related morbidity and mortality, knowledge and attitudes, sociocultural adaptation, economic impacts on the hospitality sector, and health inequalities. Assessment of each outcome in Scotland was based on a combination of secondary analyses of routine health, behavioural and economic data, and a portfolio of eight research projects commissioned to address specific questions. The research studies focused on intermediate impacts up to one year after the implementation of the legislation, but routine data will also be monitored over a longer period, in the first instance for three years.

1.6.1 Compliance

Public compliance with the smoke-free legislation has been high from the time of implementation in all jurisdictions in the UK, and acceptance has increased over time, particularly among smokers.[5,6] Smoke levels in a sample of 41 pubs and bars in Scotland, measured as $PM_{2.5}$ levels (small particulate matter, 90% of which in indoor air comes from tobacco smoke) in indoor air fell by 86% from a mean of 246 to 20 $\mu g\ m^{-3}$ within 2 months of the legislation coming into effect.[7] Similar changes have occurred in England,[6] as indeed they have in other jurisdictions where comprehensive smoke-free legislation has been introduced.[8–12] Inspection data indicate that nearly 2 years post-legislation, 99% of premises inspected were still compliant with the requirement not to permit smoking, and that a decline in the number of inspections over time has not appreciably changed this proportion (Fig 1.1).[5] There is some evidence that compliance levels may be lower in bars located in more deprived areas, where smoking prevalence is higher[14,15] and in hospitality premises serving particular communities, such as shisha bars. However, contraventions appear in general to be minor, typically occurring around doorways. Most bar staff appear actively to enforce the law, citing fear of prosecution as their primary motivation.[15]

1.6.2 Reductions in passive smoke exposure

In addition to reductions in indoor air particulate levels described above, compliance with the legislation in Scotland was accompanied by substantial reductions

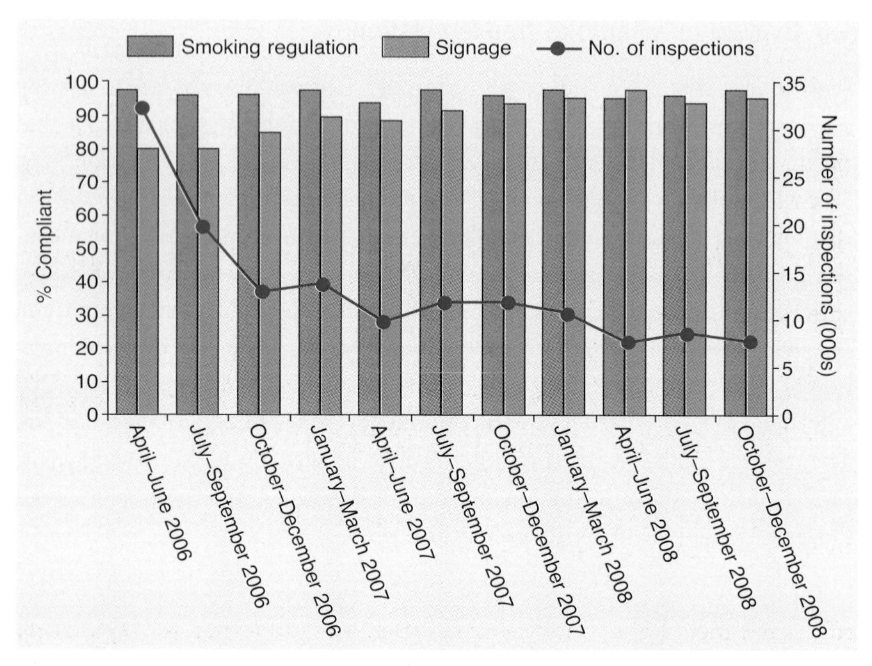

Fig 1.1 Compliance with smoke-free legislation in Scotland. Data from Hyland *et al.*[5]

in passive smoke exposure in bar workers who were occupationally exposed pre-legislation. Semple and colleagues found an 89% reduction in concentrations of salivary cotinine (a nicotine metabolite, a specific marker of tobacco smoke exposure) in a cohort of 126 non-smoking bar workers, which fell from a geometric mean of 2.9 ng ml^{-1} at baseline to 0.41 ng ml^{-1} 1 year after legislation.[16] As part of the same study, a subset of bar workers wore personal $PM_{2.5}$ monitors for the duration of a shift before and 2 months after legislation. Mean exposure fell from 202 to 28 μg m^{-3}, representing an 86% reduction in personal $PM_{2.5}$ exposure during a full shift (Fig 1.2). Similar reductions in salivary cotinine in workers from the hospitality sector after smoke-free legislation in other jurisdictions have also been reported, for example among workers from Ireland, Norway and New York.[17–19] Extrapolating from recommendations by a Department of the Environment expert panel on air quality standards,[11] Semple and colleagues have argued that a $PM_{2.5}$ concentration of 65 μg m^{-3} or more is equivalent to the highest level of outdoor air pollution – air quality band level four.[20]

1.6.3 Improvements in respiratory health

A longitudinal study of non-smoking bar workers from Dundee assessed respiratory symptoms and lung function immediately before the legislation came into

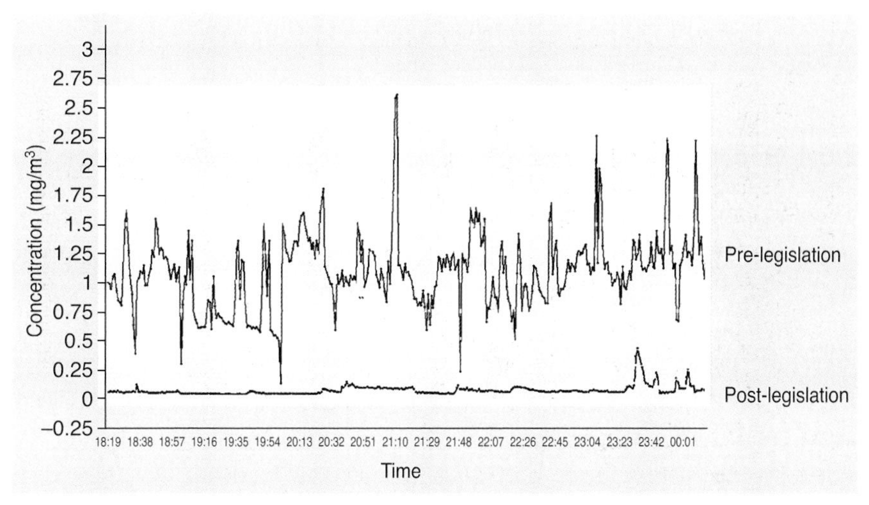

Fig 1.2 Personal full shift exposure of a bar worker to particulates ($PM_{2.5}$) pre and post Scottish legislation. Data from Semple *et al.*[16]

effect, and then again 1 and 2 months later. The proportion of respondents reporting either respiratory or sensory symptoms fell from 79% at baseline to 47% 2 months later. In addition, there was a 5% absolute improvement in lung function, as measured by forced expiratory volume in one second (FEV_1), which increased from an average of 97% to 102% of the predicted value for age, sex and height.[21] However, seasonal factors, including differences in temperature and occurrence of respiratory viral infections, may also have contributed to these changes. A larger national study of Scottish bar workers followed up participants for a longer period of 12 months, thus reducing possible seasonal confounding, and found that self-reported improvements in respiratory and sensory symptoms were maintained 1 year after workplaces had become smoke-free.[22] During this period, the proportion of non-smoking bar workers reporting phlegm production fell from 33% to 14%, irritated eyes from 39% to 11%, and sore throat from 44% to 25%. Improvements were also observed in the respiratory health of bar workers who smoked, with the proportion reporting wheeze falling from 48% immediately before the ban to 31% 1 year later, and the proportion reporting irritated eyes falling from 35% to 25%. Measures of FEV_1 and forced vital capacity (FVC) were also obtained from bar workers participating in the Scottish study, but, unlike a similar Irish study which found a 3% increase in FVC (as well as 3% increase in peak expiratory flow and 2% increase in total lung capacity),[23] no improvement in either FEV_1 or FVC was observed in the Scottish study.[24] Improvements in the lung function of bar workers from San Francisco[25] and Norway[26] have also been reported. However, as neither followed participants up for a full year post-baseline measurement, seasonal factors cannot be ruled out as an explanation of these observed improvements.

1.6.4 Reduction in hospital admissions for coronary heart disease

There is now a substantial body of epidemiological evidence linking passive smoke exposure with the development of coronary heart disease,[27] and clinical studies demonstrating immediate impacts of passive smoking on the cardiovascular system, including pro-thrombotic platelet aggregation and oxidative stress – in otherwise healthy volunteers.[28,29] In addition, there are now 13 published studies reporting a reduction in hospital admissions for myocardial infarction and related acute conditions, ranging from 13% to 40%, following the introduction of smoke-free legislation in the USA, Canada, Italy and Scotland.[30–42] However, a weakness of these studies was that 12 out of 13 relied on retrospective analysis of routine hospital data and, with the exception of two studies,[33,42] were not able to ascertain either individual smoking status or exposure to passive smoke.

A prospective study of hospital admissions to nine general hospitals for acute coronary syndrome in Scotland[39] was carried out using a standard case definition of chest pain with raised troponins I or T, and assessed individual passive smoke exposure by interview and admission blood cotinine levels. Comparing a 10–month period from June to March before legislation with the same period post-legislation, the study found an overall reduction in admissions by 17%, with a 20% reduction in non-smokers and a 14% reduction in smokers. The 17% reduction compares with an underlying trend of a 3% annual decline in admissions for acute myocardial infarction in the 10 years leading up to the legislation. There has been much debate about the size of the effect observed in these studies, but using published relative risk data and applying assumptions about reductions in smoking prevalence and exposure to passive smoke, Richiardi and colleagues estimate that a reduction of between 5% and 15% might be expected to occur.[43] This estimate range is consistent with the results from two recent meta-analyses. The first included 11 studies (from 10 locations) and reported a 17% reduction overall (95% CI 8–25%).[44] The second included 11 published and three unpublished studies and found a 17% reduction (95% CI 13–20%) 12 months post-ban.[45] Both meta-analyses found an increase in effect size over time.

1.6.5 Changes in smoking prevalence and quitting smoking

A systematic review of the impact of smoke-free regulations has suggested that making workplaces smoke-free may prompt quit attempts, reduce smoking prevalence, and reduce tobacco consumption in those who continue to smoke.[46] In Scotland, calls to Smokeline – the national smoking helpline – increased dramatically in the months leading up to smoke-free legislation but then returned to the original call rate or lower. Short-term increases in over-the-counter (OTC) nicotine replacement therapy sales were also observed in the lead-up to the legislation, but again these were maintained only for a few months after the legislation was introduced.[47] This suggests that the prospect of smoke-free legislation and initial impact may have triggered quit attempts in a number of smokers, but that this effect was relatively short-lived. Data from the Scottish Household Survey[48] are consistent with this interpretation, since the rate of decline in smoking prevalence over the years immediately before and after the legislation was introduced, from 26.2% in 2005 to 25.0% in 2006 and 24.7% in 2007, is similar to the underlying trend before the legislation.

1.7 Gaps and inconsistencies in the legislation

As set out in the Department of Health one-year review of the legislation, 'The primary aim of the legislation was to protect workers and the general public from exposure to the harmful effects of passive smoke exposure'.[6] This aim has largely been achieved in enclosed workplaces and public places. However, significant passive smoke exposure occurs in workplaces where smoking is still allowed, and a number of other gaps and inconsistencies in the legislation result in continued avoidable exposure. Examples of these fall into the following broad categories.

1.7.1 Failures in compliance

Although overall compliance with the legislation has been high from the outset, there were some determined opponents, particularly in the licensed trade. These were dealt with through enforcement measures where repeated offences occurred. The areas where breaches of the legislation still occur include commercial vehicles, where enforcement is difficult; in major public entertainment venues such as sports grounds and music festivals, where smoking sometimes occurs in covered seating areas and on covered stages; and in particular premises such as shisha bars.

1.7.2 Continued smoking in exempted areas

Smoking continues to take place legally in designated bedrooms in hotels, hostels and halls of residence, care homes, mental health units, and prison cells. In all of these circumstances, tobacco smoke will inevitably pervade passageways, staircases and other common areas, and will present a health hazard to staff, other residents, and guests. The legislation is thus failing to protect employees and the public fully in these areas. The legislation does not place a limit on the proportion of designated non-smoking bedrooms, and some hotels and members' clubs have taken the business decision not to designate any bedrooms as non-smoking. That some care homes, perhaps concerned about possible fire risks, have not designated any bedrooms for smoking indicates that more progress in reducing the extent to which smoking persists in these exempted areas could be made. The exemption for performing artists in England represents a persistent health risk to theatre audiences and staff.

1.7.3 Smoking in places not enclosed or substantially enclosed

Since the introduction of the smoke-free legislation, smokers have tended to congregate around entrances and exits to smoke-free premises and under structures which are not substantially enclosed. Smoking in such places has always taken place, but the exposure to tobacco smoke, albeit in the open air, is a source of complaints of exposure from the public, from employees such as security staff required to work in these locations, and from occupants of nearby buildings polluted as a result. Many businesses, particularly in the hospitality trade, have sought to build non-enclosed shelters or other structures to accommodate staff, customers and other visitors who want to smoke, without contravening the legislation. In some cases, close proximity to sheltering walls can prevent effective ventilation, and hence also cause passive exposure through drift of smoke into smoke-free premises.

1.7.4 Smoking in places not covered by the legislation

Private motor vehicles that are not workplaces are exempt from the legislation of major significance, since ambient levels of smoke in vehicles can be extremely high – higher than those typically encountered in bars and restaurants before becoming smoke-free.[49] Legislation making cars smoke-free has been introduced successfully in several US jurisdictions and Australian states,[50] and proposals for an extension of the legislation to private vehicles, particularly for those carrying children, has attracted public support in the UK (see Chapter 8).

In September 2007, the Driving Standards Agency (DSA) updated the UK Highway Code and added smoking to a list of distractions from safe driving which included listening to loud music, reading maps, inserting audio disks or cassettes, tuning a radio, arguing with passengers or other road users, and eating and drinking. At police discretion, a fixed penalty notice can now be issued to people who smoke while driving. In addition, Section 26 (1a) of the Road Safety Act 2006 amends the Road Traffic Act 1988 and makes it an offence to breach the requirement to control a vehicle by 'not driving a motor vehicle in a position which does not give proper control or a full view of the road and traffic ahead, or not causing or permitting the driving of a motor vehicle by another person in such a position'. A driver who loses control of a vehicle due to smoking is thus potentially open to prosecution under this legislation.

Smoking in private homes remains the main source of passive smoke exposure in the UK and is currently exempt from the legislation. Effective means of reducing exposure in the home are therefore urgently required, and approaches to this are discussed at length in the following chapters of this report.

1.8 Summary

- Smoke-free legislation in the UK has been highly effective in reducing exposure to passive smoke at work and in public places.
- Smoke-free legislation has realised some substantial health benefits, and in particular a marked reduction in hospital patients admitted with coronary heart disease.
- There are some persisting inconsistencies and gaps in the application of the legislation that could easily be resolved by changes or extensions to existing regulations.
- Experience elsewhere indicates that extension of smoke-free policies to a wider range of public places can be popular and successful.
- However, the legislation does not address exposure to passive smoke in the home and in other private places such as cars.
- New approaches are therefore needed to address this persistent and substantial source of passive smoke exposure.

References

1 Lader D, Meltzer H. *Smoking related behaviour and attitudes, 2002.* London: Office for National Statistics, 2003.

2 Department of Health. *Smoking kills.* White Paper on tobacco. London: The Stationery Office, 1998.

3 Bull S, MacGregor J, Gray I. Implementation of smokefree legislation in England. London: LACORS, 2008. www.cieh.org/library/Knowledge/Public_health/Smoking_in_the_workplace/ LACORS_CIEH_Smokefree_Guidance_2nd_Edition_-_JAN_09_.pdf

4 Haw SJ, Gruer L, Amos A *et al.* Legislation on smoking in enclosed public places: how will we evaluate the impact? *J Public Health* 2006;28(1):24–30.
5 Hyland A *et al.* the impact of smoke free legislation in Scotland: results from the scottish international tobacco policy evaluation project. *Eur J Public Health* 2009;Doi:10.1093/eurpub/ckn141.
6 Department of Health. *Smoke-free England – one year on.* London: DH, 2008.
7 Semple S, Creely KS, Naji A *et al.* Second hand smoke levels in Scottish pubs: the effect of smoke-free legislation. *Tob Control* 2007;16:127–32.
8 Travers M, Cummings K, Hyland A *et al.* Indoor air quality in hospitality venues before and after the implementation of a Clean Indoor Air Law – Western New York, 2003. *MMWR Morb Mortal Wkly Rep* 2004;53(44):1038–41.
9 Gilpin EA, White M, White V *et al. Tobacco control successes in California: A focus on young people, results from the California Tobacco surveys, 1990–2002.* La Jolla, CA: University of California, San Diego, 2003. http://libraries.ucsd.edu/ssds/pub/CTS/cpc00007/2002FINAL_ RPT.pdf
10 Fong GT, Hyland A, Borland R. Reductions in tobacco smoke pollution and increases in support for smoke-free public places following the implementation of comprehensive smoke-free workplace legislation in the Republic of Ireland: findings from the ITC Ireland/UK Survey. *Tob Control* 2006;15(Suppl 3):iii51–8.
11 Valente P, Forastiere F, Bacosi. Exposure to fine and ultrafine particles from secondhand smoke in public places before and after the smoking ban, Italy 2005. *Tob Control* 2007; 16(5):312–17.
12 Fernando D, Fowles J, Woodward A *et al.* Legislation reduces exposure to second-hand tobacco smoke in New Zealand bars by about 90%. *Tob Control* 2007;16(4):235–8
13 Scottish Government. *Clearing the Air* website. Smoke-free Legislation: National Compliance Data. www.clearingtheairscotland.com/latest/index.html
14 Richmond L, Haw S, Pell J. Impact of socioeconomic deprivation and type of facility on perceptions of the Scottish smoke-free legislation. *J Public Health* 2007;29:376–8.
15 Eadie D, Heim D, MacAskill S *et al.* A qualitative analysis of compliance with smoke-free legislation in community bars in Scotland: implications for public health. *Addiction* 2008: 103;1019–26.
16 Semple S, MacCalman L, Atherton Naji A *et al.* Bar workers' exposure to second-hand smoke: The effect of Scottish smoke-free legislation on occupational exposure. *Ann Occup Hyg* 2007;51(7):571–80.
17 Allwright S, Paul G, Greiner B *et al.* Legislation for smoke-free workplaces and health of bar workers in Ireland: before and after study. *BMJ* 2005;331,1117.
18 Ellingsen D, Fladseth G, Daae H *et al.* Airborne exposure and biological monitoring of bar and restaurant workers before and after the introduction of a smoking ban. *J Environ Monit* 2006;8:362–8.
19 Farrelly MC, Nonnemaker J, Chou R *et al.* Changes in hospitality workers' exposure to secondhand smoke following the implementation of New York's smoke-free law. *Tob Control* 2005;14(4):236–41.
20 COMEAP statement on banding of air quality, 2007. www.advisorybodies.doh.gov.uk/comeap/statementsreports/airpol9.htm
21 Menzies D, Nair A, Williamson PA *et al.* Respiratory symptoms, pulmonary function, and markers of inflammation among bar workers before and after a legislative ban on smoking in public places. *JAMA* 2006;296(14):1742–8.

22 Ayres JG, Semple S, MacCalman L *et al.* Bar workers' Health and Environmental Tobacco Smoke Exposure (BHETSE): symptomatic improvement in bar staff following smoke-free legislation in Scotland. *Occup Environ Med* 2009; 0:1–8. doi: 10.1136/oem.2008.040311
23 Goodman P, Agnew M, McCaffrey M *et al.* Effects of the Irish smoking ban on respiratory health of bar workers and air quality in Dublin pubs. *Am J Respir Crit Care Med* 2007;175: 840–5.
24 Ayres J, Personal Communication, 2009.
25 Eisner MD, Smith AK, Blanc PD. Bartenders' Respiratory Health After Establishment of Smoke-Free Bars and Taverns. *JAMA* 1998;280(22):1909–14.
26 Skogstad M, Kjaerheim K, Fladseth G *et al.* Cross shift changes in lung function among bar and restaurant workers before and after implementation of a smoking ban. *Occup Environ Med*; 2006;63(7):482–7.
27 US Department of Health and Human Services. *The health consequences of involuntary exposure to tobacco smoke: a report of the Surgeon General.* Atlanta, USA: Department of Health and Human Services, Centers for Disease Control and Prevention, Coordinating Center for Health Promotion, National Center for Chronic Disease Prevention and Health Promotion, Office on Smoking and Health. Washington, DC, US Government Printing Office, 2006.
28 Barnoya J, Glantz S. Cardiovascular effects of secondhand smoke: nearly as large as smoking. *Circulation* 2005;111,2684–98.
29 Schmid P, Karanikas G, Kritz HP *et al.* Passive smoking and platelet thromboxane. *Thromb Res* 1996;81:451–60.
30 Sargent RP, Shepard RM, Glantz SA. Reduced incidence of admissions for myocardial infarction associated with public smoking ban: before and after study. *BMJ* 2004; 328(7446):977–80.
31 Bartecchi C, Alsever RN, Nevin-Woods C *et al.* Reduction in the incidence of acute myocardial infarction associated with a citywide smoking ordinance. *Circulation* 2006; 114:1490–6.
32 Barone-Adesi F, Vizzini L, Merletti F, Richiardi L. Short-term effects of Italian smoking regulation on rates of hospital admission for acute myocardial infarction. *Eur Heart J* 2006; 27:2468–72.
33 Seo DC, Torabi MR. Reduced admissions for acute myocardial infarction associated with a public smoking ban: Matched controlled study. *J Drug Educ* 2007;37:217–26.
34 Khuder SA, Milz S, Jordan T *et al.* The impact of a smoking ban on hospital admissions for coronary heart disease. *Prev Med* 2007;45:3–8.
35 Juster HR, Loomis BR, Hinman TM *et al.* Declines in hospital admissions for acute myocardial infarction in New York state after implementation of a comprehensive smoking ban. *Am J Public Health* 2007;97:2035–9.
36 Lemestra M, Neudorf C, Opondo J. Implications of a public smoking ban. *Can J Public Health* 2008;99:62–5.
37 Cesaroni G, Forastiere F, Agabiti N *et al.* Effect of the Italian smoking ban on population rates of acute coronary events. *Circulation* 2008;117:1183–8.
38 Vasselli S, Papini P, Gaelone D *et al.* Reduction incidence of myocardial infarction associated with a national legislative ban on smoking. *Minerva Cardioangiol* 2008;56:197–203.
39 Pell JP, Haw S, Cobbe SM *et al.* Smokefree legislation and hospitalizations for acute coronary syndrome. *NEJM* 2008;359:482–91.
40 Alsever RN, Thomas WM, Nevin-Woods C *et al.* Reduced hospitalizations for acute myocardial infarction after implementation of a smoke-free ordinance – City of Pueblo, Colorado, 2002–2006. *CDC MMWR Morb Mortal Wkly Rep* 2009;57:1373–7.

41 Shetty KD, DeLeire T, White C, Bhattacharya J, *Changes in U.S. hospitalization and mortality rates following smoking bans.* NBER Working Paper 14790. www.nber.org/papers/w14790

42 Barnett R, Pearce J, Moon G. Assessing the effect of the introduction of the New Zealand Smokefree Environment Act 2003 on acute myocardial infarction hospital admissions in Christchurch, New Zealand. *Aust NZ J Public Health* 2009; 33:515–20.

43 Richiardi L, Vizzini L, Merletti F, Barone-Adesi F. Cardiovascular benefits of smoking regulations: The effect of decreased exposure to passive smoking. *Prev Med* 2009;48: 167–72.

44 Meyers, DG, Neuberger JS, He J. Cardiovascular Effect of Bans on Smoking in Public Places: A systematic review and meta-analysis. *J Am Coll Cardiol* 2009; 54:1249–55.

45 Lightwood JM, Glantz SA. Declines in acute myocardial infarction after smoke-free laws and individual risk attributable to secondhand smoke. *Circulation* 2009;DOI: 10.1161/CIRCULATIONAHA.109.870691

46 Fichtenberg CM, Glantz SA. Effect of smoke-free workplaces on smoking behaviour: systematic review. *BMJ* 2002;325:188.

47 Lewis SA, Haw SJ, McNeill AD. The impact of the 2006 Scottish smoke-free legislation on sales of nicotine replacement therapy. *Nicotine Tob Res* 2008;10:1789–92.

48 Scottish Government. *Scottish Household Survey.* www.scotland.gov.uk/Topics/Statistics/16002

49 Jones MR, Navas-Acien A, Yuan J, Breysse PN. Secondhand tobacco smoke concentrations in motor vehicles: a pilot study. *Tob Control* 2009;18:399–404.

50 Thomson G, Wilson N. Public attitudes to laws for smoke-free private vehicles: a brief review. *Tob Control* 2009 Aug;18(4):256–61.

2 Passive smoking in UK children

2.1 Introduction

As outlined in Chapter 1, smoke-free legislation has now resulted in substantial improvements in indoor air quality and reductions in exposure to passive smoke in most workplaces and enclosed public places in the UK. However, the legislation does not extend to homes and other private places where the majority of exposure occurs. Our earlier report on smoke-free policy demonstrated that passive smoking in the home is a major source of exposure in children, particularly young children.[1] Unlike most adults, they have little control over their home environment, and are therefore generally unable to remove themselves from areas of passive smoke exposure.[2] Young children are also at a higher risk of passive smoke exposure compared with adults. After exposure to similar levels of ambient tobacco smoke, cotinine levels in children are about 70% higher than those in adults, probably because children have higher breathing rates.[3]

Even before the introduction of smoke-free legislation, progressive reductions in levels of passive smoke exposure among non-smoking children aged 11–15 living in the UK had been occurring since the late 1980s.[1,4] At the time that smoke-free legislation was being debated in England, concern was expressed, notably by the then secretary of state for health John Reid, that making public places smoke-free might displace smoking back to the home, and that exposure of children and other dependents might consequently increase. In this chapter, we examine data concerning passive smoke exposure in children in England, updating and extending the results in our earlier report[1] by expanding the age range of children studied, and including data from after the implementation of smoke-free legislation. We also summarise data on exposure of children and adults to passive smoking before and after implementation of smoke-free legislation in other UK jurisdictions.

2.2 English study data and methods

The data analysed and presented in the following sections (2.2.1 to 2.2.4) come from salivary cotinine measures in non-smoking children aged 4–15 years participating in the Health Survey for England (HSE). The HSE is an annual cross-sectional survey of individuals living in a sample of private households, designed to be representative of the population living in private households in England in terms of age, gender, geographic area and socio-demographic circumstances.[5] All adults (those aged 16 and over) and up to two children in all selected households are interviewed and asked a series of questions to determine sociodemographic factors, parent and carer smoking behaviours, and the presence or absence of smoking in the home on most days. Saliva samples for cotinine estimation have been collected from all children aged 4–15 in the core survey every year since 1996, except for 1999, 2000 and 2004. Cotinine is agreed to be the best available quantitative indicator of nicotine intake, and hence passive smoke exposure, over the preceding 2–3 days.[6] Cotinine levels are directly related to the extent of passive smoking exposure sustained, though levels above 12 ng/ml are widely accepted to be indicative of active smoking.[7] Children with levels above 12 ng/ml, or those who self-report as active smokers, were therefore considered active smokers and excluded from the analysis.

The predictors of passive smoke exposure in children, including the effects of parent and carer smoking, whether there was smoking in the home on most days (based on the response from a parent or other adult living in the household), family sociodemographic status, and the age, gender and ethnicity of the child on children's salivary cotinine have been analysed in pooled data from 1996 to 2006, using univariate and multivariate regression models.[8] Exposure to carer smoking was defined as a parent reporting that the child was looked after for more than two hours a week by someone who smokes while looking after them. For analysis of time trends in children's cotinine levels, parental smoking and smoking in the home, and determinants of smoking in the home, we added data for 2007, the year in which smoke-free legislation was implemented in England, but there were insufficient data to allow a detailed comparison of levels before and after 1 July 2007. More extensive details of the methods used in the analyses are provided elsewhere.[8–9]

2.2.1 Predictors of passive smoke exposure in children

The strongest individual predictors of passive smoke exposure in children as measured by salivary cotinine were whether parents or carers were smokers, and whether people smoked inside the home (Table 2.1). Relative to geometric mean levels of cotinine of 0.24 ng/ml in children whose parents were both non-smokers, children whose father smoked had mean cotinine levels 2.9 times higher (0.71 ng/ml); those whose mother smoked had levels 6.4 times higher (1.55 ng/ml); and those whose parents both smoked had levels 8.9 times higher (2.14 ng/ml). Cotinine concentrations were 5.4 times higher in children whose carers smoked (1.71 ng/ml) compared to those who did not (0.32 ng/ml) (Fig 2.1). Children from households in which someone smoked inside on most days had cotinine levels 7.3 times higher (1.78 ng/ml) than those of children from smoke-free households (0.25 ng/ml).

Passive smoke exposure was higher in younger children (1.4 times higher at age 4 than at age 15 – see Fig 2.2), and also in white children (1.5 times higher than in black or Asian children). In relation to various measures of socio-economic status (Table 2.1), cotinine levels were 3.1 times higher in children living in households headed by semi-skilled or unskilled manual workers than in households headed by professional or managerial workers, 2.7 times higher in those living in households whose head was unemployed than employed, and 3.9 times higher in

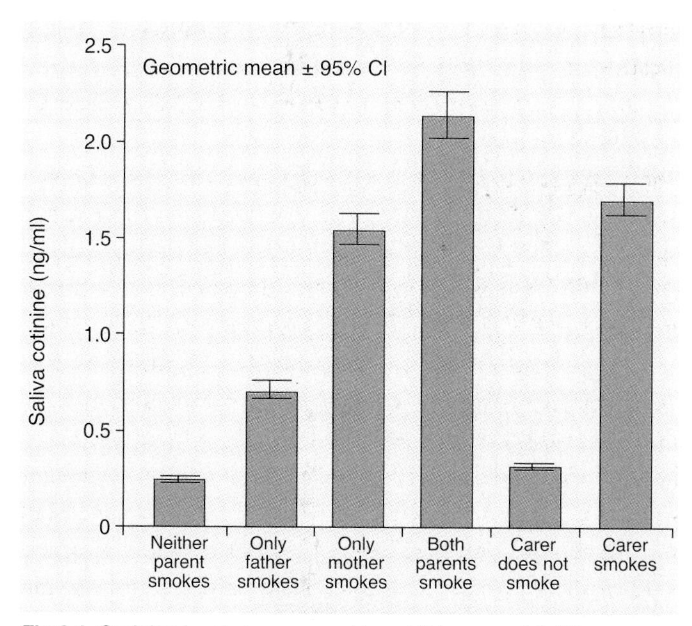

Fig 2.1 Cotinine levels in non-smoking children aged 4–15 years according to smoking status of parents and carers (pooled data from 1996–2006).

Table 2.1 Factors influencing geometric mean cotinine levels in non-smoking children aged 4–15 years in univariate and multivariate regression.

Predictor		Sample size	Cotinine (ng/ml)	Univariate regression/ multiplicative change (95% CI)‡		R^2 (%)	Multivariate regression/ multiplicative change (95% CI)‡			
							4–15 year olds[b]		4–12 year olds[c]	
Year		12,743	–	0.94	(0.93, 0.94)	2.3	0.96	(0.95, 0.96)	0.96	(0.95, 0.96)
Age		12,743	–	0.97	(0.96, 0.98)	0.5	0.98	(0.97, 0.98)	0.96	(0.95, 0.97)
Gender	Male[a]	6,367	0.46	–		<0.01	Not significant – dropped from model		–	–
	Female	6,376	0.47	1.02	(0.97, 1.07)				1.07	(1.02, 1.12)
Social class of head of household	I and II (professional and management)	4,953	0.28	–	–	8.6	–	–	–	–
	III (skilled manual and non-manual)	4,914	0.55	1.94	(1.83, 2.05)		1.14	(1.09, 1.20)	1.12	(1.06, 1.19)
	IV and V (semi-skilled and unskilled manual)	2,396	0.88	3.12	(2.91, 3.34)		1.29	(1.21, 1.37)	1.25	(1.16, 1.34)

continued

Table 2.1 Factors influencing geometric mean cotinine levels in non-smoking children aged 4–15 years in univariate and multivariate regression – *continued.*

Predictor		Sample size	Cotinine (ng/ml)	Univariate regression/ multiplicative change (95% CI)‡		R^2 (%)	Multivariate regression/ multiplicative change (95% CI)‡ 4–15 year olds[b]		4–12 year olds[c]	
Employment status of head of household	Employed[a]	10,166	0.39	–	–	6.3	–	–	–	–
	Unemployed	788	1.04	2.69	(2.42, 2.98)		1.31	(1.20, 1.43)	1.26	(1.14, 1.39)
	Other (including looking after home)	1,602	0.98	2.54	(2.36, 2.75)		1.41	(1.31, 1.51)	1.36	(1.26, 1.47)
Highest education status achieved by either parent	Higher education qualification[a]	5,032	0.28	–	–	9.0	–	–	–	–
	School level (or other) qualifications*	6,164	0.56	1.97	(1.87, 2.08)		1.23	(1.18, 1.29)	1.23	(1.16, 1.30)
	No qualification	1,503	1.09	3.85	(3.55, 4.18)		1.49	(1.38, 1.61)	1.47	(1.34, 1.60)
Ethnicity**	White[a]	11,345	0.48	–	–	0.5	–	–	–	–
	Black or Asian	990	0.32	0.67	(0.61, 0.73)		0.83	(0.77, 0.90)	0.91	(0.83, 0.99)
Parental smoking status	Neither parent smokes[a]	7,904	0.24	–	–	34.7	–	–	–	–
	Father only smokes	1,239	0.71	2.94	(2.74, 3.16)		1.36	(1.26, 1.48)	1.36	(1.24, 1.49)

continued over

Table 2.1 Factors influencing geometric mean cotinine levels in non-smoking children aged 4–15 years in univariate and multivariate regression – *continued.*

Predictor		Sample size	Cotinine (ng/ml)	Univariate regression/ multiplicative change (95% CI)‡		R^2 (%)	Multivariate regression/ multiplicative change (95% CI)‡			
							4–15 year olds[b]		4–12 year olds[c]	
	Mother only smokes	2,259	1.55	6.42	(6.06, 6.79)		2.11	(1.96, 2.28)	2.01	(1.85, 2.21)
	Both parents smoke	1,223	2.14	8.89	(8.26, 9.55)		2.95	(2.70, 3.23)	2.80	(2.52, 3.10)
Someone smokes most days inside the home?	No[a]	8,645	0.25	–	–	38.6	–	–	–	–
	Yes	4,096	1.78	7.27	(6.96, 7.59)		3.09	(2.87, 3.32)	2.56	(2.35, 2.79)
Carer smoking (>2 hrs per week) †	No[a]	6,921	0.32	–	–	23.9			–	–
	Yes	2,366	1.71	5.39	(5.07, 5.73)				1.67	(1.56, 1.78)

[a] Baseline category.
[b] n=11,645. Includes all variables listed other than those indicated as dropped from model and carer smoking.
[c] n=8,448.
*Also includes qualifications obtained outside the UK, Nursery Nurse Examination Board, clerical and commercial qualifications.
† Only asked to those aged 4–12 years (and could not therefore be included in the multivariate model for 4- to 15-year-olds).
‡ The multiplicative change in geometric mean cotinine compared with the baseline category (for continuous variables, year and age, it is the multiplicative change in geometric mean cotinine for each unit increase in year or age). Each multiplicative change was obtained by taking the exponential of the regression coefficient associated with the predictor. Values under 1 therefore represent a decline in geometric mean cotinine.
**Those classed as other ethnicities were excluded from the analysis due to their very small numbers.

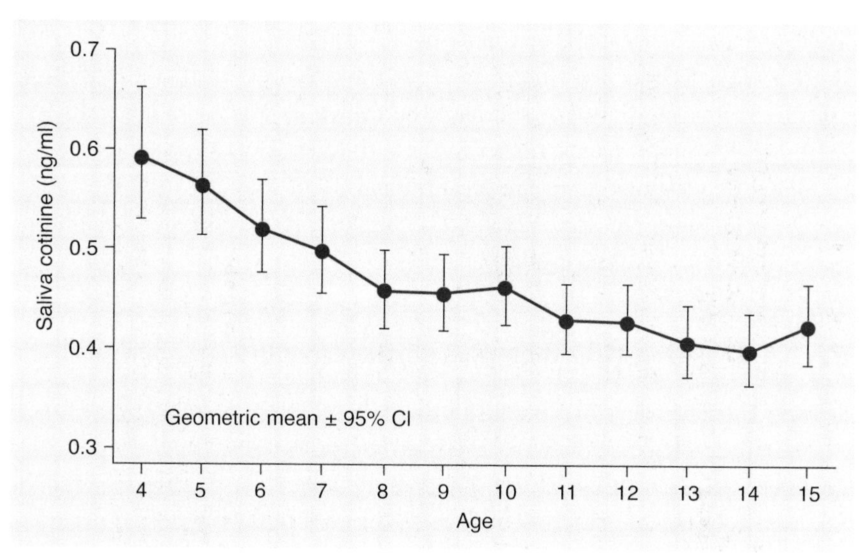

Fig 2.2 Geometric mean saliva cotinine in non-smoking children by age in years (pooled data from 1996–2006).

children whose parents had no qualifications than in children whose parents had completed higher education.

In the multivariate models to assess the independent association of potential predictors with cotinine levels, the effects of parental and carer smoking, and of smoking in the home, remained significant but their impacts were less significant than those estimated in the univariate models (Table 2.1). In 4- to 15-year olds, the most important predictors remained parental smoking status, whether someone smokes inside the home, ethnicity, and the various measures of socio-economic status (social class, parental education, employment of the head of household). The model for 4- to 12-year-olds, which also included carer smoking (not asked in those aged over 12), was very similar, although carer smoking and gender were also significant (Table 2.1). This analysis indicated that collectively these variables 'explained' just under half of the variation in children's cotinine levels.[8]

Importantly, these findings suggest that modifiable factors (whether the child lives in a home where smoking occurs regularly, whether the parents smoke, and whether the child is looked after by carers that smoke) have by far the greatest influence on children's exposure to passive smoke. The association between socio-economic status and children's exposure is unsurprising, given that lower socio-economic status is closely linked with higher smoking prevalence. Nevertheless, the persistent independent and significant effects of the socio-economic status predictors in the multivariate model indicate that children from poorer backgrounds have higher exposure even after allowing for any differences in the likelihood that their parents or carers smoke, or that someone smokes regularly in their home. There are a number of possible reasons for this. Community exposure, for example by frequenting more venues allowing smoking and where more people smoke, may be higher in these children. Home exposure may also be higher due to, for example, a greater intensity of smoking in homes where regular smoking occurs and fewer home smoking restrictions. These children may also spend more time inside the home.

2.2.2 Trends over time in passive smoke exposure

Salivary cotinine levels in children in the HSE fell progressively, by a mean of 0.4 ng/ml (nearly 70%), between 1996 (geometric mean 0.59 ng/ml) and 2007 (geometric mean 0.19 ng/ml; see Fig 2.3 and Table 2.2). The biggest decrease occurred between 2005 and 2006 (from 0.38 ng/ml to 0.24 ng/ml), a period of fairly intense media campaigns and public debates about passive smoking in the period preceding the introduction of smoke-free legislation. The extent of this decline differs, however, according to the sociodemographic characteristics of the child (Fig 2.4), whether the child's parents smoke, and whether smoking is allowed in the home (Table 2.2, Fig 2.5), in that the absolute reduction in exposure between 1996 and 2007 was greatest among the children who were most exposed at the outset. This was confirmed in a separate analysis which examined absolute changes in measured exposure in the 11 years leading up to the smoke-free legislation.[8] In line with the data displayed in Fig 2.4, absolute declines in median

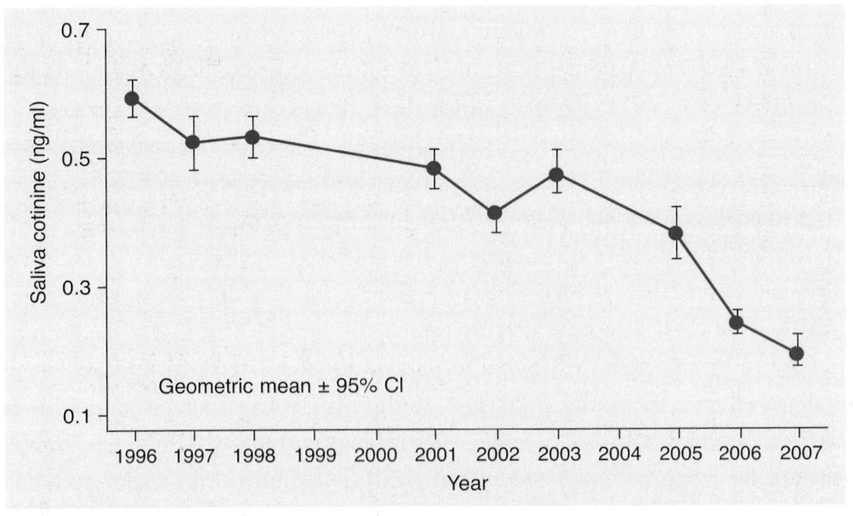

Fig 2.3 Trends in geometric mean saliva cotinine in non-smoking children aged 4–15 years, 1996–2007.

Table 2.2 Geometric mean cotinine levels in non-smoking children aged 4–15 years by number of parents who smoke and whether someone smokes in the home on most days.

Year	All children combined		No smoking in home on most days: No parent smokes		1 parent smokes		2 parents smoke		All children		Smoking in home on most days: No parent smokes		1 parent smokes		2 parents smoke		All children	
	Mean	95% CI	Mean	95% CI	Mean	95% CI	Mean	95% CI	Mean	95% CI	Mean	95% CI	Mean	95% CI	Mean	95% CI	Mean	95% CI
1996	0.59	0.56–0.62	0.29	0.27–0.31	0.39	0.32–0.46	1.12	0.69–1.82	0.30	0.28–0.32	1.00	0.78–1.28	1.81	1.67–1.95	2.85	2.58–3.15	1.97	1.85–2.10
1997	0.52	0.48–0.56	0.26	0.24–0.28	0.37	0.28–0.48	1.49	0.71–3.15	0.27	0.25–0.29	0.88	0.55–1.41	1.75	1.56–1.97	2.56	2.21–2.95	1.85	1.68–2.03
1998	0.52	0.49–0.56	0.24	0.23–0.26	0.44	0.34–0.57	0.91	0.51–1.65	0.26	0.24–0.28	0.66	0.46–0.94	1.77	1.61–1.93	2.61	2.31–2.94	1.83	1.70–1.98
2001	0.48	0.45–0.51	0.25	0.23–0. 26	0.41	0.33–0.51	0.89	0.60–1.33	0.26	0.25–0.28	0.79	0.57–1.09	1.70	1.53–1.88	2.34	1.96–2.79	1.73	1.59–1.89
2002	0.41	0.37–0.46	0.20	0.18–0.22	0.27	0.20–0.37	0.94	0.48–1.81	0.21	0.19–0.23	0.79	0.43–1.48	1.56	1.34–1.82	2.95	2.51–3.46	1.78	1.58–2.02
2003	0.47	0.44–0.51	0.25	0.23–0.27	0.37	0.29–0.46	0.63	0.40–0.99	0.26	0.25–0.28	1.08	0.74–1.57	1.71	1.52–1.93	1.92	1.63–2.26	1.69	1.54–1.86
2005	0.38	0.34–0.42	0.21	0.19–0.23	0.41	0.29–0.58	0.61	0.25–1.46	0.23	0.21–0.26	0.38	0.17–0.81	1.44	1.18–1.76	2.01	1.52–2.66	1.41	1.19–1.67
2006	0.24	0.22–0.26	0.12	0.11–0.13	0.31	0.25–0.39	0.38	0.20–0.72	0.14	0.13–0.15	0.67	0.35–1.25	1.41	1.21–1.64	1.81	1.42–2.31	1.42	1.25–1.62
2007	0.19	0.17–0.22	0.10	0.09–0.10	0.32	0.22–0.46	0.25	0.07–0.96	0.11	0.10–0.12	0.24	0.08–0.71	1.35	1.05–1.72	2.18	1.42–3.35	1.38	1.12–1.72
All years	0.44	0.43–0.45	0.22	0.21–0.22	0.37	0.34–0.40	0.70	0.57–0.87	0.23	0.23–0.24	0.80	0.69–0.92	1.67	1.61–1.74	2.46	2.33–2.60	1.75	1.70–1.81

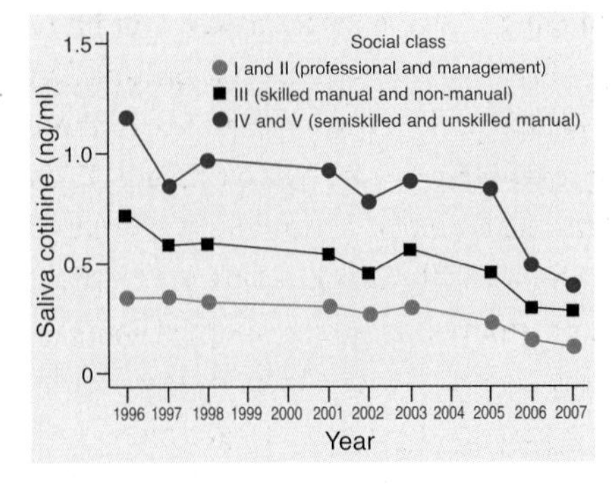

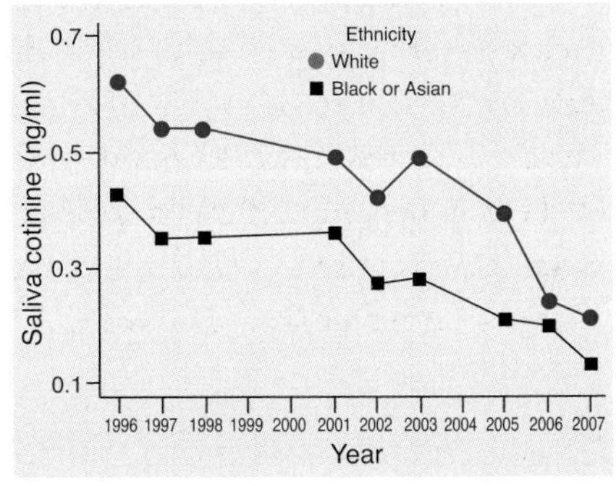

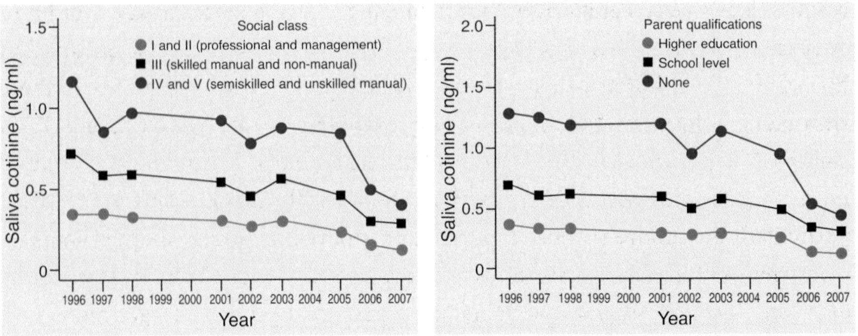

Parent qualifications chart: Higher education; School level; None.

Fig 2.4 Trends in geometric mean cotinine in non-smoking children aged 4–15 years by social class of head of household, highest educational qualification of parents and ethnicity (pooled data from 1996–2007).

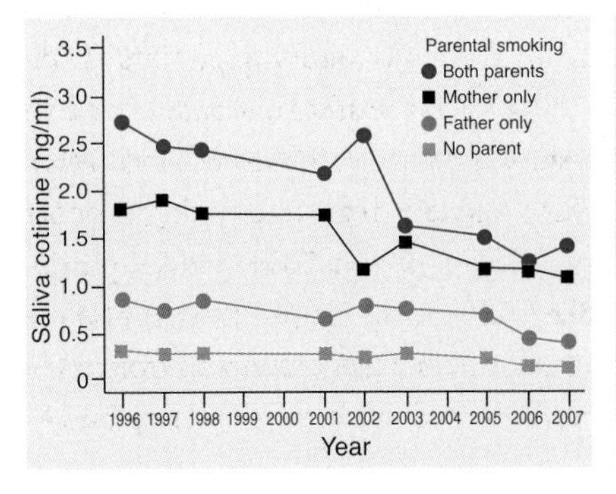

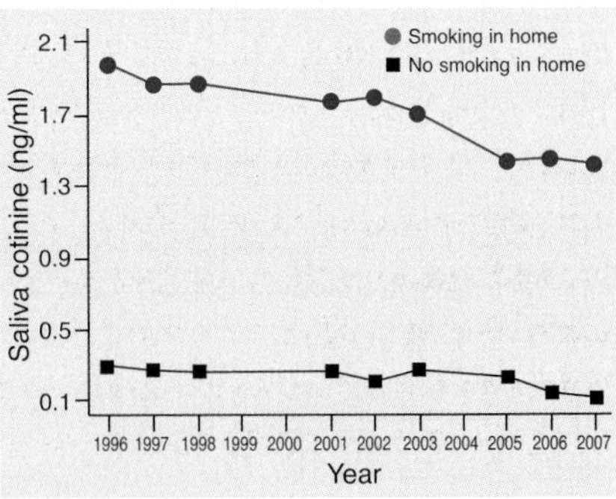

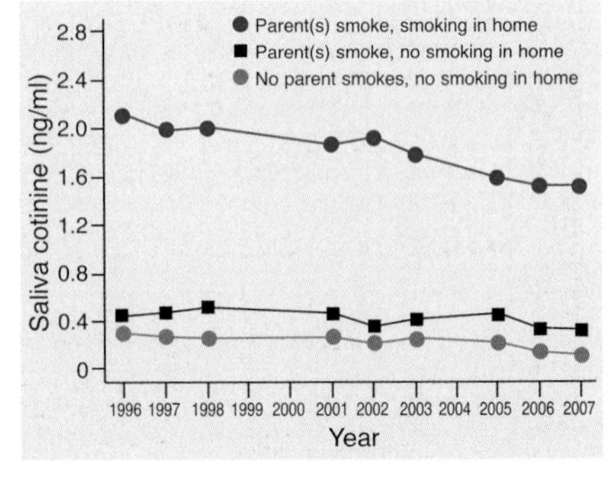

Fig 2.5 Geometric mean cotinine levels (ng/ml) over time for non-smoking children aged 4–15 years by parental smoking status, whether someone smokes in the home on most days, and parental smoking. Parents' smoke includes children for whom one or both parents smoke (pooled data from 1996–2007).

cotinine levels were significantly higher in children from semiskilled or unskilled occupation households compared to professional or managerial occupation households, in children whose parents had no qualifications compared to those with higher education qualifications, and in white compared to black and Asian children.[8] Exposure was also shown to have fallen most in children with one or more parents who were smokers, and, consistent with the data shown in Fig 2.5, particularly in children whose parents both smoked or whose mother smoked, compared with children with non-smoking parents. These declines in absolute exposure were not associated with marked relative changes between groups.[8]

Overall, these results demonstrate that passive smoking in children has declined markedly over recent years in England, and that absolute inequalities in exposure have also reduced in the years leading up to the smoke-free legislation. These reductions in exposure are likely to be attributable in part to reductions in the prevalence of adult smoking in the general population (and thus in the proportion of parents smoking), but other factors may also be involved. These factors are explored further in the next section.

2.2.3 Trends in parental smoking and smoking in the home

Figure 2.6 shows trends in the proportions of non-smoking children living with smoking and non-smoking parents between 1996 and 2007, and illustrates declines in the proportion of children living with two smoking parents (from 11% to 5%), little change in the number living with one smoking parent, and an increase in the percentage living with no smoking parents (from 60% to 69%). The proportion of children living in a home without regular smoking indoors has also increased markedly over time from 64% in 1996 to 78% in 2007, particularly among children whose parents smoke (Table 2.3). The proportion of these homes among households where one parent smokes almost doubled from 21% in 1996 to 37% in 2007. There was an even more marked increase among homes

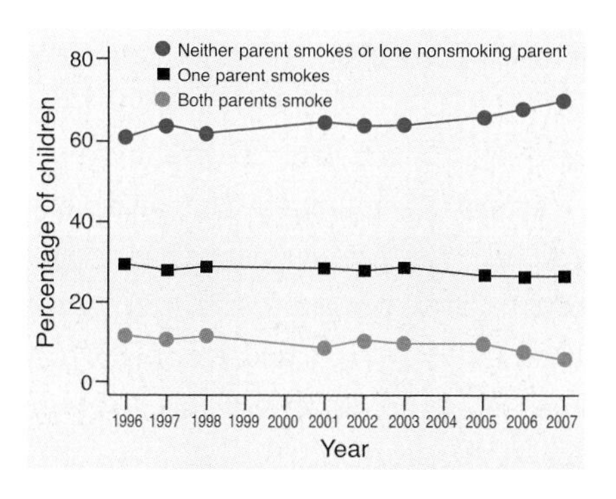

Fig 2.6 Proportion of non-smoking children aged 4–15 years living with smoking and non-smoking parents by year (pooled data from 1996–2007).

Table 2.3 Percentage of children aged 4–15 years living in a smoke-free home, by year and parental smoking habits.

Year	All children (%)	Neither parent smokes or lone non-smoking parent (%)	One parent smokes (%)	Both parents smoke (%)
1996	64	95	21	6
1997	66	96	19	9
1998	64	96	19	8
2001	69	97	23	10
2002	68	96	25	12
2003	69	96	26	17
2005	73	97	32	26
2006	77	98	38	26
2007	78	99	37	21

in which both parents smoke, from 6% in 1996 to 21% in 2007 having no regular smoking indoors, although clearly the majority of homes of smoking parents still allow smoking indoors.

These findings indicate that increases over time in both the proportion of children living with non-smoking parents, and in homes where regular smoking does not occur (including homes of smoking and non-smoking parents), are likely to have contributed to the decline in children's passive smoke exposure. While home smoking restrictions are still more prevalent in homes with non-smoking parents, the increasing proportion of smoking parents who have elected not to smoke in the home is notable and likely to have had an important impact.

Nevertheless, important differences in avoidable exposure persist, with exposure remaining far greater in children of smokers and those living in homes that allow regular smoking (Fig 2.5). It is noteworthy that children of both smokers and non-smokers living in homes where regular smoking does not occur have much lower levels of passive smoke exposure (Fig 2.5 and Table 2.2). Thus, if we compare children of non-smoking parents who live in a household allowing smoking with those living in one that does not, we see that their geometric mean cotinine levels are almost four times higher (0.80 ng/ml compared with 0.22 ng/ml over the 12-year period as a whole – Table 2.2). However, children of smokers living in homes where regular smoking does not occur still have higher levels of passive smoke exposure than children of non-smoking parents (Fig 2.7).

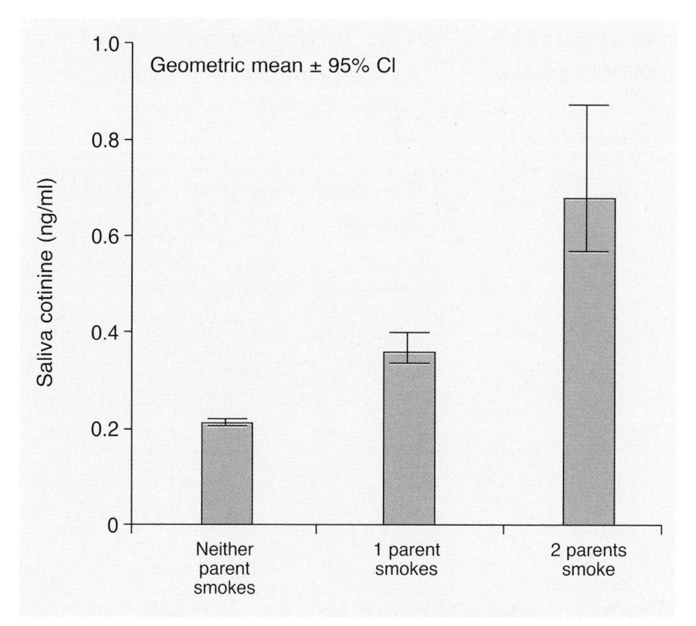

Fig 2.7 Cotinine levels in non-smoking children aged 4–15 years living in homes where regular smoking does not occur, by parental smoking status (pooled data from 1996–2007).

Over time, cotinine levels have declined most in absolute terms among children living in homes allowing smoking (by 0.59 ng/ml from 1.97 ng/ml in 1996 to 1.38 ng/ml in 2007) than in homes that do not (a decline of 0.19 ng/ml, from 0.30 ng/ml to 0.11 ng/ml – Table 2.2 and Fig 2.5). However, whilst absolute differences in exposure between smoking and non-smoking homes have fallen over this 12-year period, the smaller proportional change in those living in homes that allow smoking means that relative inequalities have increased. This is consistent with the evidence emerging from Scotland on the impact of smoke-free legislation on inequalities in exposure, described further below (section 2.3).

2.2.4 Prevalence and determinants of smoking in the home

The proportion of households in which someone smokes inside on most days varies widely by parental smoking status and socio-economic status (Table 2.4). In only 3.8% of households where neither parent smokes does someone smoke inside on most days. This compares with 88% of households where both parents smoke, 81% where only the mother smokes and 65% where only the father smokes. Households where regular smoking does not occur in the home are more likely to be of higher socio-economic status, whether defined by the head

Table 2.4 Comparison of households containing non-smoking children aged 4–15 years that do and do not allow smoking inside (based on whether someone smokes inside the home on most days), by socio-economic indicators. HSE 1996–2007 combined.

Socio-economic indicator		Does someone smoke inside the home on most days? YES (no.)	YES (%)*	NO (no.)	NO (%)*	Total
Social class of head of household	I and II (professional and management)	889	16.9	4,371	83.1	5,260
	III (skilled manual and non-manual)	1,890	37.0	3,214	63.0	5,104
	IV and V (semi-skilled and unskilled manual)	1,253	50.2	1,244	49.8	2,497
Employment status of head of household	Employed	2,849	26.6	7,851	73.4	10,700
	Unemployed	461	57.2	345	42.8	806
	Other	839	50.1	835	49.9	1,674
Highest education status achieved by either parent	Higher education qualification	944	17.7	4,393	82.3	5,337
	School level qualification or other	2,377	37.0	4,053	63.0	6,430
	No qualification	880	56.7	672	43.3	1,552
Ethnicity**	White	3,845	32.5	8,002	67.5	11,847
	Black or Asian	215	20.0	861	80.0	1,076
Parental smoking status	Neither parent smokes	313	3.8	8,028	96.2	8,341
	Only father smokes	824	64.5	454	35.5	1,278
	Only mother smokes	1,931	81.3	445	18.7	2,376
	Both parents smoke	1,103	88.0	150	12.0	1,253

* % of row total

** Those classed as other ethnicities were excluded from the analysis due to their very small numbers.

of household's occupation, employment status or educational attainment, and to contain children of black or Asian ethnicity. Smoking parents living in these homes were also considerably lighter smokers (across all years combined, their usual daily cigarette consumption averaged 8.2), compared with parents from homes where regular smoking occurred (16.2 cigarettes per day), and their average cotinine was 188.8 ng/ml compared with 318.9 ng/ml. This latter finding suggests that lighter smokers may be able to implement restrictions on smoking in the home more easily than someone with a higher level of nicotine addiction, but it is also possible that restricting smoking in the home has facilitated a reduction in their cigarette consumption and nicotine intake.

2.3 Smoke-free policy and passive smoke exposure of children in Scotland

Cross-sectional surveys of nationally representative samples of 11-year-old school children in their final year in primary school[10] were carried out in January 2006 and January 2007 – before and after the Scottish legislation came into force on 26 March 2006. Geometric mean salivary cotinine levels fell significantly from 0.36 ng/ml before the legislation, to 0.22 ng/ml after legislation, a decrease of 0.14 ng/ml or about 40%. A fall of similar relative and absolute magnitude, from 0.43 ng/ml to 0.26 ng/ml, was reported in a pre- and post-legislative study of exposure in adults in Scotland.[11]

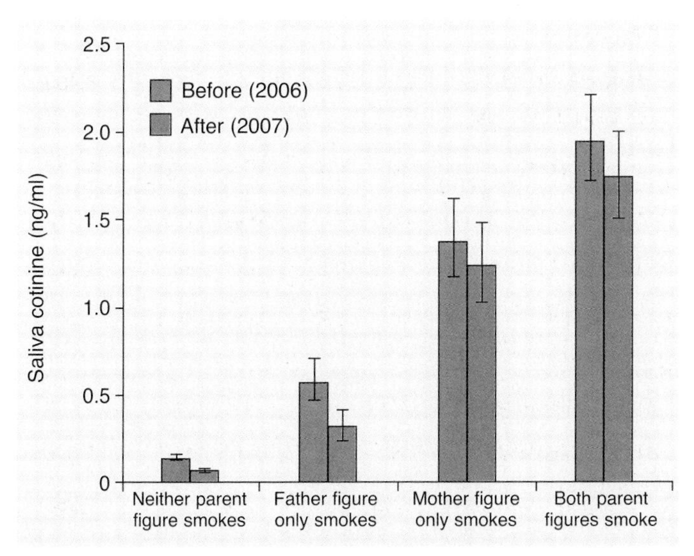

Fig 2.8 **Geometric mean salivary cotinine concentrations in Scottish 11-year-old children before and after the introduction of smoke-free legislation, by parental smoking status.**

More detailed analysis of the Scottish data reveals that the reductions were not uniform across population groups. As with the English data, exposure levels were far greater in children of smokers, particularly those whose parents both smoked or whose mother smoked, and absolute reductions in salivary cotinine tended to be larger in such children – from 1.94 ng/ml to 1.74 ng/ml (a 0.20 ng/ml decline) in children from homes where both parents smoked, from 1.38 ng/ml to 1.23 ng/ml (a 0.15 ng/ml decline) from homes where the mother smoked, 0.57 ng/ml to 0.32 ng/ml (a 0.25 ng/ml decline) from homes where the father smoked, and from 0.14 ng/ml to 0.07 ng/ml (a 0.7 ng/ml decline) from homes where neither parent smoked (Fig 2.5). However, the largest relative falls were seen in those least exposed at the outset – children living in homes where neither parent smoked (51%) or where only the father smoked (44%). A comparison of children from homes where both parents smoked with those where neither parent smoked shows that the absolute differences in mean cotinine fell from 1.8 ng/ml before the legislation to 1.67 ng/ml afterwards, but that relative differences increased from a 14-fold ratio before legislation to 25-fold after legislation.[10] Exposure levels in children of smokers thus remain high, and marked inequalities in passive smoking exposure persist.

2.4 Data from Northern Ireland

A study of non-smoking children in Northern Ireland, of similar design to the Scottish study outlined above, found a small but non-significant drop in children's geometric mean cotinine concentration following the introduction of smoke-free legislation, from 0.174 ng/ml to 0.159 ng/ml – a mean decrease of 0.015 ng/ml, or about 9%.[12] The smaller decline compared with Scotland and England may be due to Northern Ireland having much lower levels of cotinine before the legislation was introduced (0.174 ng/ml, compared with 0.36 ng/ml in Scotland). There was a reduction in self-reported passive smoke exposure in a range of public places (for example, the percentage of children who reported someone smoking in cafes or restaurants reduced from 27% to 8%), and more home smoking restrictions were observed (for example, the percentage of children who reported that smoking is allowed anywhere in their home reduced from 15% to 10%) following the introduction of legislation. These resulted in a significant increase in the proportion of children reporting they were 'never' in a location where someone else was smoking, from 8% to 12%. However, the extent of this change varied by parental smoking status. Significantly more children reported 'never' being in a smoking location if neither parent smoked, or only the father smoked, but not if only the mother or both parents smoked.

2.5 Data from Wales

A recently published study from Wales also examined changes in geometric mean salivary cotinine in children aged 10–11 from 75 Welsh primary schools immediately pre-legislation and one year later.[13] Concentrations did not fall significantly overall: mean cotinine concentrations were 0.17 ng/ml pre-legislation and 0.15 ng/ml post-legislation (compared with 0.36 ng/ml and 0.22 ng/ml respectively in Scotland). Significant movement was, however, observed from the middle (0.10–0.50 ng/ml) to lower tertile, though not from the higher end (>0.51 ng/ml) to the middle. Again, it is notable that the exposure levels in Wales were considerably lower than those in Scotland.

2.6 Data from other countries

As has been observed in England and Scotland, many other countries have experienced a gradual reduction in passive smoke exposure over recent years, probably arising from reductions in smoking prevalence, tobacco consumption, and changes in where smoking occurs.[14] Thus, there is overwhelming evidence, from a large number of jurisdictions and a recent systematic review, that restrictions on smoking in public places lead to declines in passive smoke exposure.[14] Indeed, this has been seen in every country examined, although there are variations in the extent to which population subgroups are differentially affected.[14] Importantly, such evidence also shows that the implementation of public smoking restrictions is not linked to increased exposures in other settings.[14] It is instead associated with reduced exposure to passive smoke and greater adoption of smoke-free policies in homes, with such evidence seen, for example, in the USA,[14–16] Australia,[15–16] Ireland[17] and New Zealand.[18]

2.7 Summary

- Children are particularly vulnerable to passive smoke exposure, most of which occurs in the home.
- The most important determinants of passive smoke exposure in children are whether their parents or carers smoke, and whether smoking is allowed in the home.
- Relative to children whose parents are non-smokers, passive smoke exposure in children is typically around three times higher if the father smokes, over six times higher if the mother smokes, and nearly nine times higher if both parents smoke.

- Smoking by other carers is also a significant source of passive smoke exposure.
- Children who live in households where someone smokes on most days are exposed to about seven times more smoke than children who live in smoke-free homes.
- Children who live with non-smoking parents are much more likely to live in smoke-free homes than those whose parents are smokers.
- Children from socio-economically disadvantaged backgrounds are generally more heavily exposed to smoke than other children, probably because of heavier smoking inside the family home and in other places visited by children.
- The overall level of passive smoke exposure in children has fallen substantially over recent years.
- This is probably because the number of parents and carers who smoke, and the number of parents who allow smoking inside the family home, have both fallen over this period.
- The reductions in passive smoke exposure have occurred in all sectors of society, but a significant proportion of children are still exposed, and exposure is still greatest among lower socio-economic status households.

References

1 Royal College of Physicians. *Going smoke-free: the medical case for clean air in the home, at work and in public places.* Report of a working party. London: RCP, 2005.

2 Ashley MJ, Ferrence R. Reducing children's exposure to environmental tobacco smoke in homes: issues and strategies. *Tob Control* 1998;7(1):61–5.

3 Willers S, Skarping G, Dalene M, Skerfving S. Urinary cotinine in children and adults during and after semiexperimental exposure to environmental tobacco smoke. *Arch Environ Health* 1995;50(2):130–8.

4 Jarvis MJ, Goddard E, Higgins V *et al.* Children's exposure to passive smoking in England since the 1980s: cotinine evidence from population surveys. *BMJ* 2000 Aug 5;321(7257): 343–5.

5 Health Survey for England homepage 2009. www.dh.gov.uk/en/Publicationsandstatistics/PublishedSurvey/HealthSurveyForEngland/index.htm

6 Benowitz NL. Cotinine as a biomarker of environmental tobacco smoke exposure. *Epidemiol Rev* 1996;18(2):188–204.

7 Jarvis MJ, Fidler J, Mindell J, Feyerabend C, West RJ. Assessing smoking status in children, adolescents and adults: cotinine cut-points revisited. *Addiction* 2008;103(9):1553–61.

8 Sims M, Tomkins S, Judge K *et al.* Trends in and predictors of second hand smoke exposure indexed by cotinine in children in England from 1996–2006. *Addiction* 2010; 105(3):543–53.

9 Jarvis MJ, Mindell J, Gilmore A, Feyerabend C, West R. Smoke-free homes in England: prevalence, trends and validation by cotinine in children. *Tob Control* 2009;18:491–5.

10 Akhtar PC, Currie DB, Currie CE, Haw SJ. Changes in child exposure to environmental tobacco smoke (CHETS) study after implementation of smoke-free legislation in Scotland: national cross sectional survey. *BMJ* 2007;335:545–9.

11 Haw SJ, Gruer L. Changes in exposure of adult non-smokers to secondhand smoke after implementation of smoke-free legislation in Scotland: national cross sectional survey. *BMJ* 2007;335(7619):549–52.

12 Health Promotion Agency. *Childhood exposure to tobacco smoke (CHETS) in Northern Ireland.* HPA, 2009.

13 Holliday J, Moore G, Moore L. Changes in child exposure to secondhand smoke after implementation of smoke-free legislation in Wales: a repeated cross-sectional study. *BMC Public Health* 2009;9(1):430.

14 International Agency for Research on Cancer. Reductions in exposure to secondhand smoke and effects on health due to restrictions on smoking. In: *IARC handbook of cancer prevention, tobacco control: evaluating the effectiveness of smoke-free policies,* Chapter 7. Lyon, France: WHO/IARC, 2009.

15 Borland R, Mullins R, Trotter L, White V. Trends in environmental tobacco smoke restrictions in the home in Victoria, Australia. *Tob Control* 1999;8(3):266–71.

16 Borland R, Yong HH, Cummings KM *et al.* Determinants and consequences of smoke-free homes: findings from the International Tobacco Control (ITC) Four Country Survey. *Tob Control* 2006;15 (suppl 3):iii42–50.

17 Fong GT, Hyland A, Borland R *et al.* Reductions in tobacco smoke pollution and increases in support for smoke-free public places following the implementation of comprehensive smoke-free workplace legislation in the Republic of Ireland: findings from the ITC Ireland/UK Survey. *Tob Control* 2006;15(suppl 3):iii51–8.

18 Edwards R, Thomson G, Wilson N *et al.* After the smoke has cleared: evaluation of the impact of a new national smoke-free law in New Zealand. *Tob Control* 2008;17(1):e2.

3 Effects of maternal active and passive smoking on fetal and reproductive health

3.1 Background

It has been recognised for many years that maternal smoking during pregnancy has substantial adverse effects on the fetus. There is extensive evidence from human and animal studies on the biological mechanisms of how tobacco smoke affects the female reproductive system and fetal development.[1–5] Many of the 4,000 chemicals in tobacco smoke, including nicotine and carbon monoxide, can cross the placental barrier and have a direct toxic effect on the fetus, as well as on the mother. Nicotine itself is a vasoconstrictor, causing restriction of blood flow to the placenta and the fetus. In one recent study, endothelial function, which is associated with regulating blood flow, was markedly lower in pregnant smokers compared to pregnant non-smokers.[2] Carbon monoxide binds to haemoglobin so that less oxygen is available to both mother and fetus, thus leading to fetal hypoxia, which in some instances can cause birth defects. Cadmium from tobacco smoke accumulates in the placenta and may affect fetal growth. Exposure to tobacco smoke also disrupts the formation of new blood vessels, a process integral to fetal development, including the development of the neurological system which regulates the heart and circulation.

Given the potential adverse effects of all of these biologically plausible mechanisms on fetal growth, maternal smoking in pregnancy is clearly a potential cause of major morbidity and mortality to the fetus and newborn baby. Most research on the adverse effects of smoking on the fetus has been carried out in relation to active maternal smoking, but fetal exposure also occurs as a result of maternal exposure to passive smoke. In this chapter we review the evidence available on the adverse effects of active and passive smoking among pregnant women. Where possible, we have used published definitive systematic reviews to summarise the available evidence. Where definitive reviews are not available, we have carried out our own searches and meta-analyses. For data on the effects of active maternal smoking, for which an extensive literature is available, we have, for convenience, limited our reviews to the larger published studies. For the effects of maternal passive smoke exposure, we have carried out comprehensive reviews.

3.2 Prevalence of smoking among pregnant women

In England in 2006, 32% of all expectant women smoked just before or during pregnancy, and 17% continued to smoke throughout pregnancy.[6] In Scotland, the overall prevalence of smoking during pregnancy was 23% in 2005.[7] In England, women under 20 years of age are five times as likely to smoke throughout pregnancy as women aged 30 years or over (smoking prevalence 45% and 9% respectively).[6] The prevalence of maternal smoking is strongly and inversely associated with age and occupation (an indicator of socio-economic status) (Table 3.1). Women in routine or manual work are four times as likely to smoke throughout pregnancy as women in management or professional work (smoking prevalence 29% and 7% respectively).[6] Young, socially disadvantaged women are therefore highly likely to smoke through pregnancy. Less than half of women who smoke are successful in quitting smoking before or during pregnancy.[6]

3.3 Effects of maternal active smoking on fertility and the fetus

3.3.1 Fertility

Around 25% of women of reproductive age experience infertility at some point in their lives. Infertility is usually defined as failure to achieve conception after 12 consecutive months of unprotected intercourse. A systematic review of 12 observational (cohort and case-control) studies, based on 50,166 women in total, showed that women who smoke are less likely to conceive, or take longer to conceive than non-smokers.[8] There was a 60% increase in the risk of infertility compared with non-smokers (relative risk (RR) 1.60, 95% CI 1.34 to 1.91), based on all studies; the pooled excess risk among the eight cohort studies (20,059 women) was 42% (RR 1.42, 95% CI 1.27 to 1.58).[8] Several individual studies in the review found that the risk of infertility increased with increasing cigarette consumption – evidence of a dose–response relationship. Adjustment for potential confounding factors (such as age, alcohol use, education and parity – see also section 3.6) did

Table 3.1 Smoking prevalence in pregnant women in England (2005) according to age and socio-economic status.[6]

	Percentage of women smoking	
Maternal age	**Before or during pregnancy**	**Throughout pregnancy**
≤20	68	45
21–24	49	28
25–29	29	14
30–34	23	9
35+	20	9
All	32	17
	Percentage of women smoking	
Occupational group	**Before or during pregnancy**	**Throughout pregnancy**
Routine, manual	48	29
Intermediate	30	12
Managerial, professional	19	7
Other	31	17
Never worked	33	23
All	32	17

not materially alter the risk estimates reported by several studies. There is also evidence that active smoking among men damages sperm and is associated with male sexual impotence.[1]

3.3.2 Fetal mortality

Fetal death is generally referred to as a spontaneous abortion or miscarriage if it occurs before the 20th (sometimes 24th) week of pregnancy, and perinatal mortality if it occurs between 20 weeks (or 24 weeks) of pregnancy and the first week of life. Deaths in the week after birth are classified as neonatal deaths. The association between maternal smoking and an increased risk of fetal mortality has been recognised since the late 1950s, and governmental reports from both the USA and UK have identified this as a major adverse outcome of maternal smoking since 1969, as summarised in reports from the Department of Health and Human

Services.[9,10] A 1995 systematic review and meta-analysis of the effect of maternal smoking on perinatal mortality, using data from 23 cohort studies, including 657,288 pregnancies, found a 26% increase in the risk of perinatal deaths (RR 1.26, 95% CI 1.19 to 1.34).[11] In the UK, with a prevalence of maternal smoking of about 20%, that would theoretically result in around 300 perinatal deaths per year attributable to smoking.

The 1995 review also analysed data on spontaneous abortion from seven cohort studies based on 86,632 pregnancies, and found a 24% increase in risk (RR 1.24, 95% CI 1.19 to 1.30) among smokers compared to non-smokers. In a further analysis of data from six case-control studies (10,535 pregnancies) the increase in risk of spontaneous abortion was 32% (RR 1.32, 95% CI 1.18 to 1.48).[11] Using these results, and a smoking prevalence of between 18% and 27%, the authors estimated that 3% to 7.5% of all miscarriages could be attributable to smoking.[11] Individual studies in the review that allowed for the effects of possible confounding factors (such as maternal age, previous miscarriage, alcohol consumption, education and ethnicity) still found a raised risk. There was also evidence of a dose–response relationship between cigarette consumption and risk of miscarriage. Each year in the UK, an estimated 3,000 to 5,000 miscarriages are caused by maternal smoking.[1]

3.3.3 Small for gestational age and low birth weight

Several studies have examined the association between maternal smoking and restricted fetal growth during pregnancy (intrauterine growth retardation). A measure of intrauterine growth retardation is whether the fetus is small for its gestational age, defined as being in the lowest 10% (sometimes 15%) of body weights for that gestation. These studies were reviewed in the US Surgeon General's report in 2004,[10] and indicated that pregnant women who smoked were 1.5 to 2.5 times more likely to have a baby that was small for gestational age.

Maternal smoking is an established cause of low birth weight, an important factor associated with infant morbidity and mortality. Babies from mothers who have smoked through pregnancy weigh an average of 250 g less than those from non-smoking mothers.[9,10,12] Babies are usually classified as having low birth weight if they weigh less than 2,500 g at birth. In a systematic review of 22 studies, based on data from 347,553 pregnancies, women who smoke had an 82% increase in risk (RR 1.82, 95% CI 1.67 to 1.97), compared with non-smokers, of giving birth to a low birth weight baby.[11] All but one of these studies reported statistically significant results. Each year in the UK, an estimated 14,000 to 19,000 babies are born with low birth weight attributable to maternal smoking.[1] Additional evidence that the association is causal comes from randomised trials of smoking cessation during pregnancy showing that birth weight is increased when the mother quits smoking.[12,13]

3.3.4 Premature births

Preterm delivery is usually defined as birth before 37 weeks of pregnancy. Preterm birth is a major cause of infant mortality, and can affect physical and mental development during childhood.[14,15] A systematic review of 20 prospective cohort studies, based on 65,910 pregnancies, of which 6,183 were premature, showed that maternal smoking increased the risk of having a premature birth by 27% (odds ratio (OR) 1.27, 95% CI 1.21 to 1.33).[16] There was evidence of a dose–response relationship: light or moderate smokers (fewer than 10 or sometimes 20 cigarettes per day) had a 22% increase in risk, and heavy smokers (more than 20 cigarettes per day) had a 31% excess risk. In the UK, a prevalence of maternal smoking of 20% and an OR estimate of 1.27 could lead to around 2,200 premature singleton births per year that are attributable to smoking.

3.3.5 Congenital malformations

In England and Wales in 2004, 5,677 babies born alive or stillborn had at least one birth defect (excluding those with a chromosomal abnormality), representing a birth prevalence of 9 per 1,000 each year.[17] Congenital malformations vary widely in severity, but can cause significant physical and mental morbidity to the child and parents, and result in significant and sometimes lifelong healthcare costs. It is plausible that the narrowing of blood vessels caused by substances in tobacco smoke (some of which were referred to in Section 3.1) might lead to teratogenic effects arising from ischaemia, necrosis, and ultimately resorption of body structures during early development.[18] Many research studies have examined the association between maternal smoking and a variety of congenital abnormalities, but there has not been a full systematic review in this field. We therefore provide (in Tables 3.2 to 3.8) the results of the available larger observational studies of maternal active smoking and a range of congenital anomalies,[18–49] identified from an electronic search of the medical literature (Medline 1966–2009).

3.3.5.1 All congenital abnormalities

It is unclear whether smoking is associated with an increased risk of all malformations combined (Table 3.2). The largest available study, based on over 1.4 million

Table 3.2 Studies of the association between maternal active smoking and the risk of all malformations considered together.

First author	Study type	Source	Year	Number of unaffected infants	Number of affected infants	RR	Potential confounders allowed for†
Butler 1969[20]	Cohort	British Perinatal Mortality Survey (UK)	1958	15,708	97	1.18 (0.77 to 1.80)	None
Kelsey 1978[31]	Case-control	Connecticut hospitals (USA)	1974–1976	2,968	1,369	1.10 (0.96 to 1.26)	None
Evans 1979[24]	Cohort	Cardiff Births Survey (UK)	1965–1976	65,745*	1,864	0.98 (0.89 to 1.07)	None
Shiono 1986[45]	Cohort	Kaiser Permanente Birth Defects Study (USA)	1974–1977	28,810	592 major defects	1.0 (0.8 to 1.2)	M, R A
					4,032 minor defects	0.9 (0.8 to 0.9)	as above
Malloy 1989[36]	Cohort	Missouri Birth Defects Registry (USA)	1980–1983	277,844	10,223	0.98 (0.94 to 1.03)	M, R, S, E, P
Seidman 1990[43]	Cohort	Jerusalem hospitals (Israel)	1974–1976	17,152 in total	1,767 major malformations	0.94 (0.62 to 1.43)	M, P, R, E, S, J, H
					11,183 minor malformations	1.06 (0.90 to 1.25)	as above
Van Den Eeden 1990[48]	Case-control	Washington State Birth Records (USA)	1984–1986	4,500	3,048	1.0 (0.9 to 1.1)	M, P

continued over

Table 3.2 Studies of the association between maternal active smoking and the risk of all malformations considered together – *continued.*

First author	Study type	Source	Year	Number of unaffected infants	Number of affected infants	RR	Potential confounders allowed for†
Kallen 2000[30]	Cohort	Swedish Registry of Congenital Malformations	1983–1996	1,387,192	26,619 all malformations	1.03 (1.0 to 1.06)	M, B, P, E
					25,210 (isolated)	1.02 (0.99 to 1.05)	as above
					1,409 (≥2 malformations)	1.15 (1.02 to 1.29)	as above
Morales-Suarez-Varela 2006[40]	Cohort	Danish National Birth Cohort	1997–2003	73,001	3,767	1.10 (1.0 to 1.2)	M, A

* Could have other abnormalities

† Abbreviations: A = alcohol; B = birth year or month; C = coffee; D = diabetes; E = education; G = registry; H = history of miscarriage; J = occupation; M = maternal age; O = birth order; P = parity; R = race/ethnicity; S = marital status; V = various maternal disorders.

pregnant women,[30] reported a small (3%) but statistically significant increase in risk and, among smokers of 10 or more cigarettes per day, a 34% increase in risk of having a baby with two or more malformations. However, whilst this study adjusted for a range of confounding effects, it did not control for the effect of alcohol intake. The next largest study, of 288,067 women, found no evidence of an increase in risk of congenital malformation,[36] whilst a study of 76,768 women reported in 2006[40] suggested a 10% increase in risk after allowing for maternal age and alcohol intake. The evidence is therefore inconsistent, but the absence of a clear effect on all abnormalities does not exclude significant effects on individual or subgroups of abnormality.

3.3.5.2 Heart defects

Congenital heart defects represent one of the most common and serious birth anomalies in developing countries. In England and Wales in 2004, these defects accounted for over a fifth of all congenital abnormalities, [17] and in the USA they occur in 8–10 of every 1,000 live births.[35] Surviving infants often require several operations during their lifetime. Table 3.3 shows the results of selected studies of maternal smoking and cardiovascular disease of infants at birth. The largest of these studies indicated a 15% increase in the risk of having a baby with a heart defect,[30] but this is not apparent in all the other large studies. However, the case-control study by Malik *et al*,[35] which had the greatest number of infants with a heart defect (n=3,067), reported a clear adverse effect of smoking on septal defects, with a 50% increase in risk for all types and a doubling of the risk for atrial septal defects. This study adjusted for the effects of several potential confounders, including maternal age and alcohol intake.

3.3.5.3 Musculoskeletal defects

Musculoskeletal defects of the muscles, bones and limbs include a range of problems such as missing or extra fingers or toes, missing or underdeveloped limbs, and clubfoot. They are the most common birth abnormality, and in England and Wales in 2004, constituted 34% of all congenital anomaly cases.[17] Of the studies in Table 3.4 that reported results for all such defects combined, there was little evidence of an increased risk. However, a clearer effect is seen for limb reduction defects, which include the absence or severe underdevelopment of the hands or feet (transverse limb reductions), or of the radius, tibia, ulna or fibula (longitudinal limb reductions). All of the five studies on limb reduction defects reported raised risks associated with maternal smoking,[18,19,30,45,48] with two that were

Table 3.3 Studies of the association between maternal active smoking and the risk of heart/cardiovascular defects.

First author	Study type	Source	Year	Number of unaffected infants	Number of affected infants	RR	Potential confounders allowed for†
Kelsey 1978[31]	Case-control	Connecticut hospitals (USA)	1974–1976	2,968	213 septal defects	1.05	None
Evans 1979[24]	Cohort	Cardiff Births Survey (UK)	1965–1976	67,386*	223	0.80 (0.61 to 1.05)	None
Christianson 1980[23]	Cohort	Kaiser Foundation Health Plan (USA)	1959–1966	12,054*	102	0.99 (0.67 to 1.47)	None
Shiono 1986[45]	Cohort	Collaborative Perinatal Project (USA)	1959–1966	53,512*	9 atrial septal defects	0.7 (0.2 to 3.5)	M, R, A
					62 ventricular septal defects	0.5 (0.2 to 0.96)	as above
	Cohort	Kaiser Permanente Birth Defects Study	1974–1977	33,434*	21 ventricular septal defects	1.3 (0.5 to 2.9)	as above
Malloy 1989[36]	Cohort	Missouri Birth Defects Registry (USA)	1980–1983	277,844	1,341	0.92 (0.82 to 1.05)	M, R, S, E, P
Van Den Eeden 1990[48]	Case-control	Washington State Birth Records (USA)	1984–1986	4,500	655	0.9 (0.8 to 1.2)	M, P
McDonald 1992[38]	Cohort	Several Montreal hospitals (Canada)	1982–1984	87,389	318	1.14 (0.92 to 1.40)	M, A, C, E

continued

Table 3.3 Studies of the association between maternal active smoking and the risk of heart/cardiovascular defects – *continued.*

First author	Study type	Source	Year	Number of unaffected infants	Number of affected infants	RR	Potential confounders allowed for†
Pradat 1992[41]	Case-control	Swedish Registry of Congenital Malformations	1981–1986	2,648	1,324	0.94 (0.78 to 1.14)	None
Shaw 1992[44]	Case-control	California Birth Defects Monitoring Program (USA)	1981–1983	176	141	1.21 (0.71 to 2.07)	None
Tikkanen 1992[46]	Case-control	Finnish Register of Congenital Malformations	1982–1983	756	50 atrial septal defects	0.71 (0.33 to 1.53)	M
Tikkanen 1992[47]	Case-control	Finnish Register of Congenital Malformations	1982–1983	756	90 conal defects	1.04 (0.61 to 1.76)	None
Kallen 2000[30]	Cohort	Swedish Registry of Congenital Malformations	1983–1996	1,387,192	13,266	1.15 (1.10 to 1.20)	M, I, P, E, K
Woods 2001[49]	Cohort	TriHealth Hospital system (USA)	1998–1999	18,016 in total	260	1.56 (1.12 to 2.19)	M, R, D
Cedergren 2002[22]	Case-control	Medical Birth Register (Sweden)	1982–1983	524	269	1.19 (0.84 to 1.68)	None
Cedergren 2006[21]	Cohort	Swedish Medical Birth Registry	1992–2001	764,009	6,346	0.97 (0.91 to 1.04)	None
Morales-Suarez-Varela 2006[40]	Cohort	Danish National Birth Cohort	1997–2003	73,001	746	1.2 (1.0 to 1.4)	M, A

continued over

Table 3.3 Studies of the association between maternal active smoking and the risk of heart/cardiovascular defects – *continued.*

First author	Study type	Source	Year	Number of unaffected infants	Number of affected infants	RR	Potential confounders allowed for†
Grewal 2008[26]	Case-control	California hospitals (USA)	1999–2003	691	320 cono-truncal heart defects	0.78 (0.45 to 1.34)	None
Malik 2008[35]	Case-control	National Birth Defects Prevention Study	1997–2002	773	147 cono-truncal defects	1.00 (0.81 to 1.22)	M, G, R, H, L, C
				693	302 septal defects (all)	1.50 (1.28 to 1.76)	as above
				693	97 atrial septal defects	1.98 (1.53 to 1.57)	as above
				693	138 ventricular septal defects	1.34 (1.08 to 1.65)	as above

* Could have other abnormalities.

† Abbreviations: A = alcohol; B = birth year; C = caffeine; D = diabetes; E = education; G = infant gender; H = family history of heart defects; I = body mass index; K = kidney dysgenesis of infant; L = location; M = maternal age; P = parity; R = race/ethnicity; S = marital status.

Table 3.4 Studies of the association between maternal active smoking and the risk of musculoskeletal defects.

First author	Study type	Source	Year	Number of unaffected infants	Number of affected infants	RR	Potential confounders allowed for†
Kelsey 1978[31]	Case-control	Connecticut hospitals (USA)	1974–1976	2,968	73 clubfoot	1.21	None
					50 digit anomaly#	0.69	None
Evans 1979[24]	Cohort	Cardiff Births Survey (UK)	1965–1976	66,894*	715 musculo-skeletal	0.86 (0.74 to 1.00)	None
Christianson 1980[23]	Cohort	Kaiser Foundation Health Plan (USA)	1959–1966	11,787	369 musculo-skeletal	0.77 (0.62 to 0.95)	None
Aro 1983[19]	Case-control	Finnish Registry of Congenital Malformations	1964–1977	453	453 limb reduction defects	1.3 (0.9 to 2.0)	M, A
Shiono 1986[45]	Cohort	Kaiser Permanente Birth Defects Study (USA)	1974–1977	28,810	368 clubfoot	0.7 (0.6 to 0.9)	M, R A
					73 polydactyly	1.0 (0.6 to 1.6)	as above
					34 syndactyly	0.7 (0.3 to 1.5)	as above
					17 limb reduction	2.2 (0.9 to 5.8)	as above
		Collaborative Perinatal Project (USA)	1959–1966	53,512	116 clubfoot	0.9 (0.6 to 1.3)	M, R A

continued over

Table 3.4 Studies of the association between maternal active smoking and the risk of musculoskeletal defects – *continued.*

First author	Study type	Source	Year	Number of unaffected infants	Number of affected infants	RR	Potential confounders allowed for†
Malloy 1989[36]	Cohort	Missouri Birth Defects Registry (USA)	1980–1983	277,844	3,705 musculo-skeletal	0.99 (0.92 to 1.06)	M, R, S, E, P
					980 clubfoot	1.02 (0.88 to 1.17)	as above
Van Den Eeden 1990[48]	Case-control	Washington State Birth Records (USA)	1984–1986	4,500	571 skeletal defects	1.1 (0.9 to 1.3)	M, P
					171 clubfoot	1.4 (1.0 to 2.0)	as above
					95 polydactyly	0.9 (0.6 to 1.5)	as above
					35 limb reduction	1.2 (0.6 to 2.5)	as above
McDonald 1992[38]	Cohort	Montreal hospitals (Canada)	1982–1984	89,317 in total	614 clubfoot	1.01 (0.86 to 1.19)	M, E, R, A, C
					223 musculo-skeletal	1.05 (0.80 to 1.36)	as above
Czeizel 1994[18]	Case-control	Hungarian Abnormality Registry	1975–1984	537	537 limb reduction	1.68 (1.26 to 2.24)	E, O
Reefhuis 1998[42]	Cohort	26 European Registries of Congenital Anomalies	1980–1994	7,829 chro-mosomal defects	2,905 foot defects	1.2 (1.1 to 1.3)	M, G, P, B

continued

Table 3.4 Studies of the association between maternal active smoking and the risk of musculoskeletal defects – *continued.*

First author	Study type	Source	Year	Number of unaffected infants	Number of affected infants	RR	Potential confounders allowed for†
Kallen 2000[30]	Cohort	Swedish Registry of Congenital Malformations	1983–1996	1,387,192	1,023 limb reduction	1.26 (1.11 to 1.44)	None
					3,190 digit anomaly#	0.97 (0.89 to 1.05)	None
Honein 2001[28]	Cohort	National Vital Statistics (USA)	1997–1998	6,161,506 in total	5,573 digit anomaly#	1.33 (1.23 to 1.43)	M, E, R
					3,894 clubfoot	1.62 (1.49 to 1.75)	as above
Woods 2001[49]	Cohort	TriHealth Hospital system (USA)	1998–1999	18,016 in total	14 polydactyly	1.32 (0.28 to 6.12)	M R, D
					16 foot defect	0.56 (0.07 to 4.30)	as above
Man 2006[37]	Case-control	US Natality Database (USA)	2001–2002	10,342	5,171 digital anomaly#	1.31 (1.18 to 1.45)	M, V

* Could have other abnormalities
# Missing, fused or extra fingers or toes (polydactyly, syndactyly, adactyly)
† Abbreviations: A = alcohol; B = birth year or month; C = coffee; D = diabetes; E = education; G = country registry; M = maternal age; O = birth order; P = parity; R = race/ethnicity; S = marital status; V = various maternal disorders.

statistically significant.[18,30] Together, these studies are based on 2,065 infants with limb reduction defects and 1,421,492 controls, and the pooled excess risk associated with smoking is 32% (OR 1.32, 95% CI 1.19 to 1.48). Czeizel *et al* suggested that the effect was primarily on transverse limb reductions,[23] but their analysis was limited by the smaller number of infants in this subgroup.

A large multi-centre European study based on 2,905 babies with a defect of the foot demonstrated a 20% increase in the risk of clubfoot in the babies of mothers who smoked (RR 1.20, 95% CI 1.10 to 1.30),[42] whilst a US study of 3,894 infants reported a 62% excess risk (RR 1.62, 95% CI 1.49 to 1.75).[28] Furthermore, the two studies with the largest number of infants with a digital anomaly (missing or extra fingers or toes), Honein *et al*[28] (5,573 cases) and Man *et al*[37] (5,171 cases), each reported an approximate 30% excess risk. However, the evidence was not consistent across studies. For example, there seemed to be no increase in the risk of digital anomaly in the large study from Kallen[30] (3,190 cases).

3.3.5.4 Defects of the gastrointestinal or genitourinary systems

Tables 3.5 and 3.6 summarise the larger available studies of maternal smoking and gastrointestinal or genitourinary defects of infants at birth. There does not appear to be a strong or clear effect on these anomalies, but there is a suggestion of an association with anal atresia (RR approximately 1.20), gastroschisis (RR 1.5–2.0), and perhaps kidney/urinary tract defects (RR approximately 1.2–1.5). However, further studies on these disorders are needed to provide more reliable estimates of the excess risk, and to look for the degree of consistency between studies.

3.3.5.5 Defects of the central nervous system

The most common defects of the central nervous system (CNS) are spina bifida and anencephaly. Table 3.7 shows data from selected studies of maternal smoking and CNS defects of infants at birth. There is no strong evidence of an effect on risk.

3.3.5.6 Defects of the face, eyes, ears and neck

Defects of the head (including face, eyes, ears and neck) account for 10% of all congenital anomalies in England,[17] and are a cause of significant psychological morbidity. A few large studies have reported the association between maternal smoking and defects of the face and neck, except cleft lip and palate (Table 3.8), but there is insufficient evidence of any clear effect. However, a systematic review of 25 cohort and case-control studies (from 24 reports) has shown a highly

Table 3.5 Studies of the association between maternal active smoking and the risk of gastrointestinal defects.

First author	Study type	Source	Year	Number of unaffected infants	Number of affected infants	RR	Potential confounders allowed for†
Kelsey 1978[31]	Case-control	Connecticut hospitals (USA)	1974–1976	2,968	56	1.55	None
Evans 1979[24]	Cohort	Cardiff Births Survey (UK)	1965–1976	66,894*	134	1.09 (0.78 to 1.53)	None
Christianson 1980[23]	Cohort	Kaiser Foundation Health Plan (USA)	1959–1966	11,765	391	1.38 (1.13 to 1.69)	None
Malloy 1989[36]	Cohort	Missouri Birth Defects Registry (USA)	1980–1983	277,844	961	1.11 (0.96 to 1.29)	M, R, S, E, P
Goldbaum 1990[25]	Case-control	Washington State Birth Registry (USA)	1984–1987	617	62 gastroschisis	2.0 (1.03 to 3.8)	M, B, R, S, J, P, H
Van Den Eeden 1990[48]	Case-control	Washington State Birth Records (USA)	1984–1986	4,500	35 anal atresia	0.9 (0.4 to 2.2)	M, P
					66 omphalocele	1.4 (0.8 to 2.4)	as above
McDonald 1992[38]	Cohort	Montreal hospitals (Canada)	1982–1984	89,317 in total	109 digestive, respiratory	0.97 (0.67 to 1.40)	M, E, R, A, C
Haddow 1993[27]	Cohort	Foundation for Blood Research screening (USA)	1980–1989	67,103	21 gastroschisis	2.1 (0.9 to 4.8)	M, B

continued over

Table 3.5 Studies of the association between maternal active smoking and the risk of gastrointestinal defects – *continued.*

First author	Study type	Source	Year	Number of unaffected infants	Number of affected infants	RR	Potential confounders allowed for†
Kallen 2000[30]	Cohort	Swedish Registry of Congenital Malformations	1983–1996	1,387,192	1,402	1.01 (0.89 to 1.14)	None
					410 anal atresia	1.29 (1.02 to 1.63)	M, B, P, E, K
Honein 2001[28]	Cohort	National Vital Statistics (USA)	1997–1998	6,161,506 in total	564 anal atresia	1.19 (0.94 to 1.50)	M, E, R
					1,972 omphalocele, gastroschisis	1.37 (1.22 to 1.53)	as above
Woods 2001[49]	Cohort	TriHealth Hospital system (USA)	1998–1999	18,016 in total	18	0.54 (0.07 to 4.11)	M R, D
Morales-Suarez-Varela 2006[40]	Cohort	Danish National Birth Cohort	1997–2003	73,001	214	1.3 (1.0 to 1.7)	M, A
Miller 2009[39]	Case-control	National Birth Defects Prevention Study (USA)	1997–2003	4,940	464 anal atresia	1.2 (1.0 to 1.5)	None

† Abbreviations: A = alcohol; B = birth year or month; C = coffee; D = diabetes; E = education; H = history of miscarriage; J = occupation; K = kidney dysgenesis of infant; M = maternal age; P = parity; R = race/ethnicity; S = marital status.

Table 3.6 Studies that have examined the association between maternal active smoking and the risk of defects of the genitourinary system or renal tract.

First author	Study type	Source	Year	Number of unaffected infants	Number of affected infants	RR	Potential confounders allowed for†
Evans 1979[24]	Cohort	Cardiff Births Survey (UK)	1965–1976	66,894*	134	1.09 (0.78 to 1.53)	None
Christianson 1980[23]	Cohort	Kaiser Foundation Health Plan (USA)	1959–1966	11,973	183	0.99 (0.74 to 1.33)	None
Malloy 1989[36]	Cohort	Missouri Birth Defects Registry (USA)	1980–1983	277,844	1,622	0.97 (0.86 to 1.08)	M, R, S, E, P
McDonald 1992[38]	Cohort	Montreal hospitals (Canada)	1982–1984	89,317 in total	209	1.36 (1.06 to 1.75)	M, E, R, A, C
Li 1996[33]	Case-control	Washington State Birth Defect Registry (USA)	1990–1991	369	118 urinary tract defect	2.3 (1.2 to 4.5)	E, P, L, B, U, I
Kallen 1997[29]	Cohort	Swedish Registry of Congenital Malformations	1983–1993	1,115,819*	1,202	1.04 (0.92 to 1.19)	M, P, B
					483 kidney defects**	1.22 (1.00 to 1.48)	as above
					719 other urinary tract defects	0.93 (0.79 to 1.11)	as above

continued over

Table 3.6 Studies that have examined the association between maternal active smoking and the risk of defects of the genitourinary system or renal tract – *continued.*

First author	Study type	Source	Year	Number of unaffected infants	Number of affected infants	RR	Potential confounders allowed for†
Woods 2001[49]	Cohort	TriHealth Hospital system (USA)	1998–1999	18,016 in total	288	0.93 (0.63 to 1.37)	M R, D
Morales-Suarez-Varela 2006[40]	Cohort	Danish National Birth Cohort	1997–2003	73,001	174	0.7 (0.5 to 1.0)	M, A

* Could have other abnormalities
** Kidney agenesis or dysgenesis (missing or deformed kidney)
† Abbreviations: A = alcohol; AA = anal atresia of infant; B = birth year or month; C = coffee; D = diabetes; E = education; I = income; L = county; M = maternal age; P = parity; R = race/ethnicity; S = marital status; U = use of prenatal vitamins or illicit drugs.

Table 3.7 Studies of the association between maternal active smoking and the risk of defects of the central nervous system (CNS).

First author	Study type	Source	Year	Number of unaffected infants	Number of affected infants	RR	Potential confounders allowed for†
Kelsey 1978[31]	Case-control	Connecticut hospitals (USA)	1974–1976	2,968	82#	1.36	None
Evans 1979[24]	Cohort	Cardiff Births Survey (UK)	1965–1976	66,989*	620	1.08 (0.92 to 1.26)	None
Christianson 1980[23]	Cohort	Kaiser Foundation Health Plan (USA)	1959–1966	12,054	158	0.98 (0.71 to 1.35)	None
Malloy 1989[36]	Cohort	Missouri Birth Defects Registry (USA)	1980–1983	277,844	489	1.04 (0.85 to 1.26)	M, R, S, E, P
Van Den Eeden 1990[48]	Case-control	Washington State Birth Records (USA)	1984–1986	4,500	161	0.9 (0.6 to 1.3)	M, P
McDonald 1992[38]	Cohort	Montreal hospitals (Canada)	1982–1984	89,317 in total	190 neural tube defect	1.37 (1.06 to 1.77)	M, E, R, A, C
Kallen 2000[30]	Cohort	Swedish Registry of Congenital Malformations	1983–1996	1,387,192	856**	1.00 (0.86 to 1.17)	None
Honein 2001[28]	Cohort	National Vital Statistics (USA)	1997–1998	6,161,506 in total	747 anencephaly	0.80 (0.63 to 1.03)	M, E, R
					1,563 spina bifida	1.02 (0.88 to 1.19)	as above

continued over

Table 3.7 Studies of the association between maternal active smoking and the risk of defects of the central nervous system (CNS) – *continued.*

First author	Study type	Source	Year	Number of unaffected infants	Number of affected infants	RR	Potential confounders allowed for†
Woods 2001[49]	Cohort	TriHealth Hospital system (USA)	1998–1999	18,016 in total	264	1.30 (0.91 to 1.86)	M, R, D
					11 spina bifida	0.83 (0.10 to 6.70)	as above
Morales-Suarez-Varela 2006[40]	Cohort	Danish National Birth Cohort	1997–2003	73,001	110	1.0 (0.7 to 1.6)	M, A
Grewal 2008[26]	Case-control	California hospitals (USA)	1999–2003	620	336	0.40 (0.20 to 0.78)	None

* Could have other abnormalities
# Anencephaly, spina bifida, hydrocephalus
** Anencephaly, spina bifida, encephalocele
† Abbreviations: A = alcohol; C = coffee; D = diabetes; E = education; M = maternal age; P = parity; R = race/ethnicity; S = marital status.

Table 3.8 Studies of the association between maternal active smoking and the risk of defects of the eye, face, neck and ears (not cleft lip or palate).

First author	Study type	Source	Year	Number of unaffected infants	Number of affected infants	RR	Potential confounders allowed for†
Christianson 1980[23]	Cohort	Kaiser Foundation Health Plan (USA)	1959–1966	11,684	472 eye defects	1.15 (0.96 to 1.38)	None
				12,054	120 defects of ear, face, neck	0.76 (0.52 to 1.11)	None
Malloy 1989[36]	Cohort	Missouri Birth Defects Registry (USA)	1980–1983	277,844	533 defects of ear, face, eye, neck	0.84 (0.68 to 1.02)	M, R, S, E, P
Kallen 2000[30]	Cohort	Swedish Registry of Congenital Malformations	1983–1996	1,387,192	615 eye defects	0.98 (0.81 to 1.18)	None
Morales-Suarez-Varela 2006[40]	Cohort	Danish National Birth Cohort	1997–2003	73,001	142 defects of ear, face, eye, neck	0.7 (0.5 to 1.0)	M, A

†Abbreviations: A = alcohol; E = education; M = maternal age; P = parity; R = race/ethnicity; S = marital status.

statistically significant association with cleft lip and palate.[34] Based on over 15,200 infants born with cleft lip and/or palate among 7.78 million births, the pooled increased risk associated with smoking for cleft lip, with or without a cleft palate, was 34% (RR 1.34, 95% CI 1.25 to 1.44), and the excess risk for cleft palate alone was 22% (RR 1.22, 95% CI 1.10 to 1.35). Several individual studies have also reported evidence of an exposure–response relation with increasing cigarette consumption. Most studies made allowance for potential confounding factors such as alcohol in the analysis.

3.4 Prevalence of passive smoking among pregnant women

A large study based on parents of 18,297 children born in 2000–01 in the UK indicated that 22% of non-smoking pregnant women lived with a partner who smoked throughout pregnancy,[50] and hence were potentially exposed to passive smoke. Whilst the true proportion of mothers exposed will be lower than this, since not all partners will smoke indoors, this effect will to some extent be counterbalanced by exposure to passive smoking from others in and outside the home.

3.5 Effects of maternal passive smoking on fertility and the fetus

3.5.1 Fertility

Longitudinal data from 17,733 babies in the nationally representative 1958 British birth cohort study (the National Child Development Survey) have shown in an age-adjusted analysis a significant effect of partner smoking on the time to pregnancy, which was of a similar magnitude to that of active smoking in the woman.[51] Exposure to passive smoke in 4,804 lifelong non-smoking women attending a cancer clinic has been shown to increase significantly their risk of difficulty in getting pregnant (adjusted OR 1.24, 95% CI 1.03 to 1.51).[52] The Avon Longitudinal Study of Pregnancy and Childhood (ALSPAC) conducted in the UK studied a population of 8,515 women planning pregnancy.[53] A 17% increased risk of delayed conception by more than 6 months was seen in women exposed to passive smoke (adjusted 95% CI 1.02 to 1.37), but no significant increase in risk was seen for conception delayed by more than 12 months (adjusted OR 1.14, 95% CI 0.92 to 1.42). Data from the Ontario Farm Family Health Study found significantly reduced rates of time to conception with paternal smoking (adjusted fecundity ratio (FR) 0.91, 95% CI 0.83 to 1.0).[54] Similar effect sizes were seen for paternal smoking and the risk of delayed conception within 12 months (OR 1.3, 95% CI 1.2 to 1.4).[55] However, not all studies found a significant decreased effect of paternal smoking on fecundity.[56–59]

Active smoking has also been shown to be associated with modest reductions in semen quality.[60] However, this has not directly translated to a reduction in male fertility.[57,61] It is therefore unlikely that any apparent effect of passive smoke exposure on fertility is purely due to infertility in the active smoking male.

3.5.2 Fetal mortality

We performed a systematic review and meta-analyses to assess the relationships between maternal exposure to passive smoke and the risk of adverse pregnancy outcomes, which included spontaneous abortion, perinatal morality, neonatal mortality, and stillbirth. Comprehensive searches were conducted using four electronic databases (MEDLINE, EMBASE, CAB Abstracts, PsycINFO) up to March 2009. We additionally scanned the reference lists of reviews, editorials and identified papers to identify all published comparative epidemiological studies (case-control, cross-sectional cohort) that were eligible for inclusion. Studies that assessed self-reported smoking status of the father or partner, self-reported maternal exposure to passive smoke (household, work or any exposure), or biochemically measured maternal exposure to passive smoke were included. Twenty studies were identified from the searches and included in the review. Meta-analyses using random effect models were conducted where three or more studies assessed similar outcomes and exposures; data are expressed as pooled ORs with 95% confidence intervals (CI). When assessing the impact of passive smoke on adverse pregnancy outcomes, the effect of active maternal smoking is potentially a strong confounder. Therefore, ideally the studies identified should be restricted to non-smoking women. Where possible, we have carried out sensitivity analyses to determine whether any observed effects remain when those studies that have not adequately controlled for mothers' smoking status are excluded.

3.5.2.1 Spontaneous abortion

Of the nine studies that assessed the relationship between passive smoke exposure among pregnant women and the risk of spontaneous abortion, seven were based on exposure from the baby's father (paternal smoking) and five on any exposure to passive smoke. No consistent association was seen between the risk of spontaneous abortion and exposure to smoking. There was no excess risk among seven studies based on paternal smoking (pooled OR 1.00, 95% CI 0.90 to 1.10; Fig 3.1), and a non-statistically significant increase among five studies based on passive smoke exposure from any source (pooled OR 1.21, 95% CI 0.86 to 1.70; Fig 3.2). All but one of the studies[62] assessed the effects of passive smoke

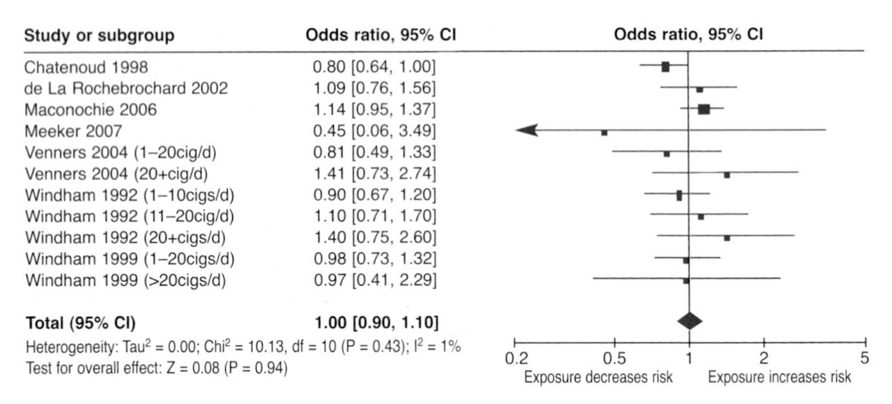

Fig 3.1 Paternal smoking and the risk of spontaneous abortion.[62,88–92]

Study or subgroup	Odds ratio, 95% CI
George 2006	1.90 [1.26, 2.86]
Meeker 2007	0.80 [0.30, 2.14]
Nakamura 2004	0.76 [0.45, 1.31]
Windham 1992	1.60 [1.22, 2.10]
Windham 1999	1.00 [0.80, 1.26]
Total (95% CI)	**1.21 [0.86, 1.70]**

Heterogeneity: $Tau^2 = 0.10$; $Chi^2 = 14.76$, df = 4 (P = 0.005); $I^2 = 73\%$
Test for overall effect: Z = 1.11 (P = 0.27)

0.2 0.5 1 2 5
Exposure decreases risk Exposure increases risk

Fig 3.2 Passive smoke exposure from any source and the risk of spontaneous abortion.[90,92–95]

exposure in either non-smoking mothers or adjusted for maternal smoking status in the analyses. Data from one further study could not be included in the meta-analysis due to lack of detailed data within the publication, which found paternal smoking of 10 or more cigarettes per day did not significantly increase risk of spontaneous abortion.[63]

3.5.2.2 Perinatal mortality

The association between perinatal or neonatal death and passive smoke exposure was assessed in five studies.[63–67] Paternal smoking was significantly associated with a 60% increased risk of perinatal mortality (adjusted OR 1.6, 95% CI 1.4 to 2.2;[66] unadjusted OR 1.57, 95% CI 1.06 to 2.33)[67] and neonatal mortality,[64,67] irrespective of whether the mother smoked. However, a further study reported no significant association between paternal smoking and perinatal mortality, but data were not presented.[65]

Three studies assessed the impact of passive smoke exposure on stillbirth. Dodds *et al* found a 65% significant increase in the risk of stillbirth in relation to passive smoke from any source (OR 1.65, 95% CI 1.01 to 2.69),[68] and a study by Uncu *et al* found a non-significant association between the risk of prenatal death and paternal smoking (OR 3.81, 95% CI 0.42 to 34.3).[69] Mishra *et al* found no significant increase in the risk of stillbirth (OR 1.05, 95% CI not reported).[70] Two further studies looked at stillbirth but combined the outcome with spontaneous abortion and showed small increased ORs, one of which was significant (adjusted OR 1.23, 95% CI 1.08 to 1.40;[52] adjusted RR 1.11, 95% CI 0.8 to 1.54).[71] Kharrazi *et al* found no significant association between passive smoke exposure and fetal death (20+ weeks gestation) (adjusted OR 1.58, 95% CI 0.78 to 3.21 per unit increase in log cotinine level).[72]

3.5.3 Small for gestational age and low birth weight

A recent systematic review and meta-analysis of epidemiological studies ascertained the association between maternal passive smoke exposure and fetal outcomes, including small for gestational age and birth weight.[73] The authors stratified their analyses based on whether passive smoke exposure was ascertained prospectively (before the outcome) or retrospectively (after the outcome). A pooled analysis of 17 studies based on smoke exposure measured prospectively found that maternal passive smoking was associated with a 33 g reduction in birth weight (95% CI 15.7 to 51.3 g; Fig 3.3). The estimate for studies that assessed exposure retrospectively was 40 g (95% CI 25.8 to 54.4 g; Fig 3.4). Of 26 studies that assessed the relationship between maternal passive smoke exposure and the risk of low birth weight (birth weight less than 2,500 g), nine assessed exposure to passive smoke prospectively and yielded a pooled estimate of increase in risk by an OR of 1.32 (95% CI 1.07 to 1.63), and the 17 studies that assessed exposure retrospectively by an OR of 1.22 (95% CI 1.08 to 1.37). The risk of small for gestational age (<10th centile) birth was significantly associated with environmental tobacco smoke (ETS) exposure in retrospective studies (OR 1.21, 95% CI 1.06 to 1.37), but not in the eight studies that used a prospectively ascertained passive smoke exposure (OR 1.05, 95% CI 0.87 to 1.28). There was no effect of ETS exposure on gestational age.[73]

Since reviews of studies of maternal active smoking report that birth weight is about 250 g lower compared to that in non-smoking pregnant women,[10] the above estimates of the effect of passive smoking (33–40 g lower) on birth weight seem disproportionately high.[77,78] However, similarly disproportionate effects of passive and active smoking have been reported in relation to cardiovascular disease, and are thought to arise from low dose effects on platelet aggregation.[74]

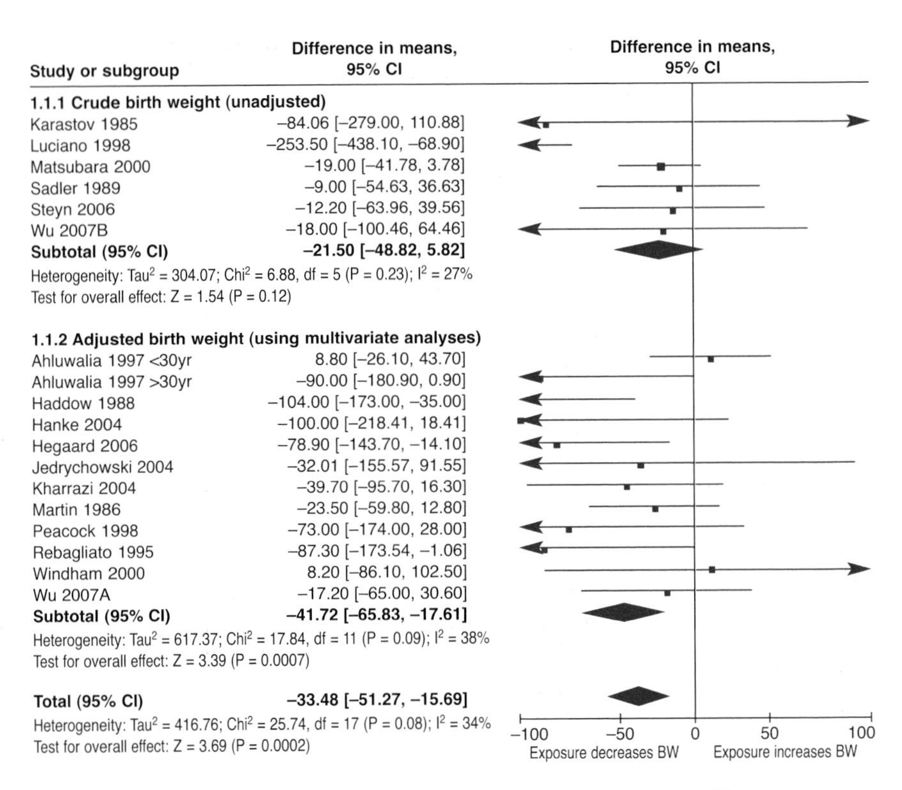

Fig 3.3 Passive smoke exposure and birth weight: prospective studies.[73]

3.5.4 Prematurity

A 2008 systematic review based on 19 epidemiological studies assessed prematurity using the proportion of premature births (defined as <37 weeks).[73] In nine studies that ascertained passive smoke exposure in the mother retrospectively, there was a significant 18% increase in the risk of prematurity with passive exposure (OR 1.18, 95% CI 1.03 to 1.35). In contrast, in eight studies which assessed passive smoke exposure in the mother prospectively, there was no significant increase in the risk of prematurity (OR 1.14, 95% CI 0.92 to 1.41).

3.5.6 Congenital malformations

We have carried out a systematic review and a series of meta-analyses similar to that for fetal mortality in section 3.5.2 above, to examine the association between maternal exposure to passive smoke and the risk of congenital malformations. Eighteen studies were identified from the searches and are included in the following analyses.

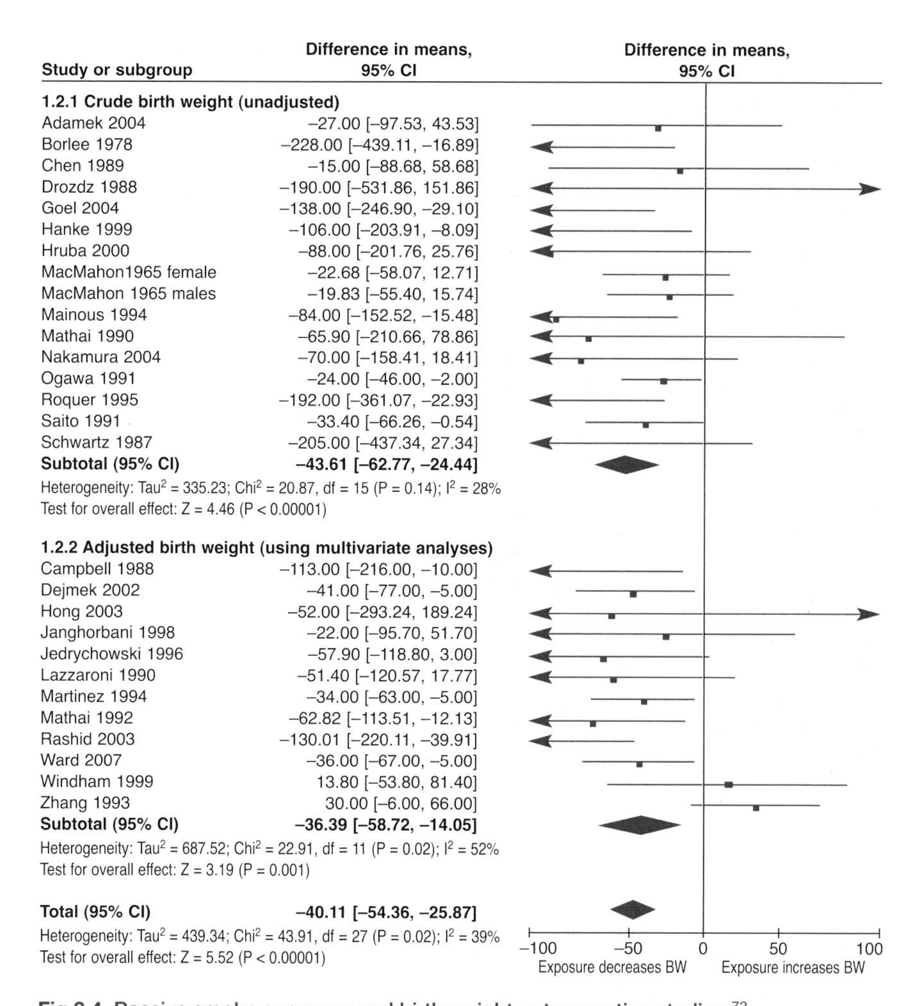

Fig 3.4 Passive smoke exposure and birth weight: retrospective studies.[73]

3.5.6.1 Any congenital malformation

Four studies reported the risk of any congenital malformations and paternal smoking.[43,63,69,75] Results from a meta-analysis of three of these studies found a 72% increased risk of any congenital malformation with paternal smoking (pooled 95% CI 1.06 to 2.78; Fig 3.5). All of the studies assessed paternal smoking exposure either in non-smoking mothers,[69,75] or found that maternal smoking was not a risk factor for the outcome.[63] The fourth study[43] could not be included in the meta-analysis because the data were not appropriately reported. However, the authors found a non-significant trend towards an increase in the incidence of major and minor congenital malformations with increasing paternal smoking level amongst non-smoking mothers.

Study or subgroup	Odds ratio, 95% CI
Mau 1974 (1–10cig/d)	1.78 [0.91, 3.48]
Mau 1974 (10+cigs/d)	2.75 [1.57, 4.83]
Uncu 2005	1.89 [0.34, 10.45]
Zhang 1992	1.21 [1.01, 1.45]
Total (95% CI)	**1.72 [1.06, 2.78]**

Heterogeneity: $Tau^2 = 0.14$; $Chi^2 = 8.35$, df = 3 (P = 0.04); $I^2 = 64\%$
Test for overall effect: Z = 2.19 (P = 0.03)

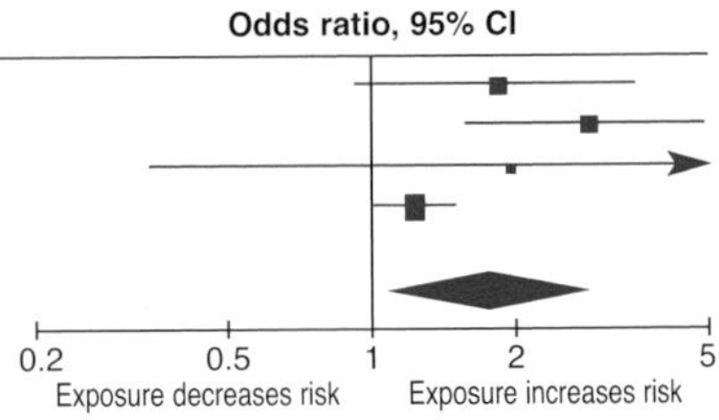

Odds ratio, 95% CI
0.2 0.5 1 2 5
Exposure decreases risk Exposure increases risk

Fig 3.5 Paternal smoke exposure and the risk of any congenital malformations.[63,69,75]

3.5.6.2 Heart defects

Five studies were identified that assessed the effect of passive smoke exposure on the risk of cardiac defects.[35,63,75–77] No significant link was seen between paternal smoking and cardiac defects,[63] conotruncal heart defects (OR 1.3, 95% CI 0.85 to 2.1),[77] pulmonic stenosis (OR 0.9, 95% CI 0.3 to 3.3),[76] atrial septal defect (OR 0.7, 95% CI 0.2 to 2.8),[76] or patent ductus arteriosis (OR 0.6, 95% CI 0.1 to 2.3).[76] Additionally, no consistent association between paternal smoking and the risk of ventricular septal defect was seen (OR 0.6, 95% CI 0.2 to 2.1; OR 2.0, 95% CI 0.9 to 4.3).[75,76] The National Birth Defects Prevention Study conducted in the US found no association between the risk of congenital heart defects and passive smoke exposure at home or in the workplace.[35]

3.5.6.3 Musculoskeletal defects

No evidence of a significant association was seen for paternal smoking and the risk of numerical deformities of extremities (OR 0.8, 95% CI 0.4 to 1.6; OR 0.5, 95% CI 0.3 to 1.0; data were not reported in one study).[63,75,76] However, for the two studies that looked at varus / valgus deformities of the feet, including club foot, conflicting results were seen (adjusted OR 0.5, 95% 0.3 to 1.0;[76] unadjusted OR 1.8, 95% CI 0.97 to 3.3).[75] Single studies looked at a range of other musculoskeletal defects including brachydactylia/adactylia (OR 1.6, 95% CI 0.4 to 6.1);[75] hip dislocation (OR 0.9, 95% CI 0.5 to 1.7); spine curvature (OR 0.9, 95% CI 0.3 to 2.8) and torticollis (OR 0.8, 95% CI 0.3 to 2.4);[76] and limb reduction defects (OR 1.2, 95% CI 0.75 to 1.9).[77] All these studies showed no significant association with paternal smoking.

3.5.6.4 Defects of the genitourinary systems

Five studies assessed the association between passive smoke exposure and the risk of hypospadias.[75,76,78–80] A pooled analysis of four studies assessing the effect of paternal smoking showed a small but non-significant increase in risk of hypospadias (pooled OR 1.43, 95% CI 0.85 to 2.38; Fig 3.6). Two of the four studies individually showed significant effects, but these did not control for active smoking in the mother.[78,80] No evidence of an association was seen between the risk of hypospadias and maternal passive exposure to smoke from the household (adjusted OR 0.7, 95% CI 0.4 to 1.1)[79] or from their working environment (adjusted OR 0.7, 95% CI 0.4 to 1.2).[79]

Study or subgroup	Odds ratio, 95% CI
Brouwers 2007	1.40 [1.03, 1.90]
Pierik 2004	3.80 [1.76, 8.19]
Savitz 1991	1.20 [0.63, 2.30]
Zhang 1992	0.79 [0.45, 1.38]
Total (95% CI)	**1.43 [0.85, 2.38]**

Heterogeneity: $Tau^2 = 0.19$; $Chi^2 = 10.71$, df = 3 (P = 0.01); $I^2 = 72\%$
Test for overall effect: Z = 1.36 (P = 0.17)

Odds ratio, 95% CI
0.1 0.2 0.5 1 2 5 10
Exposure decreases risk Exposure increases risk

Fig 3.6 Paternal smoking and the risk of hypospadias.[75,76,78,80]

The link between a risk of cryptorchidism (undescended testes) and exposure to passive smoke was assessed in four studies (Fig 3.7).[75,76,80,81] A pooled analysis of the four studies assessing the effects of paternal smoking showed a borderline significant increase of 34% in the risk of cryptorchidism (pooled OR 1.34, 95% CI 0.99 to 1.82; p=0.06). However, this effect was reduced to a non-significant 21% increase in risk when only those controlled for maternal smoking were considered (p=0.49, two studies). No significant association was seen between the risk of cryptorchidism and passive smoke from their working environment (adjusted OR 1.32, 95% CI 0.43 to 4.07).[81]

No evidence of a significant association was seen between paternal smoking and the risk of urogenital fissures,[63] urethral stenosis,[76] incompetent ureterovesical valves,[76] ureter dysplasia/agenesis,[76] polycystic kidney,[75] indeterminant sex,[75] or inguinal hernia.[76] However, a single study found a possible protective effect of paternal smoking on pyloric stenosis (adjusted OR 0.2, 95% CI 0 to 0.8).[76]

Study or subgroup	Odds ratio, 95% CI
Kurahashi 205	1.92 [1.04, 3.54]
Pierik 2004	1.20 [0.68, 2.10]
Savitz 1991	0.90 [0.51, 1.60]
Zhang 1992	1.55 [0.95, 2.54]
Total (95% CI)	**1.34 [0.99, 1.82]**

Heterogeneity: $Tau^2 = 0.02$; $Chi^2 = 3.66$, df = 3 (P = 0.30); $I^2 = 18\%$
Test for overall effect: Z = 1.88 (P = 0.06)

Odds ratio, 95% CI
0.2 0.5 1 2 5
Exposure decreases risk Exposure increases risk

Fig 3.7 Paternal smoking and the risk of cryptorchidism.[75,76,80,81]

3.5.6.5 *Defects of the central nervous system*

Six studies were identified that assessed the impact of passive smoke exposure and neural tube defects.[63,75–77,82,83] Five of these studies provided data for a meta-analysis, which showed no significant association between paternal smoking and the risk of neural tube defects (pooled OR 1.34, 95% CI 0.91 to 1.95; Fig 3.8). The remaining study reported only reported subtypes of neural tube defects;[75] they found non-significant two-fold increases in the risk of anencephaly (unadjusted OR 2.1, 95% CI 0.9 to 4.9) and spina bifida (unadjusted OR 1.9, 95% CI 0.7 to 9.4) in those exposed to paternal smoke amongst mothers who were non-smokers. Additionally, paternal smoking was not significantly associated with hydrocephalus,[75,76] microcephaly,[75] or limb paralysis.[76]

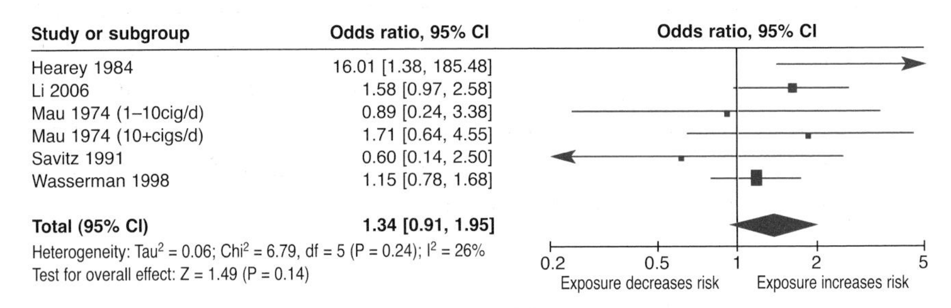

Fig 3.8 Paternal smoke exposure and the risk of neural tube defects.[63,76,77,82,83]

Two studies assessed the risk of neural tube defects in relation to exposure of passive smoke from any source.[77,82] Both of these studies found non-significant increases in the risk of neural tube defects (adjusted OR 1.60, 95% CI 0.94 to 2.73;[82] unadjusted OR 1.20, 95% CI 0.83 to 1.90).[77] Li *et al* also reported non-significant increases in the risk of anencephalus with maternal passive smoke exposure (adjusted OR 1.88, 95% CI 0.92 to 3.73), and no association with spina bifida.[82]

3.5.6.6 *Defects of the face, eyes, ears and neck*

Three studies assessed the effect of paternal smoking and the risk of orofacial malformations,[63,76,84] typically reported as cleft lip with or without cleft palate. Results from a pooled analysis found paternal smoking nearly doubled the risk of orofacial malformations (pooled OR 1.90, 95% CI 1.17 to 3.07, three studies; Fig 3.9). However, two of the studies did not adjust for maternal smoking status in their analyses,[63,84] which could have over-inflated the apparent effect. One study found passive smoke exposure from any source did not significantly increase the risk of orofacial clefts in non-smoking mothers (adjusted OR 1.1, 95% CI 0.9 to 1.3).[85]

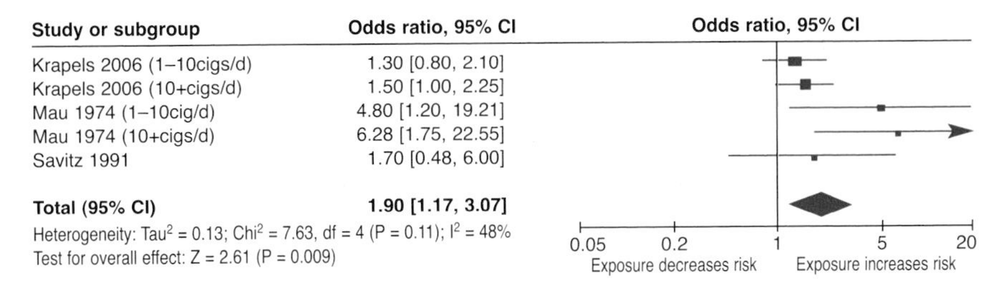

Fig 3.9 Paternal smoking and the risk of orofacial malformations.[63,76,84]

Two further studies assessed the impact of any passive smoke exposure on the risk of craniosynostosis;[76,86] no significant association was seen with paternal/home exposure in either of the studies (adjusted OR 1.3, 95% CI 0.9 to 1.9;[86] adjusted OR 0.8, 95% CI 0.2 to 2.4)[76]. Additionally, paternal smoking was not significantly associated with anomalies of the eye,[75] anomalies of the external ear,[75] microtia or absence of ear,[75] nasal bone absence,[75] refractive errors,[76] ptosis,[76] preauricular cyst,[76] branchial cyst,[76] or nasal aplasia.[76] However, data from one study suggested a protective effect of paternal smoking for strabismus, independent of maternal smoking (adjusted OR 0.7, 95% CI 0.5 to 0.9).[76]

3.5.6.7 Other congenital malformations

Two studies also looked at dermatological defects, and showed no significant effect of paternal smoking on the risk of haemangioma,[75,76] pigmentary anomalies of the skin,[75] benign melanoma/dermoid cyst,[76] or pilonidal cyst.[76] Additionally, no significant effect was seen for paternal smoking on the risk of Down's syndrome (trisomy 21),[75,76] diaphragmatic hernia,[75] or lung hypoplasia/aplasia.[75]

3.6 Bias and confounding in observational studies

Observational studies are often affected by bias and confounding, so the conclusions that can reliably be drawn from them, particularly in relation to establishing causality, partly depend on the extent to which these two features have been examined. Confounding occurs when, for example, a factor such as maternal alcohol intake is independently associated with both the exposure of interest (maternal smoking) and the disorder (eg congenital abnormalities). Many of the studies summarised in the sections above adjusted for several potential confounding factors, and most found that they did not substantially change the excess risk between maternal smoking and the disorder of interest. Wherever possible, RRs or ORs that are adjusted for common confounders have been used.

Publication bias occurs because studies in which little or no effect of an exposure is found are less likely to be published, and hence cannot be included in reviews. The effect of this bias would be to overestimate the excess risk in a meta-analysis. This could be mitigated in part by focusing on larger studies, which are generally more reliable (and thus more likely to be published whether or not they find evidence of an exposure effect). Funnel plots can also be used to determine whether bias is likely. For example, the authors who conducted the review of the association between smoking and cleft lip and palate specifically examined publication bias and found no material evidence of it.[34] The reviews described above were either based on new reviews that focused on larger studies, new full systematic reviews conducted in preparing this chapter, or published systematic reviews.

A further important potential bias in the studies discussed is that arising from misclassification, whereby some pregnant women who smoke misreport themselves as non-smokers, or underreport their cigarette consumption, due to the perceived unacceptability of smoking in pregnancy. However, such underreporting will tend to reduce any apparent effect of smoking on a disorder, and therefore result in an underestimate of the strength of the association.

Causality is difficult to establish from observational data alone, but where there is consistency of findings between studies, particularly when based on several thousand subjects, and where evidence of a dose–response relationship is seen, an association is more likely to be causal.

3.7 Limitations of the studies of maternal passive smoking

The studies of maternal passive smoking summarised above have several limitations relative to those on maternal active smoking. Although the sample sizes involved in many of the studies are substantial, they are generally smaller than those available from studies of active smoking. This matters because typical passive smoke exposure constitutes around 1% of typical active smoking exposure,[87] and although this does not necessarily translate into a 99% reduction in the risk of passive relative to active exposure,[87] the effects are necessarily likely to be substantially smaller. Identifying smaller effects requires larger sample sizes.

In the studies we have reviewed, whilst the disorders associated with maternal passive smoking are generally similar to those for maternal active smoking, namely fetal mortality and some congenital abnormalities, there is a tendency for the excess risks estimated for passive smoking to be larger than expected. For example, the pooled increase in risk for perinatal mortality is 60% for maternal passive smoking but 26% for maternal active smoking. Similarly, the pooled excess risk for all congenital abnormalities is 72% for passive smoking, compared with probably at most a 10–15% increase associated with maternal active smoking. It is likely that this difference is, at least in part, due to publication bias. Furthermore, some of the maternal passive smoking studies included mothers who themselves smoked, and this in itself could explain some of the excess risk, even though allowance was made for maternal active smoking in the original analyses.

However, in the same way that passive smoking in adults is associated with a larger than expected risk of cardiovascular disease, there could be a similar non-linear relationship between maternal passive smoking and fetal outcomes. The main value of the studies on maternal passive smoking is therefore to indicate general consistency with the adverse fetal and infant effects found with maternal active smoking, while the magnitude of the excess risks should be interpreted with caution.

3.8 Summary

- Active maternal smoking (and hence passive exposure of the fetus) causes up to about 5,000 miscarriages, 300 perinatal deaths, and 2,200 premature singleton births in the UK each year
- Passive exposure of the fetus to active maternal smoking impairs fetal growth and development, increasing the risk of being small for gestational age and reducing birth weight by about 250 g, and probably increases the risk of congenital abnormalities of the heart, limbs, and face.
- Passive exposure of the fetus to active maternal smoking also causes around 19,000 babies to be born with low birth weight in the UK each year.
- Maternal passive smoking is likely to have similar adverse effects on fetal and reproductive health, but of smaller magnitude.
- Maternal passive smoking reduces birth weight by around 30–40 g, and may also have modest effects on the risk of prematurity and being small for gestational age.
- Maternal passive smoking may reduce fertility, increase fetal and perinatal mortality, and increase the risk of some congenital abnormalities (particularly of the face and genitourinary system), though the available evidence is not yet conclusive.
- Maternal passive smoking is thus a cause of potentially significant health impacts to the fetus.
- These adverse effects are entirely avoidable.

References

1 British Medical Association. *Smoking and reproductive life: the impact of smoking on sexual, reproductive and child health.* London: BMA, 2004.

2 Quinton AE, Cook CM, Peek MJ. The relationship between cigarette smoking, endothelial function and intrauterine growth restriction in human pregnancy. *BJOG* 2008;115:780–84.

3 Rogers JM. Tobacco and pregnancy. *Reproductive Toxicology* 2009;28:152–60.

4 Talbot P. *In vitro* assessment of reproductive toxicity of tobacco smoke and its constituents. *Birth Defects Res C Embryo Today* 2008;84:61–72.

5 Werler MM, Pober BR, Holmes LB. Smoking and pregnancy. *Teratology* 1985;32:473–81.

6 The Information Centre. *Statistics on smoking: England 2006.* Office for National Statistics, 2006. www.ic.nhs.uk/statistics-and-data-collections/health-and-lifestyles/smoking/statistics-on-smoking-england-2006

7 Scottish Household Survey, *Births & maternal smoking – update up to March 2004.* ISD Scotland, 2005. www.isdscotland.org/births

8 Augood C, Duckitt K, Templeton AA. Smoking and female infertility: a systematic review and meta-analysis. *Hum Reprod* 1998;13:1532–9.

9 Department of Health and Human Services, *Women and smoking.* A report of the US Surgeon General. Rockville: DHHS, 2001.

10 Department of Health and Human Services, *The health consequences of smoking.* A report of the US Surgeon General. Rockville: DHHS, 2004.

11 DiFranza JR, Lew RA. Effect of maternal cigarette smoking on pregnancy complications and sudden infant death syndrome. *J Fam Pract* 1995;40:385–94.

12 UK Department of Health, Independent Scientific Committee on Smoking and Health. *Fourth report.* Department of Health, 1988.

13 Lumley J, Chamberlain C, Dowswell T *et al.* Interventions for promoting smoking cessation during pregnancy. *Cochrane Database Syst Rev* 2009;3(CD001055).

14 Larroque B, Ancel PY, Marret S *et al.* Neurodevelopmental disabilities and special care of 5-year-old children born before 33 weeks of gestation (the EPIPAGE study): a longitudinal cohort study. *Lancet* 2008;371:813–20.

15 Marlow N, Wolke D, Bracewell MA, Samara M, EPICure Study Group. Neurologic and developmental disability at six years of age after extremely preterm birth. *N Engl J Med* 2005;352:9–19.

16 Shah NR, Bracken MB. A systematic review and meta-analysis of prospective studies on the association between maternal cigarette smoking and preterm delivery. *Am J Obstet Gynecol* 2000;182:465–72.

17 Office for National Statistics. *Congenital anomaly statistics; notifications 2004.* Series MB3, number 19. Office for National Statistics, 2005.

18 Czeizel AE, Kodaj I, Lenz W. Smoking during pregnancy and congenital limb deficiency. *BMJ* 1994;308:1473–6.

19 Aro T, Maternal diseases, alcohol consumption and smoking during pregnancy associated with reduction limb defects. *Early Hum Dev* 1983;9:49–57.

20 Butler NR, Alberman ED. Perinatal problems. In: *The second report of the 1958 British Perinatal Mortality Survey.* London/Edinburgh: Livingstone, 1969.

21 Cedergren MI, Källén,BA, Obstetric outcome of 6346 pregnancies with infants affected by congenital heart defects. *Eur J Obstet Gynecol Reprod Biol* 2006;125:211–6.

22 Cedergren MI, Selbing AJ, Kallen BAJ. Risk factors for cardiovascular malformation – a study based on prospectively collected data. *Scand J Work Environ Health*2002;28:12–17.

23 Christianson, RE. The relationship between maternal smoking and the incidence of congenital anomalies. *Am J Epidemiol* 1980;112:684–95.

24 Evans DR, Newcombe RG, Campbell H. Maternal smoking habits and congenital malformations: a population study. *BMJ* 1979;2:171–3.

25 Goldbaum G, Daling J, Milham S, Risk factors for gastroschisis. *Teratology* 1990;42: 397–403.

26 Grewal J, Carmichael SL, Ma C, Lammer EJ, Shaw GM. Maternal periconceptional smoking and alcohol consumption and risk for select congenital anomalies. *Birth Defects Res A Clin Mol Teratol* 2008;82:519–26.

27 Haddow JE, Palomaki GE, Holman MS. Young maternal age and smoking during pregnancy as risk factors for gastroschisis. *Teratology* 1993;47:225–8.

28 Honein MA, Paulozzi LJ, Watkins ML. Maternal smoking and birth defects: validity of birth certificate data for effect estimation. *Public Health Rep* 2001;116:327–35.

29 Källén K. Maternal smoking and urinary organ malformations. *Int J Epidemiol* 1997;26: 571–4.

30 Källén K. Multiple malformations and maternal smoking. *Paediatr Perinat Epidemiol* 2000;14:227–33.

31 Kelsey JL, Dwyer T, Holford TR, Bracken MB. Maternal smoking and congenital malformations: an epidemiological study. *J Epidemiol Community Health* 1978;32: 102–7.

32 Li DK. Maternal history of subfertility and the risk of congenital urinary tract anomalies in offspring. *Epidemiology* 1999;10:80–2.

33 Li DK, Mueller BA, Hickok DE *et al.* Maternal smoking during pregnancy and the risk of congenital urinary tract anomalies. *Am J Pub Health* 1996;86:249–53.

34 Little J, Cardy A, Munger RG. Tobacco smoking and oral clefts: a meta-analysis. *Bull World Health Organ* 2004;82:213–18.

35 Malik S, Cleves MA, Honein MA *et al.* Maternal smoking and congenital heart defects. *Pediatrics* 2008;121:e810–16.

36 Malloy MH, Kleinman JC, Bakewell JM, Schramm WF, Land GH. Maternal smoking during pregnancy: no association with congenital malformations in Missouri 1980–83. *Am J Pub Health* 1989;79:1243–6.

37 Man LX, Chang B. Maternal cigarettes smoking during pregnancy increases the risk of having a child with a congenital digital anomaly. *Plast Reconstr Surg* 2006;117:301–8.

38 McDonald AD, Armstrong BG, Sloan M. Cigarette, alcohol, and coffee consumption and congenital defects. *Am J Pub Health* 1992;82:91–3.

39 Miller EA, Manning SE, Rasmussen SA, Reefhuis J, Honein MA. Maternal exposure to tobacco smoke, alcohol and caffeine, and risk of anorectal atresia: National Birth Defects Prevention Study 1997-2003. *Paediatr Perinat Epidemiol* 2009;23:9–17.

40 Morales-Suarez-Varela MM, Bille C, Christensen K, Olsen J. Smoking habits, nicotine use, and congenital malformations [see comment]. *Obstet Gynecol* 2006;107:51–7.

41 Pradat P. A case-control study of major congenital heart defects in Sweden – 1981–1986. *Eur J Epidemiol* 1992;8:789–96.

42 Reefhuis J, De Walle HE, Cornel MC. Maternal smoking and deformities of the foot: results for the EUROCAT Study. European Registries of Congenital Anomalies. *Am J Pub Health* 1998;88:1554–5.

43 Seidman DS, Ever-Hadani P, Gale R. Effect of maternal smoking and age on congenital anomalies. *Obstet Gynecol* 1990;76:1046–50.

44 Shaw GM, Malcoe LH, Swan SH, Cummins SK, Schulman J. Congenital cardiac anomalies relative to selected maternal exposures and conditions during early pregnancy. *Eur J Epidemiol* 1992;8:757–60.

45 Shiono PH, Klebanoff MA, Berendes HW. Congenital malformations and maternal smoking during pregnancy. *Teratology* 1986;34:65–71.

46 Tikkanen J, Heinonen OP. Risk factors for atrial septal defect. *Eur J Epidemiol* 1992;8: 509–12.

47 Tikkanen J, Heinonen OP. Risk factors for conal malformations of the heart. *Eur J Epidemiol* 1992;8:48–57.

48 Van den Eeden SK, Karagas MR, Daling JR, Vaughan TL. A case-control study of maternal smoking and congenital malformations. *Paediatr Perinat Epidemiol* 1990;4:147–55.

49 Woods SE and Raju U. Maternal smoking and the risk of congenital birth defects: a cohort study. *J Am Board Fam Pract* 2001;14:330–4.

50 Ward C, Lewis S, Coleman T. Prevalence of maternal smoking and environmental tobacco smoke exposure during pregnancy and impact on birth weight: retrospective study using Millennium Cohort. *BMC Public Health* 2007;7:81.

51 Joffe M, Li Z. Male and female factors in fertility. *Am J Epidemiol* 1994;140:921–9.

52 Peppone LJ, Piazza KM, Mahoney MC *et al.* Associations between adult and childhood secondhand smoke exposures and fecundity and fetal loss among women who visited a cancer hospital. *Tob Control* 2009;18:115–20.

53 Hull MGR, North K, Taylor H, Farrow A, Lord CL, the Avon Longitudinal Study of Pregnancy and Childhood Study Team. Delayed conception and active and passive smoking. *Fertil Steril* 2000;74:725–33.

54 Curtis KM, Savitz DA, Arbuckle TE. Effects of cigarette smoking, caffeine consumption, and alcohol intake on fecundability. *Am J Epidemiol* 1997;146:32–41.

55 Suonio S, Saarikoski S, Kauhanen O *et al.* Smoking does affect fecundity. *Eur J Obstet Gynecol Reprod Biol* 1990;34.

56 Baird DD, Wilcox AJ. Cigarette smoking associated with delayed conception. *JAMA* 1985; 253:2979–83.

57 Bolumar F, Olsen J, Boldsen J, the European Study Group on Infertility and Subfecundity. Smoking reduces fecundity: A European multicenter study on infertility and subfecundity. *Am J Epidemiol* 1996;143:578–87.

58 De Mouzon J, Spira A, Schwartz D. A prospective study of the relation between smoking and fertility. *Int J Epidemiol* 1988;17:378–84.

59 Florack EIM, Zielhuis GA, Rolland R. Cigarette smoking, alcohol consumption, and caffeine intake and facundability. *Prev Med* 1994;23:175–80.

60 Vine MF. Smoking and male reproduction: a review. *Int J Androl* 1996;19:323–37.

61 Hughes EG, Brennan BG. Does cigarette smoking impair natural or assisted fecundity? *Fertil Steril* 1996;66:679–89.

62 Maconochie N, Doyle P, Prior S, Simmons R. Risk factors for first trimester miscarriage – Results from a UK-population-based case-control study. *BJOG* 2007;114:170–86.

63 Mau G and Netter P. The effects of paternal cigarette smoking on perinatal mortality and the incidence of malformations. *Dtsch Med Wochenschr* 1974;99:1113–18.

64 Comstock GW, Lundin FE. Parental smoking and perinatal mortality. *Am J Obstet Gynecol* 1967;98:708–18.

65 Gaizauskiene A, Padaiga Z, Basys V, Grigorjev G, Mizeriene R. Risk factors of perinatal mortality in Lithuania, 1997-1998. *Scand J Public Health* 2003;31:137–42.

66 Gaizauskiene A, Padaiga Z, Starkuviene S, Mizeriene R. Prediction of perinatal mortality at an early stage of pregnancy. *Scand J Public Health* 2007;35:564–9.
67 Yerushalmy J. The relationship of parents' cigarette smoking to outcome of pregnancy – implications as to the problem of inferring causation from observed associations. *Am J Epidemiol* 1971;93:443–56.
68 Dodds L, King WD, Fell DB *et al.* Stillbirth risk factors according to timing of exposure. *Ann Epidemiol* 2006;16:607–13.
69 Uncu Y, Ozcakir A, Ercan I, Bilgel N, Uncu G. Pregnant women quit smoking; what about fathers? Survey study in Bursa region, Turkey. *Croat Med J* 2005;46:832–7.
70 Mishra V, Retherford RD, Smith KR. Cooking smoke and tobacco smoke as risk factors for stillbirth. *Int J Environ Health Res* 2005;15:397–410.
71 Ahlborg G, Bodin L. Tobacco smoke exposure and pregnancy outcome among working women. *Am J Epidemiol* 1991;133:338–47.
72 Kharrazi M, DeLorenze GN, Kaufman FL *et al.* Environmental tobacco smoke and pregnancy outcome. *Epidemiology* 2004;15:660–70.
73 Leonardi-Bee J, Smyth A, Britton J, Coleman T. Environmental tobacco smoke and fetal health: systematic review and meta-analysis. *Arch Dis Child Fetal Neonatal Ed* 2008;93: F351-F361.
74 Pechacek TF, Babb S. How acute and reversible are the cardiovascular risks of secondhand smoke? *BMJ* 2004; 328:980–3.
75 Zhang J, Savitz DA, Schwingl PJ, Cai W-W. A case-control study of paternal smoking and birth defects. *Int J Epidemiol* 1992;21:273–8.
76 Savitz DA, Schwingl PJ, Keels MA. Influence of paternal age, smoking, and alcohol consumption on congenital anomalies. *Teratology* 1991;44:429–40.
77 Wasserman CR, Shaw GM, O'Malley CD, Tolarova MM, Lammer EJ. Parental cigarette smoking and risk of congenital anomalies of the heart, neural tube, or limb. *Teratology* 1996;53:261–7.
78 Brouwers MM, Feitz WFJ, Roelofs LAJ *et al.* Risk factors for hypospadias. *Eur J Pediatr* 2007;166:671–8.
79 Carmichael SL, Shaw GM, Laurent C, Lammer EJ, Olney RS, the National Birth Defects Prevention Study. Hypospadias and maternal exposures to cigarette smoke. *Paediatr Perinat Epidemiol* 2005;19:406-412.
80 Pierik FH, Burdorf A, Deddens JA, Juttmann RE, Weber RFA. Maternal and paternal risk factors for cryptorchidism and hypospadias: a case-control study in newborn boys [see comment]. *Environ Health Perspect* 2004;112:1570–6.
81 Kurahashi N, Kasai S, Shibata T *et al.* Parental and neonatal risk factors for cryptorchidism. *Med Sci Monit* 2005;11:CR274–83.
82 Li Z, Ren A, Zhang L, Guo Z, Li Z. A population-based case-control study of risk factors for neural tube defects in four high-prevalence areas of Shanxi province, China. *Paediatr Perinat Epidemiol* 2006;20:43–53.
83 Hearey CD, Harris JA, Usatin MS *et al.* Investigation of a cluster of anencephaly and spina bifida. *Am J Epidemiol* 1984;120:559–64.
84 Krapels IPC, Zielhuis, GA, Vroom F *et al.* Periconceptional health and lifestyle factors of both parents affect the risk of live-born children with orofacial clefts. *Birth Defects Res A Clin Mol Teratol* 2006;76:613–20.
85 Honein MA, Rasmussen SA, Reefhuis J *et al.* Maternal smoking and environmental tobacco smoke exposure and the risk of orofacial clefts. *Epidemiology* 2007;18: 226–33.

86 Carmichael SL, Ma C, Rasmussen SA *et al.* Craniosynostosis and maternal smoking. *Birth Defects Res A Clin Mol Teratol* 2008;82:78–85.

87 Royal College of Physicians. *Going smoke-free: the medical case for clean air in the home, at work and in public places.* Report of a working party. London: RCP, 2005.

88 Chatenoud L, Parazzini F, Di Cintio E *et al.* Paternal and maternal smoking habits before conception and during the first trimester: relation to spontaneous abortion. *Ann Epidemiol* 1998;8:520–6.

89 De La Rochebrochard E, Thonneau P. Paternal age and maternal age are risk factors for miscarriage: reuslts of a multicentre European study. *Hum Reprod* 2002;17:1649–56.

90 Meeker JD, Missmer SA, Vitonis AF, Cramer DW, Hauser R. Risk of spontaneous abortion in women with childhood exposure to parental cigarette smoke. *Am J Epidemiol* 2007; 166:571–5.

91 Venners SA, Wang X, Chen C *et al.* Paternal smoking and pregnancy loss: a prospective study using a biomarker of pregnancy. *Am J Epidemiol* 2004;159:993–1001.

92 Windham GC, Swan SH, Fenster L. Parental cigarette smoking and the risk of spontaneous abortion. *Am J Epidemiol* 1992;15:1394–1403.

93 George L, Granath F, Johansson ALV, Anneren G, Cnattingius S. Environmental tobacco smoke and risk of spontaneous abortion [see comment]. *Epidemiology* 2006;17:500–5.

94 Nakamura MU, Alexandre SM, Kuhn dos Santos JF *et al.* Obstetric and perinatal effects of active and/or passive smoking during pregnancy. *Sao Paulo Med J* 2004;122:94–8.

95 Windham GC, Von Behren J, Waller K, Fenster L. Exposure to environmental and mainstream tobacco smoke and risk of spontaneous abortion. *Am J Epidemiol* 1999;149: 243–7.

4 Health effects of passive smoking in children

4.1 Introduction

The health effects of passive smoking on children have been the subject of extensive research over recent years, and the evidence has been the subject of several systematic reviews. Of particular note, in the late 1990s, Cook, Strachan and Anderson published a series of definitive systematic reviews and meta-analyses[1–8] commissioned for the 1998 UK Government Scientific Committee on Tobacco and Health (SCOTH) report.[9] Revised versions of these reviews also provided estimated effects of passive smoking on child health for the 2004 revision of the SCOTH report[10] and, with extension of literature searches to 2001, formed the basis of the analyses presented in the 2006 US Surgeon General's report on involuntary exposure to tobacco smoke.[11] The US Surgeon General's report concluded that the available evidence was sufficient to infer a causal association between passive smoking and sudden infant death syndrome, lower respiratory illness, middle ear disease, asthma in school-aged children, and impairment of lung function.[11]

Since the estimates used in these reports are based on literature searches that are now several years out of date, we have updated the systematic reviews and meta-analyses of passive smoking effects on lower respiratory illness, middle ear disease, asthma, wheeze, sudden infant death syndrome and lung function, in order to provide contemporary best estimates of the magnitude of the impact of passive smoking on these aspects of child health. In the light of recent reports linking passive smoking to an increased risk of meningitis, we have also carried out a systematic review and meta-analysis of studies of this association.

4.2 Methods

Search methods were typically based on those described for the 1997 and 1998 systematic reviews and meta-analyses by Cook, Strachan and Anderson.[1,3–5,8] We used comprehensive search strategies of MEDLINE, EMBASE, PsycINFO, CAB Abstracts and other relevant databases, using search terms identified and modified from the original reviews[1,3–5,8] (where available) to identify all published comparative epidemiological studies (case-control, cross-sectional and cohort) assessing the relationship between passive smoke exposure and: lower respiratory infection (bronchitis, pneumonia, bronchiolitis, acute respiratory infection); middle ear disease (acute otitis media, recurrent otitis media, otitis media with effusion, chronic otitis media); hearing impairment including hearing loss, deafness, glue ear, and surgery related to middle ear including adenotonsillectomy, tonsillectomy, adenoidectomy, and grommet insertion; asthma; wheeze; and lung function reported since the Cook *et al* reviews, and for all meningitis reports. For sudden infant death, for which an updated search was published in 2005,[12] we searched for papers published since this later date. For each outcome, we also scanned and checked reference lists from original research papers and review articles for further relevant studies. No language restrictions were applied during the searching, but we have chosen to report only results from studies written in English.

For wheeze and asthma, for which a very large number of cross-sectional, case-control and longitudinal studies are now available, we restricted our reviews to papers of relatively high evidence level, comprising only longitudinal cohort studies in which children were known to have been free of asthma or wheeze at the start of the study; passive smoke exposure information was collected before ascertainment of asthma or wheeze outcomes; and these outcomes occurred before the age of 18 years. We categorised the various exposures measured in the different studies as smoking by the mother during pregnancy (prenatal maternal smoking), smoking by the mother after pregnancy (maternal smoking), smoking by the father (paternal smoking) and smoking by any household member (household smoking). For sudden infant death, we explored the effect of smoking by the father or other household smoking in families in which the mother did not smoke, but for brevity have not included data on these restricted analyses for other outcomes.

As in the previous review, we limited our analysis of lower respiratory infection to episodes occurring in the first three years.[5] For middle ear disease, asthma, wheeze, lung function and meningitis, studies of children up to age 18 were included. However, because of the large number of studies now available, we grouped our analyses of asthma and wheeze into three age ranges (0–2, 3–4 and 5–8 years).

Two researchers independently reviewed the titles, abstracts and full text of all identified studies to exclude those that were not relevant to the review, and extracted data from those agreed to be suitable for inclusion. The updated systematic reviews were carried out in accordance with the Meta-analysis Of Observational Studies in Epidemiology (MOOSE) guidelines.[13] We extracted adjusted estimates of association where available, and otherwise extracted or estimated unadjusted (crude) ORs from the publications. Estimates of relative risk were then generated by meta-analyses of pooled results from studies grouped according to the sources of passive smoke exposure, using random effect models in STATA Version 10 software.

4.3 Sudden infant death syndrome

The 1997 Anderson and Cook review included 39 publications[1] and the Mitchell and Milerad update, which included studies published up to 2005,[12] a further 27 studies. Combining the results of our updated search to January 2009 with these previous reviews yielded a total of 75 comparative epidemiological studies published in English.

In meta-analysis, prenatal maternal smoking was associated with an increased risk of sudden infant death (OR 2.94, pooled 95% CI 2.58 to 3.36, 73 studies),[14–85] and maternal smoking (smoking after birth) by an OR of 3.15 (95% CI 2.58 to 3.85, 16 studies – Fig 4.1).[14,16,17,20,24,25,36,44,45,48,49,51,62,80,85,86] Smoking by the father or other household member was associated with an increase in risk of sudden infant death by a ratio of 2.31 (pooled 95% CI 1.95 to 2.73, 18 studies),[14,16–20,24–26,36,44,45,49,51,52,85,87,88] but this effect was in many cases confounded by concurrent maternal smoking. In an analysis restricted to studies in which the mother did not smoke, the OR for paternal or others' smoking in the household was 1.45 (pooled 95% CI 1.07 to 1.96, eight studies – Fig 4.2).[14,17,18,20,24,49,52,87]

4.4 Lower respiratory infection

We identified 27 suitable papers published since the 31 identified in the 1997 Strachan and Cook analysis, yielding 58 studies for meta-analysis. Statistically significant increases in the risk of lower respiratory infection were seen with all measures of passive smoke exposure; for prenatal maternal smoking by an OR of

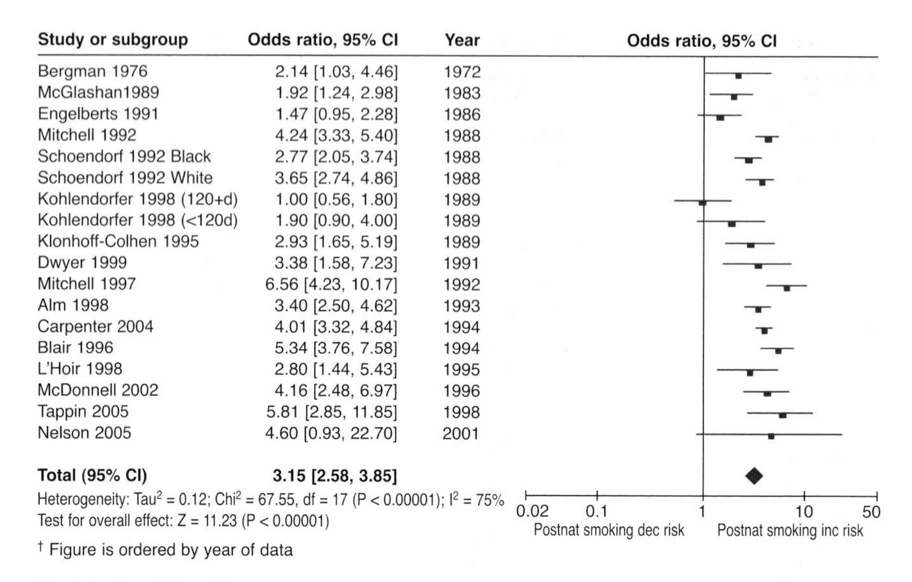

Fig 4.1 The risk of Sudden Infant Death Syndrome from postnatal maternal smoking.†

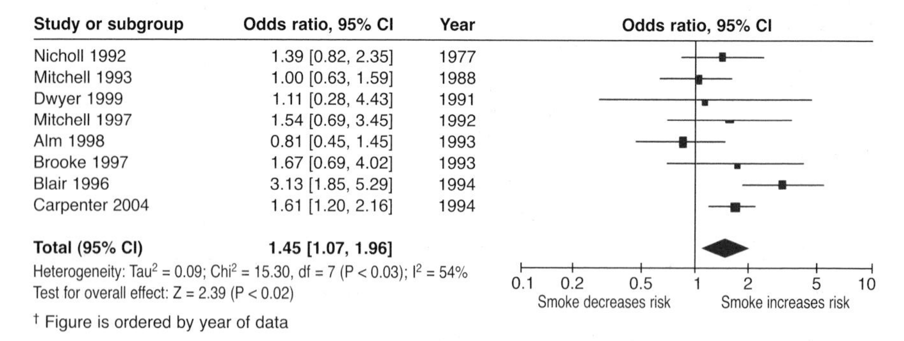

Fig 4.2 The risk of Sudden Infant Death Syndrome from paternal or other household member smoking where the mother is a non-smoker.†

1.24 (95% CI 1.10 to 1.40, nine studies),[89–97] postnatal maternal smoking by 1.58 (95% CI 1.45 to 1.73, 31 studies),[89,97–126] paternal smoking by 1.22 (95% CI 1.10 to 1.35, 21 studies),[93,97,100–104,106,107,113,114,116,117,121–123,126–130] and for household smoking by 1.54 (95% CI 1.39 to 1.70, 36 studies – Fig 4.3).[89,91,92,96,100–104,106–108,110,113,114,116,117,121,122,127,128,130–144] For smoking by both mother and father, the odds of disease were increased by 1.62 (95% CI 1.38 to 1.89, 14 studies).[101–104,113,114,116,117,121,122,126,142,145,146]

Sub-analyses based on the definition of outcome (comprising unspecified lower respiratory infection, bronchitis, bronchiolitis, pneumonia, and acute respiratory infection) found increased risks of disease were predominantly attributable to a

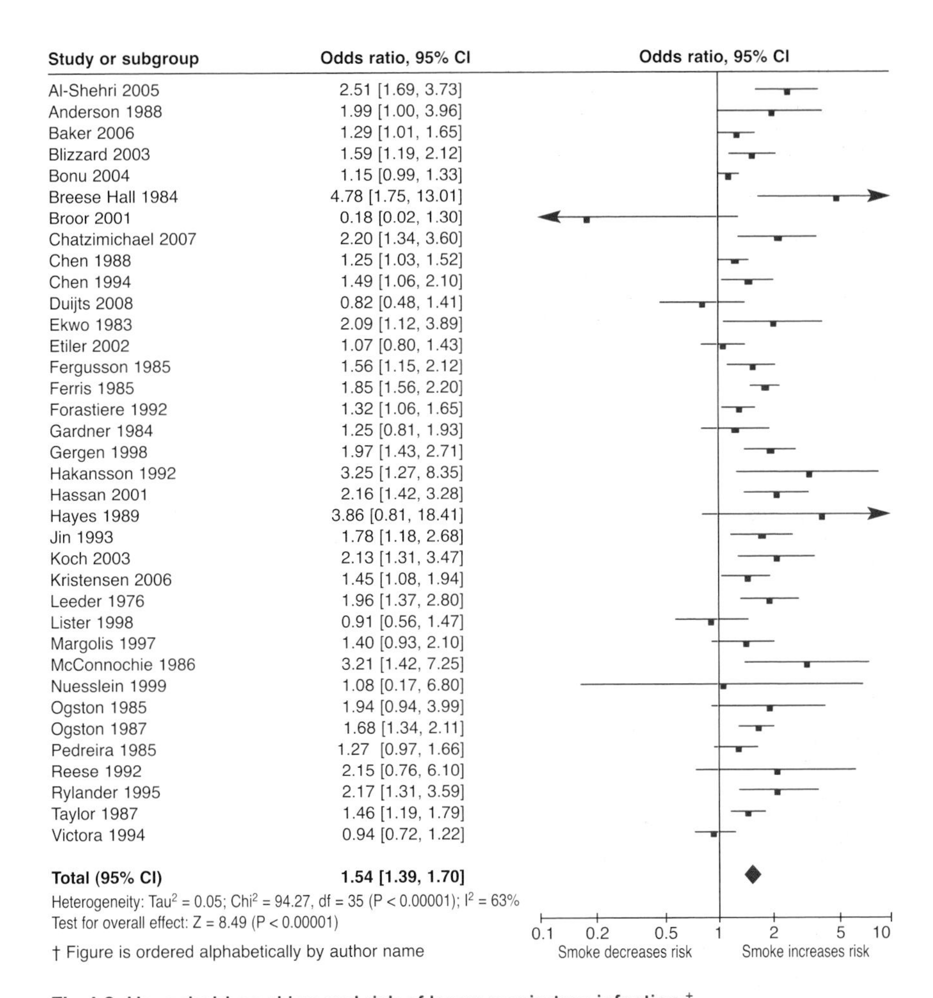

Fig 4.3 Household smoking and risk of lower respiratory infection.†

strong association between passive smoke exposure and bronchiolitis, for which the risk was increased by postnatal maternal smoking by an OR of 2.51 (95% CI 1.58 to 3.97, five studies – Fig 4.4).[110,112,116,118,126] Pooled estimates for the other categories of lower respiratory infection, with the exception of pneumonia, all identified statistically significant increases in risk with postnatal passive smoke exposure of similar magnitude (ORs ranging from 1.49–1.64 – Fig 4.4).

4.5 Wheeze and asthma

Our searches identified 61 papers, arising from 48 different longitudinal cohorts, published since the nine papers meeting the same inclusion criteria identified in

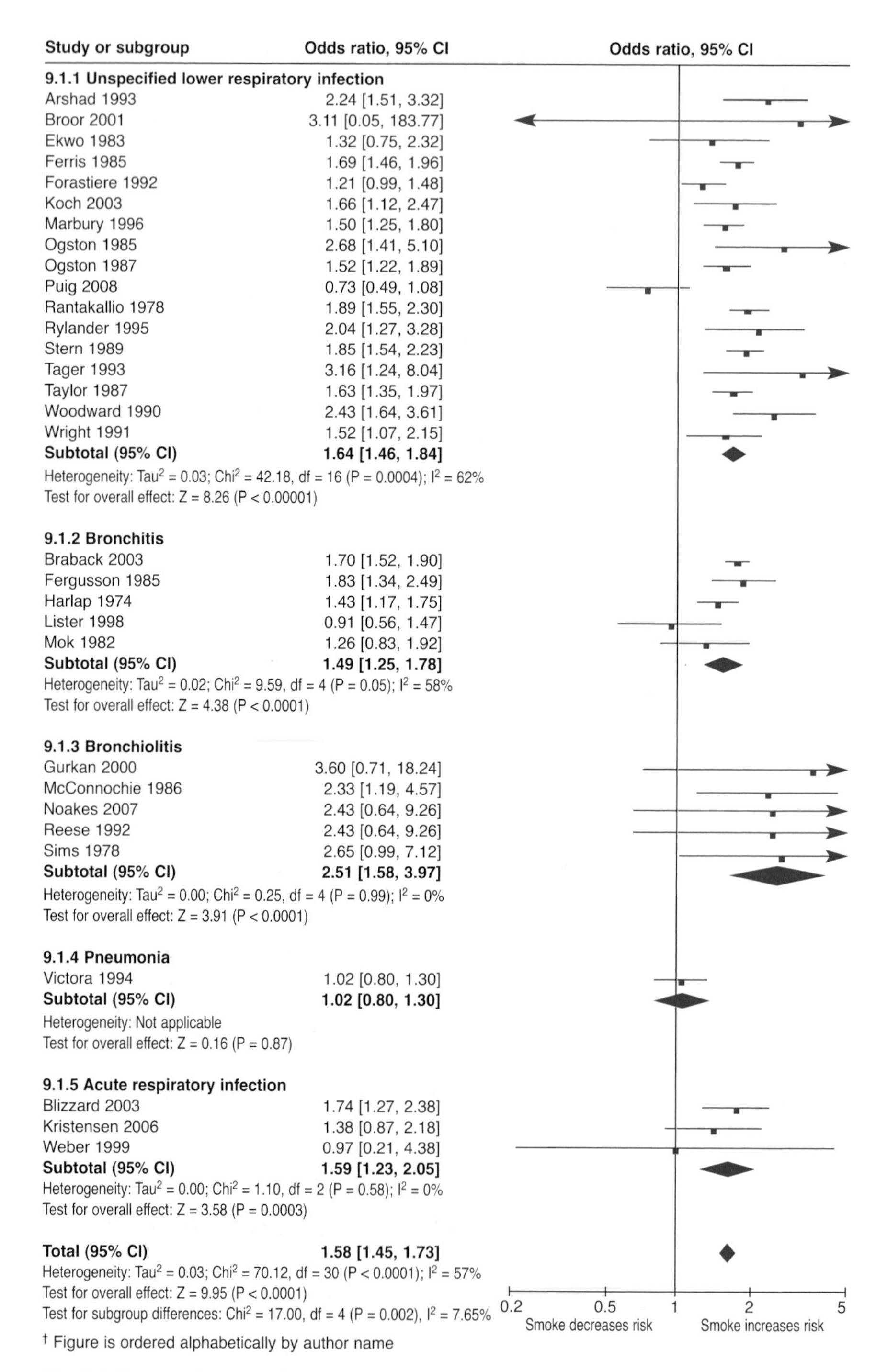

Fig 4.4 Postnatal maternal smoking and risk of subgroups of lower respiratory infection.†

the 1998 Strachan and Cook review,[8] yielding 70 papers for potential inclusion in the current meta-analyses.

4.5.1 Passive smoking and wheeze

The estimated effects of passive smoke exposure and wheeze occurring for the first time in the children in the three age ranges studied are shown in Table 4.1. With the exception of paternal smoking and wheeze occurring for the first time up to and including 2 years of age, or between 3 and 4 years of age, for which we found no relevant studies, all other measures of passive smoke exposure were associated with statistically significant increases in the risk of wheeze occurring for the first time at all ages studied, with ORs ranging from 1.25 (95% CI 1.12 to 1.40, seven studies) for prenatal maternal smoking and wheeze at age 3–4 years, and 1.72 (95% CI 1.15 to 2.58, two studies) for maternal smoking and wheeze in the first two years of life. Maternal smoking had the consistently strongest effect on wheeze at all ages.

Table 4.1 Passive smoke exposure and incidence of wheeze.

Smoking exposure	Age at outcome (years)	Number of studies	Pooled OR	95% CI	References
Prenatal maternal	≤2	11	1.44	1.20 to 1.73	93,246–255
Maternal		2	1.72	1.15 to 2.58	246,247
Paternal		0			
Household		7	1.37	1.08 to 1.73	93,248,250,251, 256–258
Prenatal maternal	3–4	7	1.25	1.12 to 1.40	246,250,259–263
Maternal		4	1.77	1.18 to 2.67	246,259,264,265
Paternal		0			
Household		4	1.06	0.88 to 1.27	250,260,262,266
Prenatal maternal	5–18	5	1.38	1.19 to 1.60	263,265,267–269
Maternal		2	1.65	1.14 to 2.41	270,271
Paternal		2	1.31	1.01 to 1.70	267,271
Household		5	1.34	1.15 to 1.56	263,271–274

4.5.2 Passive smoking and asthma

Estimated effects of passive smoking and asthma occurring for the first time in the various age ranges are shown in Table 4.2. With the exception of prenatal maternal smoking, which had a relatively strong effect on asthma occurring in the first two years (OR 1.91, 95% CI 1.43 to 2.53, four studies), the effects of passive smoke exposure on asthma were less strong than those on wheeze, with the strongest effect (for household smoking on asthma collected after 5 years old) being an OR of 1.50 (95% CI 1.13 to 1.97, four studies). Passive smoking effects were of similar magnitude for asthma at all ages studied. As for wheeze, there was limited information on the relation between paternal smoking and incident asthma.

Table 4.2 Passive smoke exposure and incidence of asthma.

Smoking exposure	Age at outcome (years)	Number of studies	Pooled OR	95% CI	References
Prenatal maternal	≤2	4	1.91	1.43 to 2.54	251,262,275,276
Maternal		1	0.70	0.04 to 11.23	112
Paternal		0			
Household		2	1.17	0.95 to 1.44	251,262
Prenatal maternal	3–4	2	1.24	0.93 to 1.64	275,277
Maternal		3	1.04	0.87 to 1.25	102,277,278
Paternal		1	1.34	1.23 to 1.46	102
Household		5	1.21	1.00 to 1.47	260,279–282
Prenatal maternal	5–18	5	1.22	1.13 to 1.32	275,283–286
Maternal		5	1.15	0.99 to 1.34	270,283,286–288
Paternal		1	0.90	0.44 to 1.83	287
Household		4	1.50	1.13 to 1.97	273,274,289,290

4.6 Middle ear infection

Our search identified 32 new studies for analysis, which in combination with the 25 papers from the 1998 Strachan and Cook review[3] yielded 58 eligible studies for inclusion in the meta-analyses. Prenatal maternal smoking was associated with an increased risk of middle ear disease by an OR of 1.11 (95% CI 0.55 to 2.24, four studies),[112,147–9] postnatal maternal smoking by 1.46 (95% CI 1.21 to 1.76, 18 studies – Fig 4.5),[108,148,150–165] paternal smoking by 1.27 (95% CI 0.97 to 1.66, 10 studies)[150,156,158–165] and household smoking by 1.35 (95% CI 1.23 to 1.49; 46 studies).[148–151,153,155,160–163,166–201]

Subgroup analyses based on the definition of outcome (comprising middle ear infection and surgery for middle ear disease) found that the increased risk arose predominantly from a relatively strong effect of passive smoke exposure on the risk of surgery for middle ear disease, for which the risk was increased by paternal smoking by an OR of 1.85 (95% CI 1.62 to 2.11, three studies)[160,162,163] and by prenatal maternal smoking by 2.90 (95% CI 1.29 to 6.53, one study).[149] Similar estimates were seen between the subgroups for postnatal maternal smoking and household smoking.

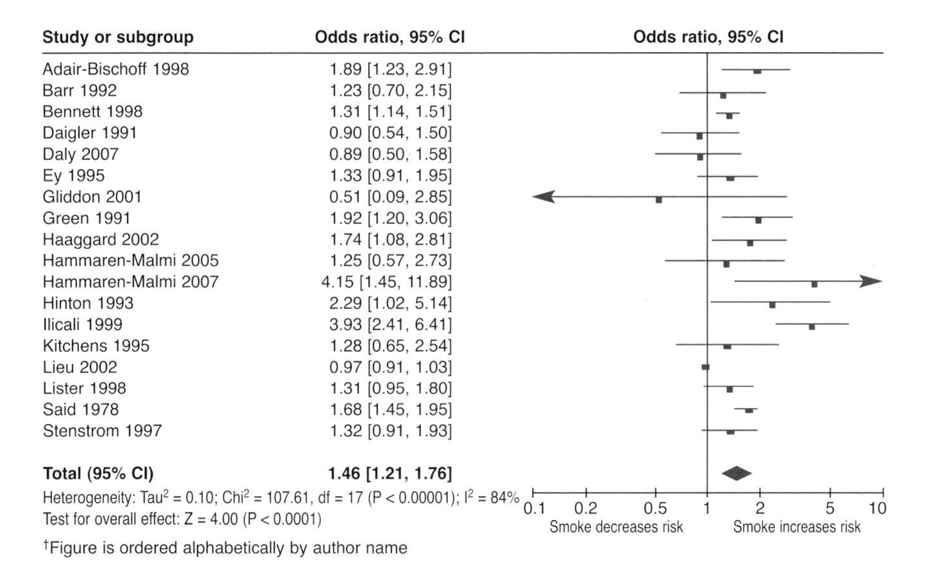

Fig 4.5 Postnatal maternal smoking and middle ear disease in children.†

4.7 Lung function

The standard and most widely used measure of airway function in adults and older children is the forced expiratory function in 1 second (FEV_1) and forced vital capacity (FVC), which are obtained by measuring volume exhaled over time after a full inspiration followed by a forced expiration carried out as quickly as possible. However, since this measure cannot be used in infants or children too young to comply with the forced expiratory manoeuvre, data on airflow in very young children are limited to measures based on external thoracic compression manoeuvres. As yet, the relationship between impairment of these measures in infants, and subsequent FEV_1 and FVC measures, is not fully defined.

4.7.1 Infants

The 1998 Cook, Strachan and Carey review included four publications which assessed the effect of parental smoking in neonates.[4] Evidence on the effect of prenatal and postnatal smoking has since been reviewed by Stocks and Dezateux in 2003,[202] who identified 21 studies assessing the effect of parental smoking on infant lung function. We identified three further relevant studies published since the 2003 review.[203–205] This total of 24 studies used a range of different and not necessarily directly comparable lung function measures, so meta-analysis was not feasible. However, the studies were generally, but not entirely, consistent in finding evidence of small reductions in measures of lung function among infants exposed to maternal smoking both before and after birth. The practical significance of these deficits as the child grows and develops into adulthood is as yet uncertain.

4.7.2 School-aged children

The 1998 review by Cook *et al* identified 42 cross-sectional studies in school-aged children and six longitudinal studies of lung function growth.[4] Our literature searches identified a further five population-based studies (two cross-sectional and three cohort studies)[206–210] with data suitable for inclusion in a further meta-analysis. This new analysis demonstrates that passive smoking is associated with a significant modest (1.02%, 95% CI 0.62 to 1.42%, 26 studies – Fig 4.6)[101,119,206–229] reduction in FEV_1, with no difference in effect between boys and girls.

4.8 Meningitis

We identified 16 studies of the effect of passive smoking on meningococcal or other bacterial meningitis:[230–245] 14 case-control studies (1,317 cases of meningococcal disease and 10,878 controls), one cohort study (47 cases out of 283,291 children), and one cross-sectional study of meningococcal carriage (82 cases out of 625 children). Fourteen studies were based on children aged ≤16 years, and two on children aged ≤18 years. Estimates of OR adjusted for potential confounders were available from nine studies. A pooled analysis of the 16 studies found that the risk of meningitis in children with one or more parent who

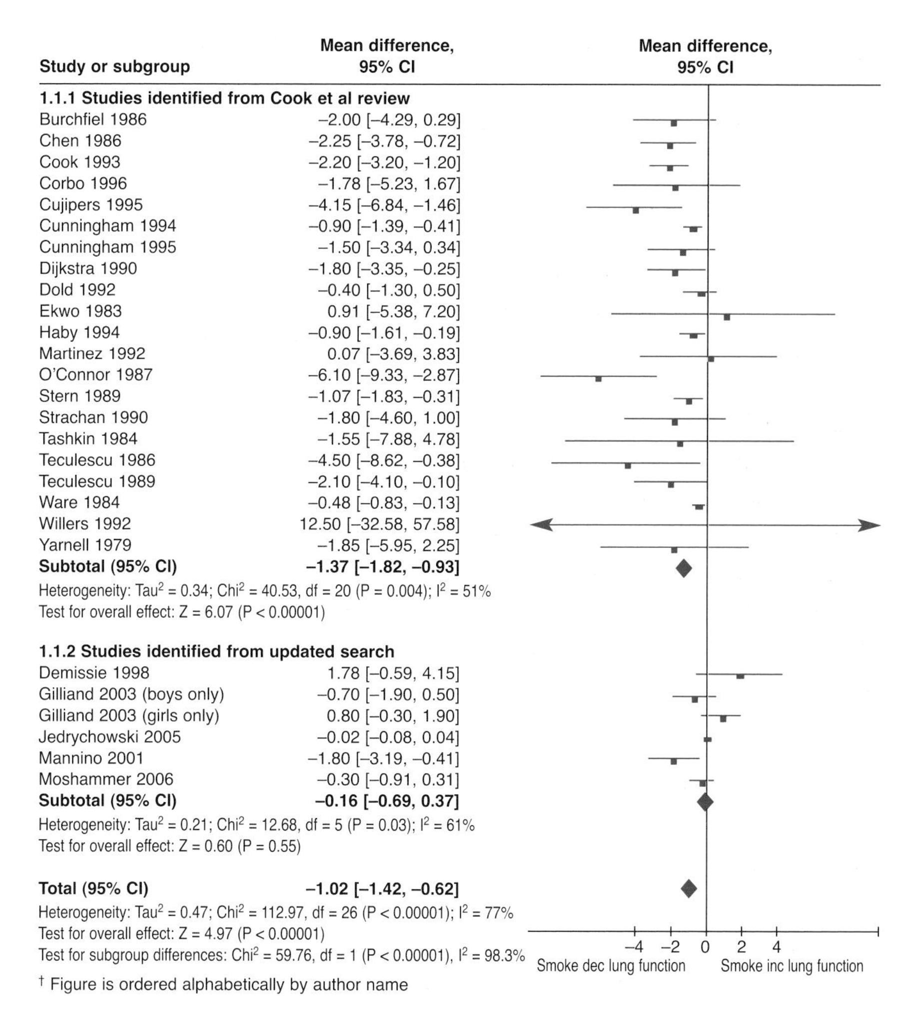

Fig 4.6 Passive smoke exposure and FEV1 (% difference) in school-aged children.†

smoked was increased by more than two-fold, with an OR of 2.30 (95% CI 1.74 to 3.06 – Fig 4.7). A subgroup analysis based on studies which presented ORs adjusted for potential confounders showed a similar magnitude of effect (OR 2.39, 95% CI 1.64 to 3.50, nine studies).[230,233,237–242,245]

Since this association was not concluded to be causal in the Surgeon General report,[11] we include a funnel plot of the published studies (Fig 4.8), which shows an asymmetrical pattern consistent with the exclusions of some smaller studies that have not demonstrated so great an increase in risk as a result of publication bias. If this is the case, then the OR of 2.30 is likely to be a modest overestimate of the true effect.

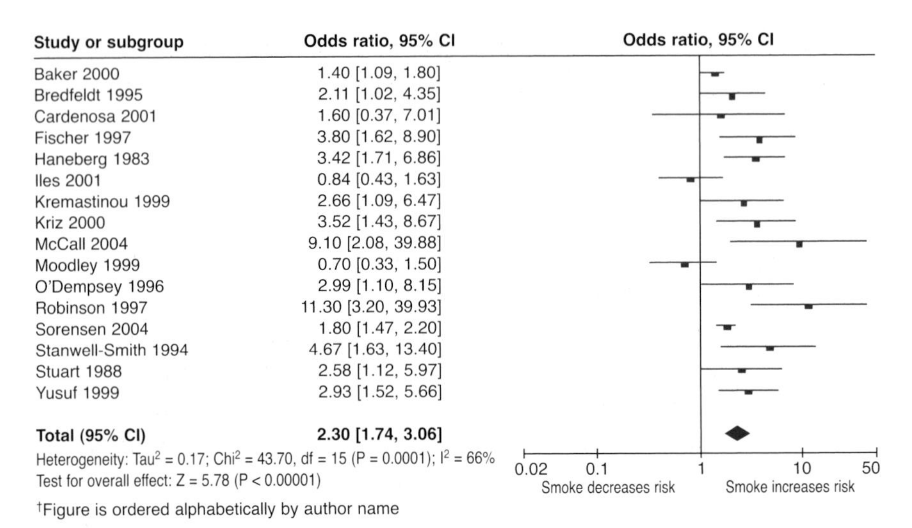

Study or subgroup	Odds ratio, 95% CI
Baker 2000	1.40 [1.09, 1.80]
Bredfeldt 1995	2.11 [1.02, 4.35]
Cardenosa 2001	1.60 [0.37, 7.01]
Fischer 1997	3.80 [1.62, 8.90]
Haneberg 1983	3.42 [1.71, 6.86]
Iles 2001	0.84 [0.43, 1.63]
Kremastinou 1999	2.66 [1.09, 6.47]
Kriz 2000	3.52 [1.43, 8.67]
McCall 2004	9.10 [2.08, 39.88]
Moodley 1999	0.70 [0.33, 1.50]
O'Dempsey 1996	2.99 [1.10, 8.15]
Robinson 1997	11.30 [3.20, 39.93]
Sorensen 2004	1.80 [1.47, 2.20]
Stanwell-Smith 1994	4.67 [1.63, 13.40]
Stuart 1988	2.58 [1.12, 5.97]
Yusuf 1999	2.93 [1.52, 5.66]
Total (95% CI)	**2.30 [1.74, 3.06]**

Heterogeneity: $Tau^2 = 0.17$; $Chi^2 = 43.70$, df = 15 (P = 0.0001); $I^2 = 66\%$
Test for overall effect: Z = 5.78 (P < 0.00001)

†Figure is ordered alphabetically by author name

Fig 4.7 Passive smoke exposure and meningitis in children.†

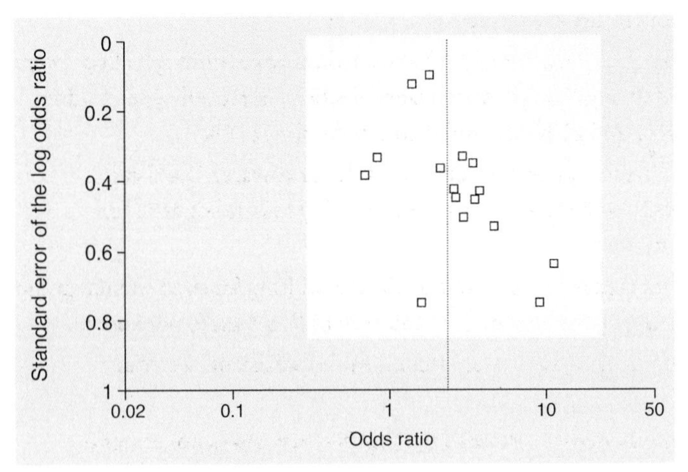

Fig 4.8 Funnel plot of 16 studies that examined the association between passive smoke exposure and meningitis in children. The dashed horizontal line indicates the pooled odds ratio (2.30).

4.9 Confounding

We have analysed results from all retrieved eligible studies, including those that adjusted for confounding and those that did not. However, the original systematic reviews[1–5] found that the associations of these outcomes with passive smoking were robust to adjustment for confounding, so we have not included adjusted estimates for the equivalent outcomes presented here.

Meningitis was not included in the above earlier systematic reviews, but our analysis found that the OR estimate based on studies that adjusted for potential confounders was actually marginally higher than the unadjusted estimate, suggesting that appreciable bias arising from confounding of the effect of passive smoking on meningitis risk is unlikely.

4.10 Summary

- Living in a household in which one or more people smoke more than doubles the risk of sudden infant death.
- Passive smoking increases the risk of lower respiratory infections in children. Smoking by the mother increases the risk by about 60%, and smoking by any household member by over 50%. Most of this increase is due to an effect on bronchiolitis, which is about 2.5 times more likely to occur in children whose mothers smoke.
- Passive smoking increases the risk of wheezing at all ages. Again, the effect is strongest for smoking by the mother, with increases in risk of 65% to 77% according to the age of the child.
- Passive smoking also increases the risk of asthma, and although effects were generally less strong than for wheeze or infection, in school-aged children the risk is increased by household smoking by about 50%.
- Passive smoking increases the risk of middle ear disease. The risk is increased by about 35% for household smoking and about 46% for smoking by the mother.
- Passive smoking results in modest impairment of lung function in infants and children. The long term practical significance of this effect is not known.
- Passive smoking appears to more than double the risk of bacterial meningitis.
- Since most mothers who smoke through pregnancy also smoke after the child is born, it is difficult to determine the relative importance of maternal smoking before and after birth on these outcomes. However, the higher ORs for postnatal maternal smoking, and the presence of effects from other household smokers, suggests that postnatal smoking is the more important.

References

1 Anderson HR, Cook DG. Passive smoking and sudden infant death syndrome: review of the epidemiological evidence. *Thorax* 1997;52:1003–9.
2 Cook DG, Strachan, DP. Health effects of passive smoking. 3. Parental smoking and prevalence of respiratory symptoms and asthma in school age children. *Thorax* 1997;52:1081–94.
3 Strachan DP, Cook DG. Health effects of passive smoking. 4. Parental smoking, middle ear disease and adenotonsillectomy in children. *Thorax* 1998;53:50–6.

4 Cook DG, Strachan DP, Carey IM. Health effects of passive smoking. 9: Parental smoking and spirometric indices in children. *Thorax* 1998;53:884–93.

5 Strachan DP, Cook DG. Health effects of passive smoking. 1. Parental smoking and lower respiratory illness in infancy and early childhood. *Thorax* 1997;52:905–14.

6 Strachan DP, Cook DG. Health effects of passive smoking. 5. Parental smoking and allergic sensitisation in children. *Thorax* 1998;53:117–23.

7 Cook DG, Strachan DP. Health effects of passive smoking. 7: Parental smoking, bronchial reactivity and peak flow variability in children. *Thorax* 1998;53:295–301.

8 Strachan DP, Cook DG. Parental smoking and childhood asthma: longitudinal and case-control studies. *Thorax* 1998;53:204–212.

9 Department of Health, Department of Health and Social Services Northern Ireland, Scottish Office Department of Health, Welsh Office. *Report of the Scientific Committee on Tobacco and Health.* London, 1998.

10 Scientific Committee on Tobacco and Health (SCOTH). *Secondhand smoke: review of evidence since 1998. Update of evidence on health effects of secondhand smoke.* London: DoH, 2004.

11 US Surgeon General. *The health consequences of involuntary exposure to tobacco smoke.* Report of the surgeon general. Atlanta: US DHHS, 2006.

12 Mitchell EA, Milerad J. Smoking and the sudden infant death syndrome. *Reviews on Environmental Health* 2006;21:81–103.

13 Stroup DF, Berlin JA, Morton SC *et al.* Meta-analysis of observational studies in epidemiology. A proposal for reporting. *JAMA* 2000;283:2008–12.

14 Alm B, Milerad J, Wennergren G *et al.* A case-control study of smoking and sudden infant death syndrome in the Scandinavian countries, 1992 to 1995. The Nordic Epidemiological SIDS Study. *Arch Dis Child* 1998;78:329–34.

15 Arnestad M, Andersen M, Vege A, Rognum TO. Changes in the epidemiological pattern of sudden infant death syndrome in southeast Norway, 1984-1998: implications for future prevention and research. *Arch Dis Child* 2001;85:108–15.

16 Bergman AB, Weisner LA. Relationship of passive cigarette-smoking to sudden infant death syndrome. *Pediatrics* 1976;58:665–8.

17 Blair PS, Fleming PJ, Bensley D *et al.* Smoking and the sudden infant death syndrome: results from 1993-1995 case-control study for the confidential inquiry into stillbirths and death in infancy. *BMJ* 1996;313:195–8.

18 Brooke H, Gibson A, Tappin D, Brown H. Case-control study of sudden infant death syndrome in Scotland, 1992–5[see comment]. *BMJ* 1997;314:1516–20.

19 Cameron MH, Williams AL. Development and testing of scoring systems for predicting infants with high-risk of sudden infant death syndrome in Melbourne. *Aust Paediatr J* 1986;Suppl:37–45.

20 Carpenter RG, Irgens LM, Blair PS *et al.* Sudden unexplained infant death in 20 regions in Europe: case control study[see comment]. *Lancet* 2004;363:185–91.

21 Chong DSY, Yip PSF, Karlberg J. Maternal smoking: an increasing unique risk factor for sudden infant death syndrome in Sweden [see comment]. *Acta Paediatr* 2004;93:471–8.

22 Cooke RW. Smoking, intra-uterine growth retardation and sudden infant death syndrome. *Int J Epidemiol* 1998;27:238–41.

23 Daltveit AK, Irgens LM, Oyen N *et al.* Circadian variations in sudden infant death syndrome: associations with maternal smoking, sleeping position and infections. The Nordic Epidemiological SIDS Study [see comment]. *Acta Paediatr* 2003;92:1007–13.

24 Dwyer T, Ponsonby AL, Couper D. Tobacco smoke exposure at one month of age and subsequent risk of SIDS – a prospective study [see comment]. *Am J Epidemiol* 1999; 149:593–602.

25 Engelberts A, *Cot death in the Netherlands: an epidemiological study*, in *VU University Press.* MD thesis, 1991.

26 Fleming PJ, Blair PS, Ward Platt M *et al.* Sudden infant death syndrome and social deprivation: assessing epidemiological factors after post-matching for deprivation. *Paediatr Perinat Epidemiol* 2003;17:272–80.

27 Getahun D, Amre D, Rhoads GG, Demissie K. Maternal and obstetric risk factors for sudden infant death syndrome in the United States. *Obstet Gynecol* 2004;103:646–52.

28 Gilbert RE, Fleming PJ, Azaz Y, Rudd PT. Signs of illness preceding sudden unexpected death in infants. *BMJ* 1990;300:1237–9.

29 Haglund B, Cnattingius S, Otterblad-Olausson P. Sudden infant death syndrome in Sweden, 1983-1990: season at death, age at death, and maternal smoking. *Am J Epidemiol* 1995;142:619–24.

30 Hauck FR, Herman SM, Donovan M *et al.* Sleep environment and the risk of sudden infant death syndrome in an urban population: The Chicago infant mortality study. *Pediatrics* 2003;111:1207–14.

31 Hilder AS. Ethnic differences in the sudden infant death syndrome: what can we learn from immigrants in the UK. *Early Hum Dev* 1994;38:143–9.

32 Hoffman HJ, Hunter JC, Ellish NJ, Janerich DT, Goldberg J. Adverse reproductive factors and the sudden infant death syndrome. In: *Sudden infant death syndrome*, New York: PMA Publishing Corp, 1988:153–7.

33 Iyasu S, Randall LL, Welty TK *et al.* Risk factors for sudden infant death syndrome among northern plains Indians. *JAMA* 2002;288:2717–23. [erratum appears in *JAMA* 2003; 289(3):303].

34 Jorch G, Schmidt-Troschke S, Bajanowski T *et al.* Risk factors for sudden infant death (SID): epidemiologic study of two German districts 1990-1992. *Monatsschr Kinderheilkd* 1994;142:45–51.

35 Karagas MR, Hollenbach KA, Hickok DE, Daling JR. Induction of labour and risk of sudden infant death syndrome. *Obstet Gynecol* 1993;81:497–501.

36 Klonoff-Cohen HS, Edelstein SL, Lefkowitz ES *et al.* The effect of passive smoking and tobacco exposure through breast milk on sudden infant death syndrome. *JAMA* 1995;273: 795–8.

37 Leach CE, Blair PS, Fleming PJ *et al.* Epidemiology of SIDS and explained sudden infant deaths. CESDI SUDI Research Group. *Pediatrics* 1999;104:e43.

38 Lewak N, van den Berg BJ, Beckwith JB. Sudden infant death syndrome risk factors: prospective data review. *Clin Pediatr* 1979;18: 404–11.

39 Li DK, Daling JR. Maternal smoking, low birth weight, and ethnicity in relation to sudden infant death syndrome. *Am J Epidemiol* 1991;134:958–64.

40 MacDorman MF, Cnattingius S, Hoffman HJ, Kramer MS, Haglund B. Sudden infant death syndrome and smoking in the United States and Sweden. *Am J Epidemiol* 1997; 146:249–57.

41 Malloy MH, Kleinman JC, Land GH, Schramm WF. The association of maternal smoking with age and the cause of infant death. *Am J Epidemiol* 1988;128:46–55.

42 Matthews T, McDonnell M, McGarvey C, Loftus G, O'Regan M. A multivariate "time based" analysis of SIDS risk factors. *Arch Dis Child* 2004;89:267–71.

43 Matthews TG, O'Brien SJ. Perinatal epidemiological characteristics of the sudden infant death syndrome in an Irish population. *Irish Medical Journal* 1985;78:251–3.

44 McDonnell M, Mehanni M, McGarvey C, Oregan M, Matthews TG. Smoking: the major risk factor for SIDS in Irish infants. *Irish Medical Journal* 2002;95:111–13.

45 McGlashan ND. Sudden infant deaths in Tasmania, 1980–1986: a seven year prospective study. *Soc Sci Med 1989*;29:1015–26.

46 McLoughlin A. Sudden infant deaths in Tameside. *Health Visitor* 1988;61:235–7.

47 Menihan CA, Phipps M, Weitzen S. Fetal heart rate patterns and sudden infant death syndrome. *Journal of Obstetric, Gynecologic, and Neonatal Nursing* 2006;35:116–22.

48 Mitchell EA, Taylor BJ, Ford RP *et al.* Four modifiable and other major risk factors for cot death: the New Zealand study. *Journal of Paediatrics and Child Health* 1992;28:S3–8.

49 Mitchell EA, Tuohy PG, Brunt JM *et al.* Risk factors for sudden infant death syndrome following the prevention campaign in New Zealand: a prospective study. *Pediatrics* 1997;100:835–40.

50 Murphy J, Newcombe R, Sibert JR. The epidemiology of sudden infant death syndrome. *J Epidemiol Community Health* 1982;36:17–21.

51 Nelson T, To K-F, Wong Y-Y *et al.* Hong Kong case-control study of sudden unexpected infant death. *New Zealand Medical Journal* 2005;118:U1788.

52 Nicholl JP, O'Cathain A. Antenatal smoking, postnatal passive smoking, and sudden infant death syndrome. In: Alberman P (ed), *Effects of smoking on the fetus, neonate and child.* Oxford: Oxford Medical Publications, 1992:138–49.

53 Nilsen ST, Laerdal A. Krybbedod og royking i svangerskapet. *Tidsskr Nor Laegeforen* 1991; 111:3493–5.

54 Petru E, Einspieler C, Rosanelli K *et al.* Are there pre- or perinatal risk factors for sudden infant death syndrome? *Geburtshilfe Frauenheilkd* 1989;49:494–7.

55 Pinho APS, Aerts D, Nunes ML. Risk factors for sudden infant death syndrome in a developing country. *Rev Saude Publica* 2008;42:396–401.

56 Poets CF, Schlaud M, Kleemann WJ *et al.* Sudden infant death and maternal cigarette smoking: results from the Lower Saxony Perinatal Working Group. *Eur J Pediatr* 1995;154: 326–9.

57 Pollack HA. Sudden infant death syndrome, maternal smoking during pregnancy, and the cost-effectiveness of smoking cessation intervention. *Am J Public Health* 2001;91:432–6.

58 Ponsonby AL, Dwyer T, Kasi SV, Cochrane JA. The Tasmanian SIDS case-control study; univariable and multivariable risk factor analysis. *Paediatr Perinat Epidemiol* 1995;9: 256–72.

59 Rintahaka PJ, Hirvonen J. The epidemiology of sudden infant death syndrome in Finland in 1969-1980. *Forensic Sci Int* 1986;30:219–33.

60 Schellscheidt J, Ott A, Jorch G. Epidemiological features of sudden infant death after a German intervention campaign in 1992. *Eur J Pediatr* 1997a;156:655–60.

61 Schellscheidt J, Oyen N, Jorch G. Interactions between maternal smoking and other prenatal risk factors for sudden infant death syndrome (SIDS). *Acta Paediatr* 1997b; 86:857–63.

62 Schoendorf KC, Kiely JL. Relationship of sudden infant death syndrome to maternal smoking during and after pregnancy. *Pediatrics* 1992;90:905–8.

63 Smith GCS, Pell JP, Dobbie R. Risk of sudden infant death syndrome and week of gestation of term birth. *Pediatrics* 2003;111:1367–71.

64 Stebbens VA, Alexander JR, Southall, DP. Pre and perinatal clinical characteristics of infants who suffer sudden infant death syndrome. *Biol Neonate* 1987;51:129–137.

65 Steele R and Langworth JT. The relationship of antenatal and postnatal factors to sudden unexpected death in infancy. *Can Med Assoc J* 1966;94:1165–71.
66 Taylor JA, Sanderson M. A reexamination of the risk factors for the sudden infant death syndrome. *J Pediatr* 1995;126:887–91.
67 Toro K, Sotonyi P. Distribution of prenatal and postnatal risk factors for sudden infant death in Budapest. *Scand J Prim Health Care* 2001;19:178–80.
68 VandenBerg M. Smoking during pregnancy and post-neonatal death. *New Zealand Medical Journal* 1985;98:1075–8.
69 Vennemann MM, Findeisen M, Butterfass-Bahloul T *et al.* Modifiable risk factors for SIDS in Germany: results of GeSID. *Acta Paediatr* 2005;94:655–60.
70 Victora CG, Nobre LC, Lombardi C *et al.* Epidemiologic picture of sudden infant death in cities of Rio Grande do Sul (Brazil). *Rev Saude Publica* 1987;21:490–6.
71 Wierenga H, Brand R, Geudeke T *et al.* Prenatal risk factors for cot death in very preterm and small for gestational age infants. *Early Hum Dev* 1990;23:15–26.
72 Wigfield R, Fleming PJ, The prevalence of risk factors for SIDS: Impact of an interaction campaign. In: Rognum TO (ed), *Sudden infant death syndrome. New trends for the nineties.* Oslo: Scandinavian University Press, 1995:124–8.
73 Wisborg K, Kesmodel U, Henriksen TB, Olsen SF, Secher NJ. Exposure to tobacco smoke in utero and the risk of stillbirth and death in the first year of life. *Am J Epidemiol* 2001; 154:322–7.
74 Zotti ME, Replogle WH, Sappenfield WM. Prenatal smoking and birth outcomes among Mississippi residents. *Journal of the Mississippi State Medical Association* 2003;44:3–9.
75 Blair PS, Platt MW, Smith IJ, Fleming PJ, Group SSR. Sudden Infant Death Syndrome and the time of death: factors associated with night-time and day-time deaths. *Int J Epidemiol* 2006;35:1563–9.
76 Bulterys M. Passive tobacco exposure and sudden infant death syndrome [letter]. *Pediatrics* 1993;92:205–6.
77 Einspieler C. Case-control study of SIDS between 1982–93 in Austria. Cited in: Mitchell EA, Milerad J. Smoking and the sudden infant death syndrome. *Reviews on Environmental Health* 2006;21:81–103.
78 Haglund B, Cnattingius S. Cigarette smoking as a risk factor for sudden infant death syndrome: a population-based study. *Am J Public Health* 1990;80:29–32.
79 Irwin KL, Mannino S, Daling J. Sudden infant death syndrome in Washington State; why are Native Americans at greater risk than white infants? *J Pediatr* 1992;121:242–7.
80 Kohlendorfer U, Kiechl S, Sperl W. Sudden infant death syndrome: risk factor profiles for distinct subgroups [see comment]. *Am J Epidemiol* 1998;147:960–8.
81 Naeye RL, Ladis B, Drage JS. Sudden infant death syndrome: a prospective study. *Am J Dis Child* 1976;130:1207–12.
82 Schrauzer GN, Rhead WJ, Saltzstein SL. Sudden infant death syndrome: plasma vitamin E level and dietary factors. *Ann Clin Lab Sci* 1975;5:31–7.
83 Kraus JF, Bulterys M. The epidemiology of sudden infant death syndrome. In: Kiely M (ed), *Reproductive and perinatal epidemiology.* Florida: CRC Press, 1990:219–49.
84 Nordstrom ML, Cnattingius S, Haglund B. Social differences in Swedish infant mortality by cause of death, 1983 to 1986. *Am J Public Health* 1993;83:26–30.
85 l'Hoir MP. *Cot death: Risk factors and prevention in the Netherlands in 1995-1996.* Utrecht: Elinkwijk BV, 1998.
86 Tappin D, Ecob R, Brooke H. Bedsharing, roomsharing, and sudden infant death syndrome in Scotland: a case-control study [see comment]. *J Pediatr* 2005;147:32–7.

87 Mitchell EA, Ford RP, Stewart AW *et al.* Smoking and the sudden infant death syndrome. *Pediatrics* 1993;91:893–6.
88 Lee NNY, Chan YF, Davis DP, Lau E, Yip DC. Sudden infant death syndrome in Hong Kong: confirmation of low incidence. *BMJ* 1989;298:721–2.
89 Blizzard L, Ponsonby A-L, Dwyer T, Venn A, Cochrane JA. Parental smoking and infant respiratory infection: how important is not smoking in the same room with the baby? *Am J Public Health* 2003;93:482–8.
90 Carroll KN, Gebretsadik T, Griffin MR *et al.* Maternal asthma and maternal smoking are associated with increased risk of bronchiolitis during infancy [see comment]. *Pediatrics* 2007;119:1104–12.
91 Duijts L, Jaddoe VWV, Hofman A *et al.* Maternal smoking in prenatal and early postnatal life and the risk of respiratory tract infections in infancy. The Generation R study. *Eur J Epidemiol* 2008;23:547–55.
92 Gergen PJ, Fowler JA, Maurer KR, Davis WW, Overpeck MD. The burden of environmental tobacco smoke exposure on the respiratory health of children 2 months through 5 years of age in the United States: Third National Health and Nutrition Examination Survey, 1988 to 1994. *Pediatrics* 1998;101:E8.
93 Haberg SE, Stigum H, Nystad W, Nafstad P. Effects of pre- and postnatal exposure to parental smoking on early childhood respiratory health. *Am J Epidemiol* 2007;166:679–86.
94 Koehoorn M, Karr CJ, Demers PA *et al.* Descriptive epidemiological features of bronchiolitis in a population-based cohort. *Pediatrics* 2008;122:1196–203.
95 Latzin P, Frey U, Roiha HL *et al.* Prospectively assessed incidence, severity, and determinants of respiratory symptoms in the first year of life. *Pediatr Pulmonol* 2007;42: 41–50.
96 Nuesslein TG, Beckers D, Rieger CH. Cotinine in meconium indicates risk for early respiratory tract infections. *Hum Exp Toxicol* 1999;18:283–90.
97 Puig C, Sunyer J, Garcia-Algar O *et al.* Incidence and risk factors of lower respiratory tract illnesses during infancy in a Mediterranean birth cohort. *Acta Paediatr* 2008;97:1406–11.
98 Arshad SH, Stevens M, Hide DW. The effect of genetic and environmental factors on the prevalence of allergic disorders at the age of two years. *Clin Exp Allergy* 1993;23:504–11.
99 Braback L, Bjor O, Nordahl G. Early determinants of first hospital admissions for asthma and acute bronchitis among Swedish children. *Acta Paediatr* 2003;92:27–33.
100 Broor S, Pandey RM, Ghosh M *et al.* Risk factors for severe acute lower respiratory tract infection in under-five children. *Indian Pediatr* 2001;38:1361–9.
101 Ekwo EE, Weinberger MM, Lachenbruch PA, Huntley WH. Relationship of parental smoking and gas cooking to respiratory disease in children. *Chest* 1983;84:662–8.
102 Fergusson DM and Horwood LJ. Parental smoking and respiratory illness during early childhood: a six-year longitudinal study. *Pediatr Pulmonol* 1985;1:99–106.
103 Ferris BG Jr, Ware JH, Berkey CS *et al.* Effects of passive smoking on health of children. *Environ Health Perspect* 1985;62:289–95.
104 Forastiere F, Corbo GM, Michelozzi P *et al.* Effects of environment and passive smoking on the respiratory health of children. *Int J Epidemiol* 1992;21:66–73.
105 Harlap S, Davies AM. Infant admissions to hospital and maternal smoking. *Lancet* 1974; 1:529–32.
106 Koch A, Molbak K, Homoe P *et al.* Risk factors for acute respiratory tract infections in young Greenlandic children. *Am J Epidemiol* 2003;158:374–84.
107 Kristensen IA, Olsen J. Determinants of acute respiratory infections in Soweto – a population-based birth cohort. *S Afr Med J* 2006;96:633–40.

108 Lister SM, Jorm LR. Parental smoking and respiratory illnesses in Australian children aged 0-4 years: ABS 1989-90 National Health Survey results. *Aust N Z J Public Health* 1998; 22:781–6.

109 Marbury MC, Maldonado G, Waller L. The indoor air and children's health study: methods and incidence rates. *Epidemiology* 1996;7:166–74.

110 McConnochie KM, Roghmann KJ. Parental smoking, presence of older siblings, and family history of asthma increase risk of bronchiolitis. *Am J Dis Child* 1986;140:806–12.

111 Mok JY, Simpson H. Outcome of acute lower respiratory tract infection in infants: preliminary report of seven-year follow-up study. *BMJ (Clin Res Ed)* 1982;285:333–7.

112 Noakes P, Taylor A, Hale J *et al.* The effects of maternal smoking on early mucosal immunity and sensitization at 12 months of age. *Pediatr Allergy Immunol* 2007;18:118–27.

113 Ogston SA, Florey CD, Walker CH. The Tayside infant morbidity and mortality study: effect on health of using gas for cooking. *BMJ (Clin Res Ed)* 1985;290:957–60.

114 Ogston SA, Florey CD, Walker CH. Association of infant alimentary and respiratory illness with parental smoking and other environmental factors. *J Epidemiol Community Health* 1987;41:21–5.

115 Rantakallio P. Relationship of maternal smoking to morbidity and mortality of the child up to the age of five. *Acta Paediatr Scand* 1978;67:621–31.

116 Reese AC, James IR, Landau LI, Lesouef PN. Relationship between urinary cotinine level and diagnosis in children admitted to hospital. *Am Rev Respir Dis* 1992;146:66–70.

117 Rylander E, Pershagen G, Eriksson M, Bermann G. Parental smoking, urinary cotinine, and wheezing bronchitis in children. *Epidemiology* 1995;6:289–93.

118 Sims DG, Downham MA, Gardner PS, Webb JK, Weightman, D. Study of 8-year-old children with a history of respiratory syncytial virus bronchiolitis in infancy. *BMJ* 1978; 1:11–14.

119 Stern B, Raizenne M, Burnett R. Respiratory effects of early childhood exposure to passive smoke. *Environ Int* 1989;15:29–34.

120 Tager IB, Hanrahan JP, Tosteson TD *et al.* Lung function, pre- and post-natal smoke exposure, and wheezing in the first year of life. *Am Rev Respir Dis* 1993;147:811–7.

121 Taylor B, Wadsworth J. Maternal smoking during pregnancy and lower respiratory tract illness in early life. *Arch Dis Child* 1987;62:786–91.

122 Victora CG, Fuchs SC, Flores JA, Fonseca W, Kirkwood B. Risk factors for pneumonia among children in a Brazilian metropolitan area. *Pediatrics* 1994;93:977–85.

123 Weber MW, Milligan P, Hilton S *et al.* Risk factors for severe respiratory syncytial virus infection leading to hospital admission in children in the Western Region of The Gambia. *Int J Epidemiol* 1999;28:157–62.

124 Woodward A, Douglas RM, Graham NM, Miles H. Acute respiratory illness in Adelaide children: breast feeding modifies the effect of passive smoking. *J Epidemiol Community Health* 1990;44:224–30.

125 Wright AL, Holberg C, Martinez FD, Taussig LM. Relationship of parental smoking to wheezing and nonwheezing lower respiratory tract illnesses in infancy. Group Health Medical Associates. *J Pediatr* 1991;118:207–14.

126 Gurkan F, Kiral A, Dagli E, Karakoc F. The effect of passive smoking on the development of respiratory syncytial virus bronchiolitis. *Eur J Epidemiol* 2000;16:465–8.

127 Chen Y. Environmental tobacco smoke, low birth weight, and hospitalization for respiratory disease. *Am J Respir Crit Care Med* 1994;150:54–8.

128 Chen Y, Li WX, Yu SZ, Qian WH. Chang-Ning epidemiological study of children's health: I: Passive smoking and children's respiratory diseases. *Int J Epidemiol* 1988;17:348–55.

129 El-Sawy IH, Nasr FMK, Mowafy EWE, Sharaki OAM, Bakey AMA. Passive smoking and lower respiratory tract illnesses in children. *East Mediterr Health J* 1997;3:425–34.

130 Jin C, Rossignol AM. Effects of passive smoking on respiratory illness from birth to age eighteen months, in Shanghai, People's Republic of China. *J Pediatr* 1993;123:553–8.

131 Al-Shehri MA, Sadeq A, Quli K. Bronchiolitis in Abha, Southwest Saudi Arabia: viral etiology and predictors for hospital admission. *West Afr J Med* 2005;24:299–304.

132 Anderson LJ, Parker RA, Strikas RA *et al.* Day-care center attendance and hospitalization for lower respiratory tract illness. *Pediatrics* 1988;82:300–8.

133 Baker RJ, Hertz-Picciotto I, Dostal M *et al.* Coal home heating and environmental tobacco smoke in relation to lower respiratory illness in Czech children, from birth to 3 years of age. *Environ Health Perspect* 2006;114:1126–32.

134 Bonu S, Rani M, Jha P, Peters DH, Nguyen SN. Household tobacco and alcohol use, and child health: an exploratory study from India. *Health Policy* 2004;70:67–83.

135 Breese Hall C, Hall WJ, Gala CL, MaGill FB, Leddy JP. Long-term prospective study in children after respiratory syncytial virus infection. *J Pediatr* 1984;105:358–64.

136 Chatzimichael A, Tsalkidis A, Cassimos D *et al.* The role of breastfeeding and passive smoking on the development of severe bronchiolitis in infants. *Minerva Pediatr* 2007; 59:199–206.

137 Etiler N, Velipasaoglu S, Aktekin M. Incidence of acute respiratory infections and the relationship with some factors in infancy in Antalya, Turkey. *Pediatr Int* 2002;44:64–9.

138 Gardner G, Frank AL, Taber LH. Effects of social and family factors on viral respiratory infection and illness in the first year of life. *J Epidemiol Community Health* 1984;38:42–8.

139 Hakansson A, Carlsson B. Maternal cigarette smoking, breast-feeding, and respiratory tract infections in infancy. A population-based cohort study. *Scand J Prim Health Care* 1992;10:60–5.

140 Hassan MK, Al-Sadoon I. Risk factors for severe pneumonia in children in Basrah. *Trop Doct* 2001;31:139–41.

141 Hayes EB, Hurwitz ES, Schonberger LB, Anderson LJ. Respiratory syncytial virus outbreak on American Samoa. Evaluation of risk factors. *Am J Dis Child* 1989;143:316–21.

142 Leeder SR, Corkhill R, Irwig LM, Holland WW, Colley JR. Influence of family factors on the incidence of lower respiratory illness during the first year of life. *Br J Prev Soc Med* 1976;30:203–12.

143 Margolis PA, Keyes LL, Greenberg RA, Bauman KE, LaVange LM. Urinary cotinine and parent history (questionnaire) as indicators of passive smoking and predictors of lower respiratory illness in infants. *Pediatr Pulmonol*1997;23:417–23.

144 Pedreira FA, Guandolo VL, Feroli EJ, Mella GW, Weiss IP. Involuntary smoking and incidence of respiratory illness during the first year of life. *Pediatrics* 1985;75:594–7.

145 Maziak W, Mzayek F, al-Musharref M. Effects of environmental tobacco smoke on the health of children in the Syrian Arab Republic. *East Mediterr Health J* 1999;5:690–7.

146 Rahman MM, Rahman AM. Prevalence of acute respiratory tract infection and its risk factors in under five children. *Bangladesh Medical Research Council Bulletin* 1997;23:47–50.

147 Bener A, Eihakeem AAM, Abdulhadi K. Is there any association between consanguinity and hearing loss. *Int J Pediat Otorhinolaryngol* 2005;69:327–33.

148 Lieu JEC, Feinstein AR. Effect of gestational and passive smoke exposure on ear infections in children. *Arch Paedr Adolesc Med* 2002;156:147–54.

149 Stathis SL, O'Callaghan DM, Williams GM *et al.* Maternal cigarette smoking during pregnancy is an independent predictor for symptoms of middle ear disease at five years' postdelivery. *Pediatrics* 1999;104:e16.

150 Adair-Bischoff CE and Sauve RS. Environmental tobacco smoke and middle ear disease in preschool-age children. *Arch Paedr Adolesc Med*1998;152:127–33.

151 Barr G. Passive smoking and otitis media with effusion. *BMJ* 1992;304:382–3.

152 Bennett KE, Haggard MP. Accumulation of factors influencing children's middle ear disease: risk factor modelling on a large population cohort. *J Epidemiol Community Health* 1998;52:786–93.

153 Daly KA, Pirie PL, Rhodes KL, Hunter LL, Davey CS. Early otitis media among Minnesota American Indians: The little ears study. *Am J Public Health* 2007;97:317–22.

154 Ey JL, Holberg CJ, Aldous MB *et al.* Passive smoke exposure and otitis media in the first year of life. *Pediatrics* 1995;95:670–7.

155 Gliddon ML, Sutton GJ. Prediction of 8-month MEE from neonatal risk factors and test results in SCBU and full-term babies. *Br J Audiol* 2001;35:77–85. [erratum appears in *Br J Audiol* 2001;35(3):219]

156 Green MRE, Cooper MNK. Passive smoking and middle ear effusions in children of British Servicemen in West Germany – a point prevalence survey of outpatient attendance. *J R Army Med Corps* 1991;137:31–3.

157 Haggard MP, Gannon MM, Birkin JA *et al.* Selecting persistent glue ear for referral in general practice: A risk factor approach. *Br J Gen Pract* 2002;52:549–53.

158 Hammaren-Malmi S, Saxen H, Tarkkanen J, Mattila PS. Passive smoking after tympanostomy and risk of recurrent acute otitis media. *Int J Pediat Otorhinolaryngol* 2007;71:1305–10.

159 Hammaren-Malmi S, Tarkkanen J, Mattila PS. Analysis of risk factors for childhood persistent middle ear effusion. *Acta Otolaryngol* 2005;125:1051–4.

160 Hinton AE, Herdman RCD, Martin-Hirsch D, Saeed SR. Parental cigarette smoking and tonsillectomy in children. *Clin Otolaryngol* 1993;18:178–80.

161 Ilicali OC, Kclcj N, Deger K, Savaj I. Relationship of passive cigarette smoking to otitis media. *Arch Otolaryngol Head Neck Surg* 1999;125:758–62.

162 Kitchens GG. Relationship of environmental tobacco smoke to otitis media in young children. *Laryngoscope* 1995;105:1–13.

163 Said G, Zalokar J, Lellouch J, Patois E. Parental smoking related to adenoidectomy and tonsillectomy in children. *J Epidemiol Community Health* 1978;32:97–101.

164 Stenstrom C, Ingvarsson L. Otitis-prone children and controls: A study of possible predisposing factors. 2. Physical findings, frequency of illness, allergy, day care and parental smoking. *Acta Otolaryngol* 1997;117:696–703.

165 Diagler GE, Markello SJ, Cummings KM. The effect of indoor air pollutants on otitis media and asthma in children. *Laryngoscope* 1991;101:293–6.

166 Alho OP, Kilkku O, Oja H, Koivu M, Sorri M. Control of the temporal aspect when considering risk factors for acute otitis media. *Arch Otolaryngol Head Neck Surg* 1993; 119:444–9.

167 Apostolopoulos K, Xenelis J, Tzagaroulakis A *et al.* The point prevalence of otitis media with effusion among school children in Greece. *Int J Pediat Otorhinolaryngol* 1998;44: 207–14.

168 Bentdal YE, Karevold G, Nafstad P, Kvaerner KJ. Early acute otitis media: Predictor for AOM and respiratory infections in schoolchildren? *Int J Pediat Otorhinolaryngol* 2007; 71:1251–9.

169 Collett J-P, Larson CP, Boivin J-F, Suissa S, Pless IB. Parental smoking and risk of otitis media in pre-school children. *Can J Public Health* 1995;86:269–73.

170 Da Costa JL, Navarro A, Neves JB, Martin M. Household wood and charcoal smoke increases risk of otitis media in childhood in Maputo. *Int J Epidemiol* 2004;33:573–8.

171 Engel J, Anteunis L, Volovics A, Hendriks J, Marres E. Risk factors of otitis media with effusion during infancy. *Int J Pediat Otorhinolaryngol* 1999;48:239–49.

172 Etzel RA, Pattishall EN, Haley NJ, Fletcher RH, Henderson FW. Passive smoking and middle ear effusion among children in day care. *Pediatrics* 1992;90:228–32.

173 Froom J, Culpepper L, Green LA *et al.* A cross-national study of acute otitis media: risk factors, severity, and treatment at initial visit. Report from the International Primary Care Network (IPCN) and the Ambulatory Sentinel Practice Network (ASPN) [see comment]. *J Am Board Fam Prac* 2001;14:406–17.

174 Gryczynska D, Kobos J, Zakrzewska A. Relationship between passive smoking, recurrent respiratory tract infections and otitis media in children. *Int J Pediat Otorhinolaryngol* 1999;49:275–8.

175 Hinton AE. Surgery for otitis media with effusion in children and its relationship to parental smoking. *J Laryngol Otol* 1989;103:559–61.

176 Hinton AE, Buckley G. Parental smoking and middle ear effusions in children. *J Laryngol Otol* 1988;102:992–6.

177 Homoe P, Christensen RB, Bretlau P. Acute otitis media and sociomedical risk factors among unselected children in Greenland. *Int J Pediat Otorhinolaryngol* 1999;49:37–52.

178 Ilicali OC, Keles N, Deger K, Sagun OF, Guldiken, Y. Evaluation of the effect of passive smoking on otitis media in children by an objective method: Urinary cotinine analysis. *Laryngoscope* 2001;111:163–7.

179 Iversen M, Birch L, Lundqvist GR. Middle ear effusion in children and the indoor environment: an epidemiological study. *Arch Environ Health* 1985;40:74–9.

180 Jacoby PA, Coates HL, Arumugaswamy A *et al.* The effect of passive smoking on the risk of otitis media in Aboriginal and non-Aboriginal children in the Kalgoorlie-Boulder region of Western Australia. *Medical Journal of Australia* 2008;188:599–603.

181 Kraemer MJ, Richardson MA, Weiss NS, *et al.* Risk factors for persistent middle-ear effusions. *JAMA* 1983;249:1022–5.

182 Lasisi AO, Olaniyan FA, Muibi SA *et al.* Clinical and demographic risk factors associated with chronic suppurative otitis media. *Int J Pediat Otorhinolaryngol* 2007;71:1549–54.

183 Lee DJ, Gaynor JJ, Trapido E. Secondhand smoke and earaches in adolescents: The Florida youth cohort study. *Nicotine Tob Res* 2003;5:943–6.

184 Lubianca Neto JF, Burns AG, Lu L, Mombach R, Saffer M. Passive smoking and nonrecurrent acute otitis media in children. *Arch Otolaryngol Head Neck Surg* 1999;121:805–8.

185 Paradise JL, Rockette HE, Colborn DK *et al.* Otitis media in 2253 Pittsburgh-area infants: Prevalence and risk factors during the first two years of life. *Pediatrics* 1997;99:318–33.

186 Pukander J, Luotonen J, Timonen M, Karma P. Risk factors affecting the occurrence of acute otitis media among 2-3-year old urban children. *Acta Otolaryngology (Stockholm)* 1985;100:260–5.

187 Rasmussen F. Protracted secretory otitis media. The impact of familial factors and day-care center attendance. *Int J Pediat Otorhinolaryngol* 1993;26:29–37.

188 Rowe-Jones JM, Brockbank MJ. Parental smoking and persistent otitis media with effusion in children. *Int J Pediat Otorhinolaryngol* 1992;24:19–24.

189 Rylander R, Megevand Y. Environmental risk factors for respiratory infections. *Arch Environ Health* 2000;55:300–3.

190 Saim A, Saim L, Saim S, Ruszymah BHI, Sani A. Prevalence of otitis media with effusion amongst pre-school children in Malaysia. *Int J Pediat Otorhinolaryngol* 1997;41:21–8.

191 Salazar JC, Daly KA, Giebink GS *et al.* Low cord blood pneumococcal immunoglobulin G (IgG) antibodies predict early onset acute otitis media in infancy. *Am J Epidemiol* 1997; 145:1048–56.

192 Shiva F, Nasiri M, Sadeghi B, Padyab M. Effects of passive smoking on common respiratory symptoms in young children. *Acta Paediatr, Int J Paediatr* 2003;92:1394–7.

193 Ståhlberg M-R, Ruuskanen O, Virolainen E. Risk factors for recurrent otitis media. *Pediatr Infect Dis* 1986;5:30–2.

194 Stenstrom R, Bernard PAM, Ben-Simhon H. Exposure to environmental tobacco smoke as a risk factor for recurrent acute otitis media in children under the age of five years. *Int J Pediat Otorhinolaryngol* 1993;27:127–36.

195 Strachan DP. Impendance tympanometry and the home environment in seven-year-old children. *J Laryngol Otol* 1990;104:4–8.

196 Tainio V-M, Savilahti E, Salmenperä L. Risk factors for infantile recurrent otitis media: atopy but not type of feeding. *Pediatr Res* 1988;23:509–12.

197 Teele DW, Klein JO, Rosner B, Greater Boston Otitis Media Study Group. Epidemiology of otitis media during the first seven years of life in children in Greater Boston: A prospective, cohort study. *J Infect Dis* 1989;160:83–94.

198 Willatt DJ. Children's sore throats related to parental smoking. *Clin Otolaryngol* 1986; 11:317–21.

199 Xenellis J, Paschalidis J, Georgalas C *et al.* Factors influencing the presence of otitis media with effusion 16 months after initial diagnosis in a cohort of school-age children in rural Greece: A prospective study. *Int J Pediat Otorhinolaryngol* 2005;69:1641–7.

200 Zielhuis GA, Heuvelmans-Heinen EW, Rach GH, Van Den Broek P. Environmental risk factors for otitis media with effusion in preschool children. *Scand J Prim Health Care* 1989;7:33–8.

201 Safavi Naini A, Safavi Naini A, Vazirnezam M. Parental smoking and risk of otitis media with effusion among children. *Tanaffos* 2002;1:25–8.

202 Stocks J, Dezateux C. The effect of parental smoking on lung function and development during infancy. *Respirology* 2003;8:266–85.

203 Bisgaard H, Loland L, Holst KK, Pipper CB. Prenatal determinants of neonatal lung function in high-risk newborns. *J Allergy Clin Immunol* 2009;123:651–7.

204 Dezateux C, Lum S, Hoo A-F *et al.* Low birth weight for gestation and airway function in infancy: exploring the fetal origins hypothesis. *Thorax* 2004;59:60–6.

205 Tepper RS, Williams-Nkomo,T, Martinez T *et al.* Parental smoking and airways reactivity in healthy infants. *Am J Respir Crit Care Med* 2005;171:78–82.

206 Demissie K, Ernst P, Joseph L, Becklake MR. The role of domestic factors and day-care attendance on lung function of primary school children. *Respir Med* 1998;92:928–35.

207 Gilliland FD, Berhane K, Li Y-F, Rappaport EB, Peters JM. Effects of early onset asthma and *in utero* exposure to maternal smoking on childhood lung function. *Am J Respir Crit Care Med* 2003;167:917–24.

208 Jedrychowski W, Maugeri U, Jedrychowska-Bianchi I, Flak E. Effect of indoor air quality in the postnatal period on lung function in pre-adolescent children: a retrospective cohort study in Poland. *Public Health* 2005;119:535–41.

209 Mannino DM, Moorman JE, Kingsley B, Rose D, Repace J. Health Effects Related to Environmental Tobacco Smoke Exposure in Children in the United States: Data From the Third National Health and Nutrition Examination Survey. *Arch Pediatr Adolesc Med* 2001; 155:36–41.

210 Moshammer H, Hoek G, Luttmann-Gibson H *et al.* Parental Smoking and Lung Function in Children: An International Study. *Am J Respir Crit Care Med* 2006;173:1255–63.

211 Burchfiel CM, Higgins MW, Keller JB *et al.* Passive smoking in childhood. Respiratory conditions and pulmonary function in Tecumseh, Michigan. *Am Rev Respir Dis* 1986; 133:966–73.

212 Chen Y, Li WX. The effect of passive smoking on children's pulmonary function in Shanghai. *Am J Public Health* 1986;76:515–18.

213 Cook DG, Whincup PH, Papacosta O *et al.* Relation of passive smoking as assessed by salivary cotinine concentration and questionnaire to spirometric indices in children. *Thorax* 1993;48:14–20.

214 Corbo GM, Agabiti N, Forastiere F *et al.* Lung function in children and adolescents with occasional exposure to environmental tobacco smoke. *Am J Respir Crit Care Med* 1996; 154:695–700.

215 Cuijpers CE, Swaen GM, Wesseling G, Sturmans F, Wouters EF. Adverse effects of the indoor environment on respiratory health in primary school children. *Environ Res* 1995; 68:11–23.

216 Cunningham J, Dockery DW, Gold DR, Speizer FE. Racial differences in the association between maternal smoking during pregnancy and lung function in children. *Am J Respir Crit Care Med* 1995;152:565–9.

217 Cunningham J, Dockery DW, Speizer FE. Maternal smoking during pregnancy as a predictor of lung function in children. *Am J Epidemiol* 1994;139:1139–52.

218 Dijkstra L, Houthuijs D, Brunekreef B *et al.* Respiratory health effects of the indoor environment in a population of Dutch children. *Am Rev Respir Dis* 1990;142:1172–78.

219 Dold S, Reitmeir P, Wjst M, Von Mutius E. Effects of passive smoking on the pediatric respiratory tract. *Monatsschr Kinderheilkd* 1992;140:763–8.

220 Haby MM, Peat JK, Woolcock AJ. Effect of passive smoking, asthma, and respiratory infection on lung function in Australian children. *Pediatr Pulmonol* 1994;18:323–9.

221 Martinez FD, Cline M, Burrows B. Increased incidence of asthma in children of smoking mothers. *Pediatrics* 1992;89:21–6.

222 O'Connor GT, Weiss ST, Tager IB, Speizer FE. The effect of passive smoking on pulmonary function and nonspecific bronchial responsiveness in a population-based sample of children and young adults. *Am Rev Respir Dis* 1987;135:800–4.

223 Strachan DP, Jarvis MJ, Feyerabend C. The relationship of salivary cotinine to respiratory symptoms, spirometry, and exercise-induced bronchospasm in seven-year-old children. *Am Rev Respir Dis* 1990;142:147–51.

224 Taskin DP, Clark VA, Simmons M *et al.* The UCLA population studies of chronic obstructive respiratory disease. VII. Relationship between parental smoking and children's lung function. *Am Rev Respir Dis* 1984;129:891–7.

225 Teculescu D, Pham QT, Aubry C *et al.* Respiratory health of children and atmospheric pollution. II. Ventilatory function. *Revue de Maladies Respiratoires* 1989;6:221–8.

226 Teculescu DB, Pham QT, Varona-Lopez W *et al.* The single-breath nitrogen test does not detect functional impairment in children with passive exposure to tobacco smoke. *Bulletin Europeen de Physiopathologie Respiratoire* 1986;22:605–7.

227 Ware JH, Dockery DW, Spiro AR, Speizer FE, Ferris BGJ. Passive smoking, gas cooking, and respiratory health of children living in six cities. *Am Rev Respir Dis* 1984;129:366–74.

228 Willers S, Attewell R, Bensryd I *et al.* Exposure to environmental tobacco smoke in the household and urinary cotinine excretion, heavy metals retention, and lung function. *Arch Environ Health* 1992;47:357–63.

229 Yarnell JW, Leger AS. Respiratory illness, maternal smoking habit and lung function in adolescent children. *Br J Dis Chest* 1979;73:230–6.

230 Baker M, McNicholas A, Garrett N *et al.* Household crowding a major risk factor for epidemic meningococcal disease in Auckland children. *Pediatr Infect Dis* 2000;19:983–90.

231 Bredfeldt R, Cain S, Schutze G, Holmes T, McGhee L. Relation between passive tobacco smoke exposure and the development of bacterial meningitis in children. *J Am Board Fam Prac* 1995;8:95–8.

232 Cardeñosa N, Domínguez A, Orcau A *et al.* Carriers of Neisseria meningitidis in household contacts of meningococcal disease cases in Catalonia (Spain). *Eur J Epidemiol* 2001;17:877–84.

233 Fischer M, Hedberg K, Cardosi P *et al.* Tobacco smoke as a risk factor for meningococcal disease. *Pediatr Infect Dis* 1997;16:979–83.

234 Haneberg B, Tønjum T, Rodahl K, Gedde-Dahl TW. Factors preceding the onset of meningococcal disease, with special emphasis on passive smoking, symptoms of ill health. *NIPH Ann* 1983;6:169–73.

235 Iles K, Poplawski N, Couper R. Passive exposure to tobacco smoke and bacterial meningitis in children. *J Paediatr Child Health* 2001;37:388–91.

236 Kremastinou J, Tzanakaki G, Velonakis E *et al.* Carriage of Neisseria meningitidis and Neisseria lactamica among ethnic Greek school children from Russian immigrant families in Athens. *FEMS Immunol Med Microbiol* 1999;23:13–20.

237 Kriz P, Bobak M, Kriz B. Parental smoking, socioeconomic factors, and risk of invasive meningococcal disease in children: a population based case-control study. *Arch Dis Child* 2000;83:117–21.

238 McCall B, Neill A, Young M. Risk factors for invasive meningococcal disease in southern Queensland, 2000-2001. *Intern Med J* 2004;34:464–8.

239 Moodley J, Coetzee N, Hussey G. Risk factors for meningococcal disease in Cape Town. *S Afr Med J* 1999;89:56–9.

240 O'Dempsey T, McArdle T, Morris J *et al.* A study of risk factors for pneumococcal disease among children in a rural area of West Africa. *Int J Epidemiol* 1996;25:885–93.

241 Robinson P, Taylor K, Nolan T. Risk-factors for meningococcal disease in Victoria, Australia, in 1997. *Epidemiol Infect* 2001;127:261–8.

242 Sørensen H, Labouriau R, Jensen E, Mortensen P, Schønheyder H. Fetal growth, maternal prenatal smoking, and risk of invasive meningococcal disease: a nationwide case-control study. *Int J Epidemiol* 2004;33:816–20.

243 Stanwell-Smith R, Stuart J, Hughes A *et al.* Smoking, the environment and meningococcal disease: a case control study. *Epidemiol Infect* 1994;112:315–28.

244 Stuart JM, Cartwright KA, Dawson JA, Rickard J, Noah ND. Risk factors for meningococcal disease: a case control study in south west England. *Community Med* 1988;10.

245 Yusuf H, Rochat R, Baughman W *et al.* Maternal cigarette smoking and invasive meningococcal disease: a cohort study among young children in metropolitan Atlanta, 1989-1996. *Am J Public Health* 1999;89:712–17.

246 Tariq SM, Matthews SM, Hakim EA *et al.* The prevalence of and risk factors for atopy in early childhood: a whole population birth cohort study. *J Allergy Clin Immunol* 1998; 101:587–93.

247 Murray CS, Woodcock A, Smillie FI *et al.* Tobacco smoke exposure, wheeze, and atopy. *Pediatr Pulmonol* 2004;37:492–8.

248 Hagendorens MM, Bridts CH, Lauwers K *et al.* Perinatal risk factors for sensitization, atopic dermatitis and wheezing during the first year of life (PIPO study). *Clin Exp Allergy* 2005;35:733–40.

249 Henderson AJ, Sherriff A, Northstone K, Kukla L, Hruba D. Pre- and postnatal parental smoking and wheeze in infancy: cross cultural differences. Avon Study of Parents and Children (ALSPAC) Study Team, European Longitudinal Study of Pregnancy and Childhood (ELSPAC) Co-ordinating Centre. *Eur Respir J* 2001;18:323–9.

250 Jedrychowski W, Perera FP, Maugeri U *et al.* Length at birth and effect of prenatal and postnatal factors on early wheezing phenotypes. Krakow epidemiologic cohort study. *Int J Occup Med Environ Health* 2008;21:111–19.

251 Lannero E, Wickman M, Pershagen G, Nordvall L. Maternal smoking during pregnancy increases the risk of recurrent wheezing during the first years of life (BAMSE). *Respir Res* 2006;7:3.

252 Linneberg A, Simonsen JB, Petersen J, Stensballe LG, Benn CS. Differential effects of risk factors on infant wheeze and atopic dermatitis emphasize a different etiology. *J Allergy Clin Immunol* 2006;117:184–9.

253 Park JH, Gold DR, Spiegelman DL, Burge HA, Milton DK. House dust endotoxin and wheeze in the first year of life [see comment]. *Am J Respir Crit Care Med* 2001;163:322–8.

254 Young S, Arnott J, O'Keeffe PT, Le Souef PN, Landau LI. The association between early life lung function and wheezing during the first 2 yrs of life. *Eur Respir J* 2000;15:151–7.

255 Stein RT, Holberg CJ, Sherrill D *et al.* Influence of parental smoking on respiratory symptoms during the first decade of life: the Tucson Children's Respiratory Study. *Am J Epidemiol* 1999;149:1030–7.

256 Mallol J, Andrade R, Auger F *et al.* Wheezing during the first year of life in infants from low-income population: a descriptive study. *Allergol Immunopathol (Madr)* 2005;33: 257–63.

257 Sangsupawanich P, Chongsuvivatwong V, Mo-Suwan L, Choprapawon C. Relationship between atopic dermatitis and wheeze in the first year of life: analysis of a prospective cohort of Thai children. *J Investig Allergol Clin Immunol* 2007;17:292–6.

258 Yang KD, Ou CY, Chang JC *et al.* Infant frequent wheezing correlated to Clara cell protein 10 (CC10) polymorphism and concentration, but not allergy sensitization, in a perinatal cohort study. *J Allergy Clin Immunol* 2007;120:842–8.

259 Sherriff A, Peters TJ, Henderson J, Strachan D, Alspac Study Team. Avon Longitudinal Study of Parents and Children. Risk factor associations with wheezing patterns in children followed longitudinally from birth to 3(1/2) years. *Int J Epidemiol* 2001;30:1473–84.

260 Johansson A, Ludvigsson J, Hermansson G. Adverse health effects related to tobacco smoke exposure in a cohort of three-year olds. *Acta Paediatr* 2008;97:354–7.

261 Lewis S, Richards D, Bynner J, Butler N, Britton J. Prospective study of risk factors for early and persistent wheezing in childhood. *Eur Respir J* 1995;8:349–56.

262 Magnusson LL, Olesen AB, Wennborg H, Olsen J. Wheezing, asthma, hayfever, and atopic eczema in childhood following exposure to tobacco smoke in fetal life. *Clin Exp Allergy* 2005;35:1550–6.

263 Midodzi WK, Rowe BH, Majaesic CM, Saunders LD, Senthilselvan A. Predictors for wheezing phenotypes in the first decade of life. *Respirology* 2008;13:537–45.

264 Calam R, Gregg L, Simpson A, *et al.* Behavior problems antecede the development of wheeze in childhood: a birth cohort study. *Am J Respir Crit Care Med* 2005;171:323–7.

265 Martinez FD, Wright AL, Taussig LM *et al.* Asthma and wheezing in the first six years of life. The Group Health Medical Associates. *N Engl J Med* 1995;19;332:133–8.

266 Lemanske RF Jr, Jackson DJ, Gangnon RE *et al.* Rhinovirus illnesses during infancy predict subsequent childhood wheezing [see comment]. *J Allergy Clin Immunol* 2005;116: 571–7.

267 Nicolaou NC, Simpson A, Lowe LA *et al.* Day-care attendance, position in sibship, and early childhood wheezing: a population-based birth cohort study. *J Allergy Clinical Immunol* 2008;122:500–6.

268 Lewis SA, Britton JR. Consistent effects of high socioeconomic status and low birth order, and the modifying effect of maternal smoking on the risk of allergic disease during childhood. *Respir Med* 1998;92:1237–44.

269 Keil T, Lau S, Roll S *et al.* Maternal smoking increases risk of allergic sensitization and wheezing only in children with allergic predisposition: Longitudinal analysis from birth to 10 years. *Allergy* 2009;64:445–51.

270 Ronmark E, Perzanowski M, Platts-Mills T, Lundback B. Incidence rates and risk factors for asthma among school children: a 2-year follow-up report from the obstructive lung disease in Northern Sweden (OLIN) studies. *Respir Med* 2002;96:1006–13.

271 De Bilderling G, Chauhan AJ, Jeffs JAR *et al.* Gas cooking and smoking habits and the risk of childhood and adolescent wheeze. *Am J Epidemiol* 2005;162:513–22.

272 Kurukulaaratchy RJ, Matthews S, Arshad SH. Does environment mediate earlier onset of the persistent childhood asthma phenotype? *Pediatrics* 2004;113:345–50.

273 Oddy WH, Holt PG, Sly PD *et al.* Association between breast feeding and asthma in 6 year old children: findings of a prospective birth cohort study. *BMJ* 1999;319: 815–19.

274 Genuneit J, Weinmayr G, Radon K *et al.* Smoking and the incidence of asthma during adolescence: results of a large cohort study in Germany. *Thorax* 2006;61:572–8.

275 Karmaus W, Dobai AL, Ogbuanu I, *et al.* Long-term effects of breastfeeding, maternal smoking during pregnancy, and recurrent lower respiratory tract infections on asthma in children. *J Asthma* 2008;45:688–95.

276 Yuan W, Fonager K, Olsen J, Sorensen HT. Prenatal factors and use of anti-asthma medications in early childhood: a population-based Danish birth cohort study [see comment]. *Eur J Epidemiol*2003;18:763–8.

277 Tariq SM, Hakim EA, Matthews SM, Arshad SH. Influence of smoking on asthmatic symptoms and allergen sensitisation in early childhood. *Postgrad Med J* 2000;76:694–9.

278 Miller JE. Predictors of asthma in young children: does reporting source affect our conclusions? *Am J Epidemiol* 2001;154:245–50.

279 Bergmann RL, Edenharter G, Bergmann KE, Lau S, Wahn U. Socioeconomic status is a risk factor for allergy in parents but not in their children. *Clin Exp Allergy* 2000;30:1740–5.

280 Milner JD, Stein DM, McCarter R, Moon RY. Early infant multivitamin supplementation is associated with increased risk for food allergy and asthma. *Pediatrics* 2004;114:27–32.

281 Horwood LJ, Fergusson DM, Shannon FT. Social and familial factors in the development of early childhood asthma. *Pediatrics* 1985;75:859–68.

282 Jaakkola JJ, Nafstad P, Magnus P. Environmental tobacco smoke, parental atopy, and childhood asthma. *Environ Health Perspect* 2001;109:579–82.

283 Bacopoulou F, Veltsista A, Vassi I *et al.* Can we be optimistic about asthma in childhood? A Greek cohort study. *J Asthma* 2009;46:171–4.

284 Jaakkola JJK and Gissler M. Maternal smoking in pregnancy, fetal development, and childhood asthma. *Am J Public Health* 2004;94:136–40.

285 Mamun AA, Lawlor DA, Alati R *et al.* Increasing body mass index from age 5 to 14 years predicts asthma among adolescents: evidence from a birth cohort study. *Int J Obes* 2007;31:578–83.

286 Alati R, Al Mamun A, O'Callaghan M, Najman JM, Williams GM. *In utero* and postnatal maternal smoking and asthma in adolescence. *Epidemiology* 2006;17:138–44.
287 Chan-Yeung M, Hegele RG, Mich-Ward H *et al.* Early environmental determinants of asthma risk in a high-risk birth cohort. *Pediatr Allergy Immunol* 2008;19:482–9.
288 Gold DR, Damokosh AI, Dockery DW, Berkey CS. Body-mass index as a predictor of incident asthma in a prospective cohort of children. *Pediatr Pulmonol* 2003;36:514–21.
289 Arshad SH, Kurukulaaratchy RJ, Fenn M, Matthews S. Early life risk factors for current wheeze, asthma, and bronchial hyperresponsiveness at 10 years of age. *Chest* 2005;127:502–8.
290 Zejda JE, Kowalska M. Risk factors for asthma in school children – results of a seven-year follow-up. *Cent Eur J Public Health* 2003;11:149–54.

5 How much disease in children is caused by passive smoking?

5.1 Introduction

The systematic reviews and meta-analyses summarised in Chapter 4 provide contemporary estimates of the extent to which the risks of a range of common childhood diseases and outcomes are increased in children who are passively exposed to tobacco smoke, compared with those who are not. They do not, however, provide estimates of the numbers of children who become ill as a result of passive smoking, or the magnitude of the burden on health service provision that results from these illnesses. To provide this information, it is necessary to combine estimates of relative risk in exposed children with estimates of the incidence of the diseases of interest, the degree of health service use that these diseases generate, and the number of children who are exposed.

In this chapter we have used data from a range of sources to generate estimates of the burden of disease caused by passive smoking in UK children. The estimates are inevitably approximate, since they depend on a number of assumptions about the representativeness of the data sources we have used, and also on the representativeness of the relative risk estimates presented in Chapter 4 to the various age-groups, exposure categories and outcome measures involved. They are also limited predominantly to the more common diseases caused by passive smoking; the list of outcomes studies is not exhaustive. However, they give an indication of the likely order of magnitude of the numbers of children who currently become ill or, in the case of sudden infant death syndrome, die as a result of passive smoking. They also indicate the number of primary care consultations and hospital admissions that these diseases generate. The costs of this disease burden to the NHS and wider society are estimated in Chapter 7.

5.2 Estimates of disease incidence

To obtain measures of disease incidence for lower respiratory infection, wheeze, asthma, middle ear disease and meningitis, we have used primary care data from The Health Improvement Network (THIN), a computerised database of over 5.7 million people registered with 330 general practices across England, Scotland, Wales and Northern Ireland.[1] For each individual, THIN records include demographic data, Townsend score of socio-economic deprivation (from the 2001 census), and contacts with the practice Read-coded by diagnosis. The population in THIN is broadly representative of the general population of the UK.[1] As part of a programme of research on perinatal health, we have identified a birth cohort representative of UK children with full medical records for each child and other members of their household for the period they are registered with a THIN general practice.[2,3] In this chapter, we used these data for all children born between 1988 and 2004 who were registered with the general practice within 3 months of their date of birth either up to the time they left the general practice, reached the age of 16 years, or until the end of 2004. On average, approximately 6 years of follow-up data were available for each child.

Using this birth cohort dataset, we identified the first diagnoses of wheeze occurring before the age of 3 years, of asthma occurring between the ages of 3 and 16 years, and of bacterial meningitis occurring between birth and 16 years. Our data for these outcomes therefore reflect disease incidence using time to first diagnosis. We limited the analysis of wheeze and asthma to the above age ranges on the conservative assumption that most wheezing illness in very young children will be coded as wheeze, whilst as children get older, episodes of wheezing are more likely to gain the diagnostic label of asthma. We separated the asthma outcomes into age groups 3–4 and 5–16, for consistency with the age groups used in the meta-analyses in Chapter 4.

For middle ear disease, we identified all new episodes of disease between birth and 16 years of age, defining a new episode of disease as a recorded diagnosis for middle ear disease with no other diagnoses for middle ear disease in the preceding 3 months. We used this approach to minimise the potential to erroneously count repeat consultations for the same episode of middle ear disease as a new diagnosis. We used the same approach for lower respiratory tract infections but, in accordance with the age range included in the Chapter 4 meta-analysis, we assessed only infections occurring before the age of 3 years. This means that, for our analyses of incident disease, children may have more than one diagnosis of lower respiratory tract infection or middle ear disease, but only one diagnosis of wheeze, asthma or meningitis. The incidence estimates arising from these analyses are presented in Table 5.1.

Table 5.1 Incidence of new events of disease, and of general practice contacts, for lower respiratory infection, middle ear infection, wheezing, asthma and meningitis in children in the THIN cohort.

	Age range in years	Person-years available (000s)	Events	Incidence/ 1,000 person-years	95% CI
Disease incidence					
Lower respiratory infections[a]	≤2	516	42,083	82	81 to 82
Middle ear infections[a]	0–16	1,214	171,048	141	140 to 142
Wheeze[b]	≤2	485	19,335	40	37 to 43
Asthma[b]	3–4	207	6,330	31	29 to 32
Asthma[b]	5–16	364	5,775	16	15 to 17
Meningitis[b]	0–16	1,214	301	0.25	0.22 to 0.28
Disease consultations					
Lower respiratory infections[c]	≤2	516	53,486	104	102 to 105
Middle ear infections[c]	0–16	1,214	226,141	186	185 to 188
Wheeze[c]	≤2	516	29,443	57	56 to 58
Asthma[c]	3–4	237	32,026	135	132 to 139
Asthma[c]	5–16	461	52,923	115	112 to 118
Meningitis[c]	0–16	1,214	363	0.30	0.26 to 0.34

[a] Includes multiple episodes of infection per child where a new episode of infection was considered as a diagnosis preceded by at least 3 months with no diagnoses of the same infection. Clustering of episodes by child is allowed for in calculation of confidence intervals.
[b] Based on first recorded diagnosis. Clustering of diagnoses by general practice is allowed for in calculation of confidence intervals.
[c] Includes multiple consultations per child where a consultation was considered as any general practice contact for the relevant diagnosis on a unique day – multiple consultations on the same day were counted as one consultation). Clustering of episodes by child is allowed for in calculation of confidence intervals.

5.3 General practice consultation rates

We also estimated the burden for each of these outcomes in terms of primary healthcare use, by extracting data for all general practice contacts for each of the above five disease outcomes (excluding multiple contacts on the same day) in the same age categories as the disease incidence figures, and calculating the incidence of general practice contacts for each recording of disease outcome. The resulting estimates are also presented in Table 5.1.

5.4 Disease incidence and socio-economic status

To determine whether the burden of each of our disease outcomes was related to socio-economic status, we stratified our analyses for disease incidence by quintile of the census-derived output area Townsend score of material deprivation linked to the household postcode. For each disease outcome we then generated rate ratios of disease incidence for children living in each area quintile of Townsend score in relation to the least deprived quintile. Figure 5.1 demonstrates a progressive increase in relative incidence for lower respiratory infections, wheeze, asthma and meningitis with increasing socio-economic deprivation, but not for middle ear disease.

5.5 Hospital admissions

We obtained hospital admission data for wheeze, asthma, lower respiratory tract infections, middle ear disease and meningitis for children living in England using

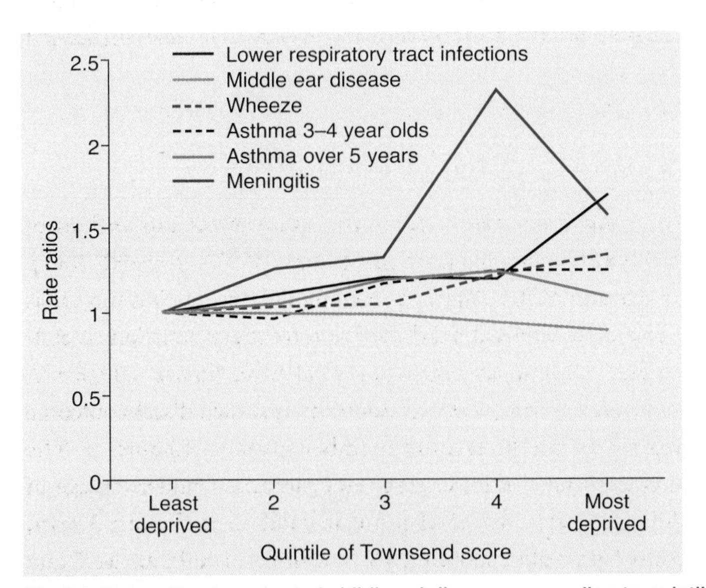

Fig 5.1 Rate ratios for selected childhood diseases according to quintile of deprivation.

Hospital Episode Statistics (HES). For middle ear disease and bacterial meningitis, data on admissions in children aged 0–14 years are available directly from the HES website.[4] Data on admissions for lower respiratory infection to age 3, and for wheeze and asthma in the age categories used above (to a maximum of 14) were obtained by request. The data are from the 2005/6 financial year, the most recent for which detailed data are available.

5.6 Notified cases of meningococcal meningitis

Approximately 65% of all cases of bacterial meningitis are caused by infection with *Neisseria meningitidis*, also known as meningococcal meningitis, and this proportion is actually higher in children.[5] In England and Wales, all laboratory-confirmed cases of invasive meningococcal disease are notified to the Health Protection Agency, and details of these cases stratified by age group and serotype are published on their website. In order to provide a figure for England and Wales, we extracted the data from this website for the year 2007/8 for all serotypes in children under the age of 15 years. This gave a total of 834 cases.[6]

5.7 Sudden infant deaths

The ONS 2008 mortality report records 176 deaths registered as being due to sudden infant death (ICD 10 code R95) in 2008 England and Wales, 167 of which were in children under the age of 1 year.[7] We restricted our analysis to children in the first year of life to reflect the age criteria used in our meta-analysis-derived relative risks.

5.8 Attributable fractions for passive smoke exposure

We used the odds ratios presented in Chapter 4 to estimate the proportions of disease attributable to passive smoking from the formula $p(OR-1)/[p(OR-1)+1]$, in which p is the proportion of the cohort exposed to passive smoking and OR is the odds ratio for disease in exposed children. We took the proportion of children exposed to be the 22% who do not live in smoke-free homes (Chapter 2, Table 2.3), and as a measure of risk, used the odds ratio for each disease outcome in relation to smoking by any household member given in Chapter 4. The attributable fractions were 11% of lower respiratory infection under the age of 3 years, 7% of middle ear disease, 8% of wheezing in children aged under 3 years, 4% of asthma in 3- to 4-year-old children, 10% of asthma in children age 5 and over, and 22% of cases of meningitis.

5.9 Morbidity and mortality attributable to passive smoking

5.9.1 New cases of disease

We took ONS data for the number of children in the relevant age-groups living in the UK in 2008[8] and multiplied these by the incidence rates in Table 5.1, and the attributable fractions in section 5.8 above, to generate the estimated number of new cases of lower respiratory infection, middle ear disease, wheeze, asthma and meningitis attributable to passive smoking in the UK each year. The figures are presented in Table 5.2, which indicates that around 165,000 new cases of these diseases in the defined age categories are caused by passive smoking in the UK each year. The majority of these are children with middle ear disease, but lower respiratory infection in young children, and asthma in school-aged children, are also particularly common. There were an estimated 600 new cases of bacterial meningitis due to passive smoking.

5.9.2 General practice consultations

Numbers of general practice contacts, estimated from consultation rates using the same approach as above, are also presented in Table 5.2. These numbers demonstrate that passive smoking in children accounts for a total of over 300,000 general practice consultations in the UK each year. The majority of these consultations are for middle ear disease. However, asthma emerges as a cause of repeated contacts with the GP, with over 100,000 consultations for asthma in children each year attributable to passive smoking.

5.9.3 Hospital admissions

The number of hospital admissions arising from the above conditions, by age, and the numbers attributable to passive smoking, are summarised in Table 5.3. The estimates are based on assumptions that the likelihood of admission to hospital with any of these diseases is not related to passive smoking, and that the odds ratios estimated in Chapter 4 are not appreciably influenced by the inclusion of children aged over 14. There is also an assumption that the proportion of repeat admissions for wheezing or asthma attributable to smoking is similar to that of first episodes of disease. The figures demonstrate that a total of around 8,500 admissions from the above conditions in the given age ranges are caused by passive smoking each year in England. The approximate figure for the UK will therefore be around 9,500.

The estimated 231 admissions in England (or 260 in the UK, extrapolating using the population estimates in Table 1.1) with meningitis attributable to

Table 5.2 Events of disease in children in the UK caused by passive smoking in the home (2008).

	Age range in years	UK population (000s)[d]	Estimated UK events[e]	Estimated relative risk for household smoking	Population attributable fraction	UK cases attributable to smoking[f]
Disease incidence						
Lower respiratory infections[a]	≤2	2,276	186,630	1.54	11%	20,500
Middle ear infections[a]	0–16	12,310	1,735,710	1.35	7%	121,400
Wheeze[b]	≤2	2,276	91,040	1.37	8%	7,200
Asthma[b]	3–4	1,424	44,140	1.21	4%	1,700
Asthma[b]	5–16	8,611	137,770	1.50	10%	13,700
Meningitis[b]	0–16	12,310	3,070	2.30	22%	600
Total incident cases						165,100
Disease consultations						
Lower respiratory infections[c]	≤2	2,276	236,700	1.54	11%	26,000
Middle ear infections[c]	0–16	12,310	2,289,660	1.35	7%	160,200
Wheeze[c]	≤2	2,276	129,730	1.37	8%	10,300
Asthma[c]	3–4	1,424	192,240	1.21	4%	7,600
Asthma[c]	5–16	8,611	990,260	1.50	10%	99,000
Meningitis[c]	0–16	12,310	3,690	2.30	22%	800
Total consultations						303,900

[a] Includes multiple episodes of infection per child where a new episode of infection was considered as a diagnosis preceded by at least 3 months with no diagnoses of the same infection.
[b] Based on 1st recorded diagnosis.
[c] Includes multiple consultations per child where a consultation was considered as any general practice contact for the relevant diagnosis on a unique day – multiple consultations on the same day were counted as one consultation.
[d] Office for National Statistics 2008 population numbers for the UK.[8]
[e] Figures are calculated by multiplying Table 5.1 disease incidence rates by the UK population for the relevant disease outcome and age group, rounded down to the nearest 10 cases.
[f] Figures are calculated by multiplying the estimated UK cases by the population attributable fraction for the relevant disease outcome and age group, rounded down to the nearest 100 cases.

Table 5.3 Hospital episodes (admissions) in children aged 0–14 in England in 2005/6 from specified diseases attributable to passive smoke exposure.

	Age group	Admissions in England	Population attributable fraction	Admissions attributable to smoking
Lower respiratory infections[a]	≤2	33,613	10%	3,361
Middle ear infections[b]	0–14	35,961	7%	2,517
Wheeze[c]	≤2	11,724	8%	938
Asthma[d]	3–4	5,910	4%	236
	5–14	12,109	10%	1,211
Meningitis[e]	0–14	1,049	22%	231
Total				**8,494**

[a] Acute bronchitis (HES Code J20), acute bronchiolitis (J21), unspecified acute lower respiratory infection (J22).
[b] Non-suppurative (H65) and suppurative and unspecified otitis media (H66).
[c] Code R062.
[d] Asthma (J45) and status asthmaticus (J46).
[e] Meningococcal meningitis (A39.0), and bacterial meningitis (G00).

passive smoking is substantially lower than the estimate of the number of cases of meningitis attributable to passive smoking seen by UK GPs each year. Since almost all cases of bacterial meningitis would normally be referred to and admitted to hospital, this discrepancy probably reflects diagnostic inaccuracy in both sources of data (see below).

5.9.4 Notified cases of meningococcal disease

Applying the 22% attributable fraction to notified cases of meningococcal disease generates an estimated 183 cases in England (or an extrapolated 206 cases in the UK) caused by passive smoking in children each year. Since this figure relates to confirmed cases of meningococcal disease, and excludes other causes of bacterial meningitis, this suggests that the HES admission figure for bacterial meningitis due to passive smoking is an underestimate.

5.9.5 Sudden infant death syndrome

The population attributable fraction for sudden infant death syndrome, estimated using the formula in 5.8 above, is also 22%. Applying this fraction to the

167 deaths in England and Wales in 2008 generates an estimate that 37 of these deaths were caused by passive smoking. By extrapolation, the total for the UK is about 40 deaths each year.

5.10 Association between morbidity and deprivation

We are unable to provide estimates of numbers of excess cases of illness due to passive smoke exposure in the home for different levels of socio-economic status, since we do not have exposure data for the social groups defined by Townsend score for which we have incidence data from THIN. However, the strong association between passive smoke exposure in the home and socio-economic status reported in Chapter 2 suggests that children living in poorer homes will have a higher level of exposure than children living in more affluent homes, and this is likely to contribute to the higher relative incidences for lower respiratory infection, asthma, wheeze and meningitis in children living in more deprived compared with less deprived areas, shown in Fig 5.1. The absence of a strong social gradient for middle ear disease, however, indicates that other factors also play an important role in the incidence of that particular disease outcome.

5.11 Summary

- A combination of data from a range of sources has allowed estimation of approximate numbers of cases of disease and consequent morbidity in children caused by passive smoking in the UK.
- We estimate that passive smoking causes around 20,500 new cases of lower respiratory tract infection in children under the age of 3 years, and 121,400 new cases of middle ear disease in children of all ages in the UK each year.
- We also estimate that passive smoking causes 22,600 new cases of wheeze and asthma in UK children each year.
- There is some inconsistency in the estimates of the numbers of cases of bacterial meningitis caused by passive smoking in the UK each year, but the true figure is likely to be at least 200.
- These cases of disease result in over 300,000 UK general practice consultations, and about 9,500 hospital admissions in the UK each year.
- Since we have studied only the more common and other selected disease outcomes, the above figures underestimate the true burdens of disease caused by passive smoking.
- Passive smoking causes around 40 sudden infant deaths in the UK each year.

- It is likely that passive smoke exposure is a significant contributor to the socio-economic gradient of incidence of most of the childhood illnesses studied.
- This entire excess disease burden is avoidable.

References

1 Bourke A, Dattani H, Robinson M. Feasibility study and methodology to create a quality evaluated database of primary care data. *Inform Prim Care* 2004;12(3):171–7.
2 Tata LJ, Lewis SA, McKeever TM *et al.* A comprehensive analysis of adverse obstetric and paediatric complications in women with asthma. *Am J Respir Crit Care Med* 2007;175: 991–7.
3 Tata L, Hubbard R, McKeever T *et al.* Fertility rates in women with asthma, eczema, and hay fever: a general population-based cohort study. *Am J Epidemiol* 2007;165:1023–30.
4 The Information Centre. Hospital Episode Statistics online. www.hesonline.nhs.uk/HES2/jsp/query_diag.jsp
5 Health Protection Agency. Statutory notifications of infectious diseases in England and Wales. Week 2009/48 week ending 27/11/2009. www.hpa.org.uk/web/HPAwebFile/HPAweb_C/1259152074332
6 Health Protection Agency. All laboratory confirmed cases of invasive meningococcal disease by serogroup, age and epidemiological year. www.hpa.org.uk/webw/HPAweb&HPAwebStandard/HPAweb_C/1234859710351?p=1201094595391
7 Office for National Statistics. Mortality Statistics – deaths registered in 2008. DR_08. 2009.
8 Office for National Statistics. The interactive population pyramid. www.statistics.gov.uk/populationestimates/flash_pyramid/default.htm

6 Effect of parent and sibling smoking on smoking uptake

6.1 Introduction

The preceding three chapters have focused on the physical harm to children, and to the unborn fetus, arising from passive smoke exposure. However, a further significant cause of damage arising from others' smoking, particularly of immediate family members, results from the impact of smoking behaviour on the likelihood that children and young people will themselves experiment with smoking, and in due course become regular smokers. The longer-term implications for the health and wealth of the individual resulting from this outcome are immense and, whilst a full review is beyond the scope of this report, they include a 50% chance of premature death with an average 10-year loss of life expectancy.[1] The younger the age of smoking uptake, the greater the harm from smoking is likely to be, since early uptake is associated with subsequent heavier smoking, higher levels of dependence, a lower likelihood of subsequent cessation, and higher mortality.[1] In this chapter, we therefore review the evidence surrounding the impact of smoking by other family members on the risk of incident smoking in the child.

6.2 Age and uptake of smoking

The majority of regular cigarette users start smoking during late childhood and early adolescence.[2] The proportion of children in England who have smoked in the past week is strongly age-related, increasing from about 1% in 11-year-olds, to 7% at age 13, and 20% by age 15.[3] Among 16- to 19-year-olds in Britain, 21% are regular (typically daily) smokers, and in 20- to 24-year-olds, 31% are regular smokers.[4] The prevalence of smoking declines with age thereafter. Thus, in England (as in many countries) the great majority of smoking experimentation and uptake occurs during teenage years.

6.3 Factors influencing smoking uptake

Uptake of smoking is associated with a wide range of risk factors,[5] which include: the ease of obtaining cigarettes;[5] smoking by friends and peer group members;[6–8] socio-economic status;[9] exposure to positive tobacco marketing and depictions in film, television and other media;[10] attitudes and behaviours in school environments;[11] and parental and sibling smoking.[5] Since exposure to smoking role models in parents, siblings and other household members is likely to be most prevalent in the homes of children who sustain passive smoke exposure, we have therefore attempted to quantify this additional behavioural effect of passive smoking on the subsequent risk of smoking uptake in the exposed child.

6.4 Studies identified

We searched for relevant studies published between 2000 and 2009 in the EMBASE, MEDLINE, PSYCInfo, and CAB Abstracts databases. The key words used to search for the exposure variables were: parent; mother; paternal; father; household; sibling; maternal; guardian; brother; sister; smoke; tobacco; cigarette; cotinine; and exp smoking; and for the outcome variable: adolescent; teenager; children; and child. We scanned the reference lists of the identified studies, and also searched the proceedings of the Society for Research on Nicotine and Tobacco (SRNT) conference for additional relevant references. We excluded five studies published in non-English languages.

The titles of the identified publications were screened by one researcher to assess the eligibility of the articles, and the abstracts of all studies with titles that appeared potentially eligible were screened independently by two researchers to identify those that appeared relevant. Full text versions of these studies were then obtained. Meta-analysis was carried out using random effect models, and presented as pooled ORs with 95% CIs for seven exposure variables: smoking by both parents, either parent, at least one parent, mother, father, household, or sibling.

A total of 58 relevant studies were included in the meta-analyses. The majority of these were carried out in the USA and Europe, and involved a range of school, family, clinical and community-based populations and settings. Most of the studies measured adolescent smoking by self report, though two used biochemical measures of cotinine in saliva.[12,13] Thirty studies assessed current smoking,[8,9,13–40] 26 studies assessed ever smoked,[12,41–65] and two studies combined current and ever-tried smokers together.[66,67]

6.5 Parental smoking

A pooled analysis of 14 studies in which exposure was determined by having one parent who smokes found that the risk of smoking in adolescence was increased by 62% (OR 1.62, 95% CI 1.49 to 1.76; Fig 6.1).[8,12,23,27,31,33,38–40,42,44,46,47,62] This effect was stronger if the parent who smoked was the mother (OR 2.19, 95% CI 1.73 to 2.79, 24 studies)[20–22,24–26,28,34,35,37,43,47,48,50,52,54,56–58,63–67] than the father (OR 1.66, 95% CI 1.42 to 1.94, 18 studies).[20–22,28,34,35,47,50,52,54,56–58,60,63–65,67]

Among children with at least one parent who smokes, the risk of smoking in the child is increased by 72% (OR 1.72, 95% CI 1.59 to 1.86, 10 studies);[13–19,30,53,61] if both parents smoke, the risk is increased almost three-fold (pooled OR 2.73, 95% CI 2.28 to 3.28, 15 studies).[8,13,20,23,27–29,31,33,34,39,44,46,47,63]

6.6 Sibling smoking

A pooled analysis of 23 studies found the effect of a sibling smoking (usually defined within the included studies as an older sibling) more than doubled the

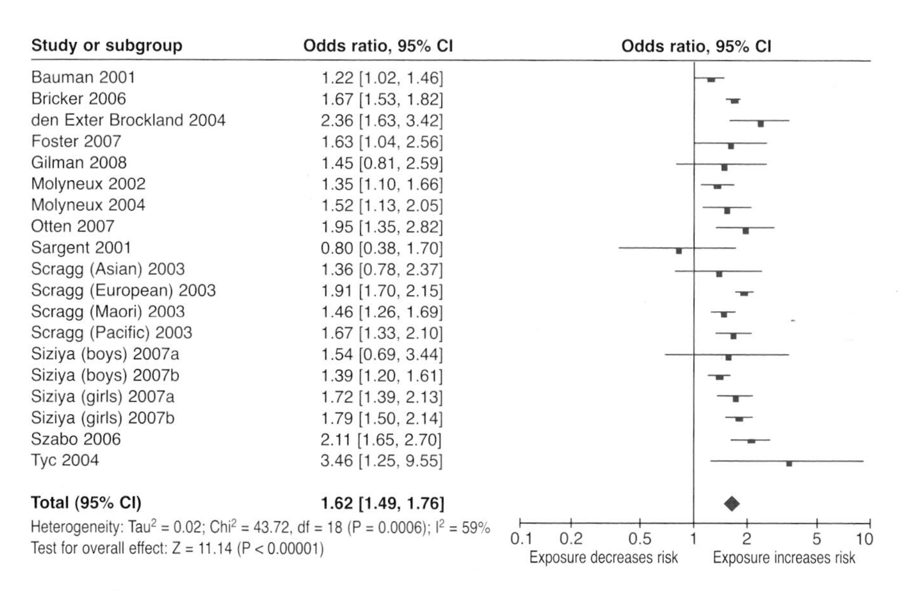

Fig 6.1 Studies of risk of adolescent smoking if either parent smokes.

risk of an adolescent smoking (pooled OR 2.30, 95% CI 1.85 to 2.86; Fig 6.2).[8,12,14,16,20–23,29–32,34,35,41,52,54–56,58,63–65]

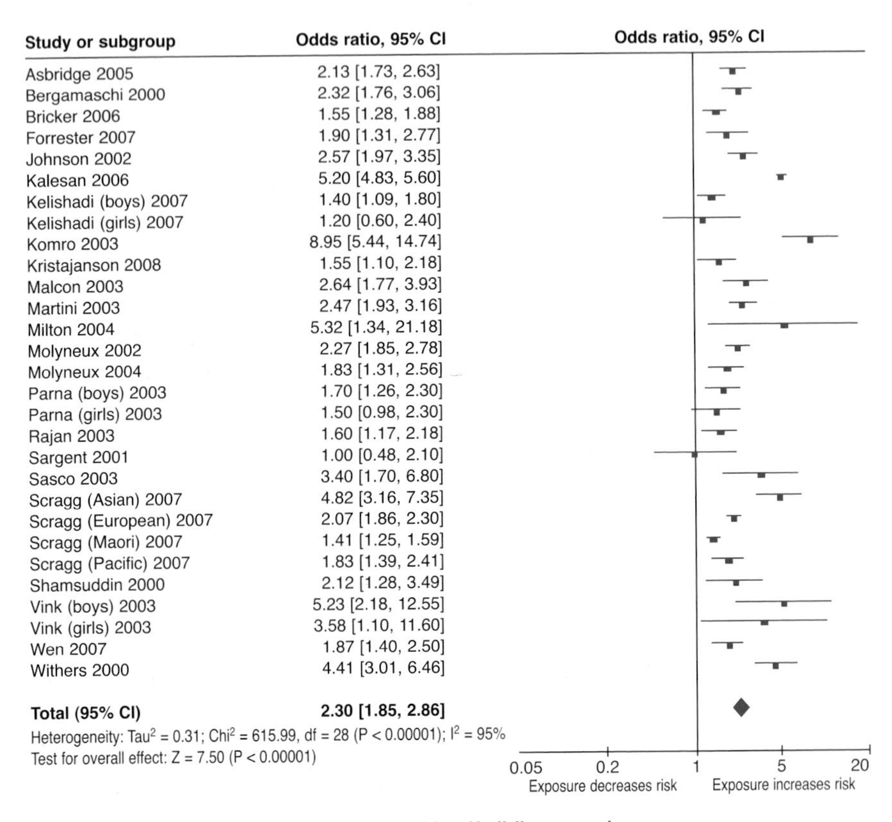

Fig 6.2 Studies of risk of adolescent smoking if siblings smoke.

6.7 Household smoking

Any household smoking (usually defined as either 'lives with a smoker' or 'an adult smokes in the home') increased the risk by an OR of 1.92 (95% CI 1.70 to 2.16, 12 studies).[9,17,33–36,45,49,51,55,58,59]

6.8 Implications of effect of family smoking on smoking uptake

The meta-analyses summarised above indicate that a young person who grows up in a family in which parents or siblings smoke is substantially more likely to become a smoker. The magnitude of this effect depends on which family member or members smoke. The available studies differ in how these exposures are categorised. At the lowest estimate of effect, arising from having only one parent who smokes, the risk of uptake is increased by about 60%. If both parents smoke, the risk is substantially higher.

The impact of smoking by any family member in these analyses inevitably has some component of confounding by exposure to other smokers both in the family and outside the home, since smokers are more likely to live with other smokers and to have other smokers in their social networks and wider social and work environments. However, collectively these influences amount to a highly significant impact on the risk that an individual child will become a smoker, and on the persistence of smoking in populations. Since exposure to family smoking is particularly common in relatively socially disadvantaged households, this effect is also likely to be an important contributor to the perpetuation of the association between smoking and social disadvantage. The harm caused to the child by smoking uptake is also likely to be substantial, since most people who become established smokers as young people will remain regular smokers for many years, and about half of those who remain smokers will die as a consequence of their smoking.[1]

6.9 Number of children who take up smoking as a result of smoking exposure in the home

Approximately 22% of children aged up to 15 live in a home that is not smoke-free (Table 2.3). Taking the estimate of the increased odds of becoming a smoker in these children to be that for household smoking, of 1.92 (Section 6.7), which also lies approximately midway in the range of ORs for different definitions of exposure, then the attributable fraction equation used in Chapter 5 generates an estimate that around 17% of smoking uptake among children up to age 15 is likely to be attributable to exposure to smoking in the home. In 2008, there were around 675,000 15-year-olds in England and Wales,[68] of whom 20% smoked.[3] A 17% attributable percentage translates into approximately 23,000 new smokers by age 15 arising from exposure to smoking in the home. This figure excludes smoking uptake arising from exposure to smokers outside the home, or uptake occurring after the age of 15.

6.10 Implications for policy

Breaking the cycle of persistent smoking passing from one generation to the next, particularly in disadvantaged families, demands measures to reduce exposure of children and young people to smoking behaviour and role models. The most effective means of ensuring that exposure to parental smoking is prevented is to maximise cessation among adult smokers. At present, smoking prevalence is highest in the young adult, and hence potentially parental, age groups.[4] Measures to prevent smoking in this young adult age group are thus likely to be especially effective in both preventing harm from passive smoking, reducing the uptake of smoking by the current generation of children and young people, and reducing the magnitude of the link between smoking and social inequality in health.

6.11 Summary

- Children growing up with parents or siblings who smoke are around 90% more likely to become smokers themselves.
- Similar, though probably less strong, influences on smoking behaviour are likely to result from exposure to smoking outside the home.
- At least 23,000 young people in England and Wales each year start smoking by the age of 15 as a result of exposure to smoking in the home, though the true total for uptake as a consequence of exposure to others' smoking is likely to be higher.
- Since uptake of regular smoking has significant health implications for the child, including a 50% likelihood of premature death if smoking continues, this represents a major health hazard to children.
- Together, these influences are likely to play a major role in perpetuating the association between social disadvantage and smoking.
- Maximising measures to reduce the prevalence of exposure of children to smokers is thus a high priority, not only to avoid harm caused by passive smoke, but also from the increased risk of smoking uptake.

References

1 Doll R, Peto R, Boreham J, Sutherland I. Mortality in relation to smoking: 50 years' observations on male British doctors. *BMJ* 2004;328:1519–33.

2 Hill KG, Hawkins JD, Catalano RF, Abbott RD, Guo, J. Family influences on the risk of daily smoking initiation. *J Adolesc Health* 2005;37:202–10.

3 The Information Centre. *Drug use, smoking and drinking among young people in England in 2008*. London: The Health and Social Care Information Centre, 2009.

4 Robinson S, Lader D. Smoking and drinking among adults. In *Office for National Statistics, 2009*. Newport: ONS, 2007.

5 Geckova A, Van Dijk JP, Van Ittersum-Gritter T *et al.* Determinants of adolescents' smoking behaviour: a literature review. *Cent Eur J Public Health* 2002;10:79–87.

6 De Vries H, Engels R, Kremers S *et al.* Parents' and friends' smoking status as predictors of smoking onset: findings from six European countries. *Health Educ Res* 2003;18: 627–36.

7 Kobus K. Peers and adolescent smoking. *Addiction* 2003;98:37–55.

8 Molyneux A, Lewis S, Antoniak M *et al.* Prospective study of the effect of exposure to other smokers in high school tutor groups on the risk of incident smoking in adolescence. *Am J Epidemiol* 2004;159:127–32.

9 Pust S, Mohnen SM, Schneider S. Individual and social environment influences on smoking in children and adolescents. *Public Health* 2008;122:1324–30.

10 Wellman RJ, Sugarman DB, DiFranza JR, Winickoff JP. The extent to which tobacco marketing and tobacco use in films contribute to children's use of tobacco. A meta-analysis. *Arch Pediatr Adolesc Med* 2006;160:1285–96.

11 Henderson M, Ecob R, Wight D, Abraham C. What explains between-school differences in rates of smoking? *BMC Public Health* 2008;8:218.

12 Bricker JB, Peterson AV Jr, Leroux BG *et al.* Prospective prediction of children's smoking transitions: role of parents' and older siblings' smoking. *Addiction* 2006;101: 128–36.

13 Fidler JA, West R, Van Jaarsveld CHM, Jarvis MJ, Wardle J. Smoking status of step-parents as a risk factor for smoking in adolescence. *Addiction* 2008;103:496–501.

14 Bergamaschi A, Gambi A, Gentilini F *et al.* Tobacco smoking among high school students in Romagna (Italy) and evaluation of a prevention campaign. *Subst Use Misuse* 2000;35: 1277–95.

15 Fisher LB, Winickoff JP, Camargo CA Jr, Colditz GA, Frazier AL. Household smoking restrictions and adolescent smoking. *Am J Health Promot* 2007;22:15–21.

16 Forrester K, Biglan A, Severson HH, Smolkowski K. Predictors of smoking onset over two years. *Nicotine Tob Res* 2007;9:1259–67.

17 Griesbach D, Amos A, Currie C. Adolescent smoking and family structure in Europe. *Soc Sci Med* 2003;56:41–52.

18 Jackson C. Perceived legitimacy of parental authority and tobacco and alcohol use during early adolescence. *J Adolesc Health* 2002;31:425–32.

19 Jackson C, Dickinson D. Cigarette consumption during childhood and persistence of smoking through adolescence. *Arch Pediatr Adolesc Med* 2004;158:1050–6.

20 Kalesan B, Stine J, Alberg AJ. The joint influence of parental modeling and positive parental concern on cigarette smoking in middle and high school students. *J Sch Health* 2006;76:402–7; quiz 438–9.

21 Kristjansson AL, Sigfusdottir ID, Allegrante JP, Helgason AR. Social correlates of cigarette smoking among Icelandic adolescents: a population-based cross-sectional study. *BMC Public Health* 2008;8:86.

22 Martini S, Sulistyowati M. *The determinants of smoking behavior among teenagers in East Java Province, Indonesia.* Health, Nutrition, and Population study paper. Washington: World Bank, 2005.

23 Molyneux A, Lewis S, Antoniak M *et al.* Is smoking a communicable disease? Effect of exposure to ever smokers in school tutor groups on the risk of incident smoking in the first year of secondary school. *Tob Control* 2002;11:241–5.

24 Moore L, Roberts C, Tudor-Smith C. School smoking policies and smoking prevalence among adolescents: multilevel analysis of cross-sectional data from Wales. *Tob Control* 2001;10:117–23.

25 O' Byrne KK, Haddock CK, Poston WSC, Mid America Heart Institute. Parenting style and adolescent smoking. *J Adolesc Health* 2002;30:418–25.

26 O'Callaghan FV, O'Callaghan M, Najman JM *et al.* Prediction of adolescent smoking from family and social risk factors at 5 years, and maternal smoking in pregnancy and at 5 and 14 years. *Addiction* 2006;101:282–90.

27 Otten R, Engels RC, Van de Ven MO *et al.* Parental smoking and adolescent smoking stages: the role of parents' current and former smoking, and family structure. *J Behav Med* 2007;30:143–54.

28 Ozawa M, Washio M, Kiyohara C. Factors related to starting and continuing smoking among senior high school boys in Fukuoka, Japan. *Asian Pacific J Cancer Prev: APJCP* 2008;9:239–45.

29 Pärna K, Rahu K, Fischer K *et al.* Smoking and associated factors among adolescents in Tallinn, Helsinki and Moscow: a multilevel analysis. *Scand J Public Health* 2003;31:350–8.

30 Rajan KB, Leroux BG, Peterson AV *et al.* Nine-year prospective association between older siblings' smoking and children's daily smoking. *J Adolesc Health* 2003;33:25–30.

31 Sargent JD, Dalton M. Does parental disapproval of smoking prevent adolescents from becoming established smokers? *Pediatrics* 2001;108:1256–62.

32 Sasco AJ, Merrill RM, Benhaim-Luzon V *et al.* Trends in tobacco smoking among adolescents in Lyon, France. *Eur J Cancer* 2003;39:496–504.

33 Scragg R, Laugesen M, Robinson E. Parental smoking and related behaviours influence adolescent tobacco smoking: results from the 2001 New Zealand national survey of 4th form students [see comment]. *N Z Med J* 2003;116:U707.

34 Scragg R, Laugesen M. Influence of smoking by family and best friend on adolescent tobacco smoking: results from the 2002 New Zealand national survey of year 10 students. *Aust N Z J Public Health* 2007;31:217–23.

35 Shamsuddin K, Haris MA. Family influence on current smoking habits among secondary school children in Kota Bharu, Kelantan. *Singapore Med J* 2000;41:167–71.

36 Simons-Morton B, Haynie DL, Crump AD, Eitel P, Saylor KE. Peer and parent influences on smoking and drinking among early adolescents. *Health Educ Behav* 2001;28:95–107.

37 Siziya S, Muula AS, Rudatsikira E. Prevalence and correlates of current cigarette smoking among adolescents in East Timor-Leste. *Indian Pediatr* 2008;45:963–8.

38 Siziya S, Ntata PR, Rudatsikira E *et al.* Sex differences in prevalence rates and predictors of cigarette smoking among in-school adolescents in Kilimanjaro, Tanzania. *Tanzania Health Res Bull* 2007b;9:190–5.

39 Szabo E, White V, Hayman J. Can home smoking restrictions influence adolescents' smoking behaviors if their parents and friends smoke? *Addict Behav* 2006;31:2298–303.

40 Tyc VL, Hadley W, Allen D *et al.* Predictors of smoking intentions and smoking status among nonsmoking and smoking adolescents. *Addict Behav* 2004;29:1143–7.

41 Asbridge M, Tanner J, Wortley S. Ethno-specific patterns of adolescent tobacco use and the mediating role of acculturation, peer smoking, and sibling smoking. *Addiction* 2005;100:1340–51.

42 Bauman KE, Carver K, and Gleiter K. Trends in parent and friend influence during adolescence. The case of adolescent cigarette smoking. *Addict Behav* 2001;26:349–61.

43 Cornelius MD, Leech SL, Goldschmidt L, Day NL. Is prenatal tobacco exposure a risk factor for early adolescent smoking? A follow-up study. *Neurotoxicol Teratol* 2005;27:667–76.

44 Den Exter Blokland EAW, Engels RCME, Hale WW 3rd, Meeus W, Willemsen MC. Lifetime parental smoking history and cessation and early adolescent smoking behavior. *Prev Med* 2004;38:359–68.

45 Elder JP, Campbell NR, Litrownik AJ *et al.* Predictors of cigarette and alcohol susceptibility and use among Hispanic migrant adolecents. *Prev Med* 2000;31:115–23.

46 Foster SE, Jones DJ, Olson AL *et al.* Family socialization of adolescent's self-reported cigarette use: the role of parents' history of regular smoking and parenting style. *J Pediatr Psychol* 2007;32:481–93.

47 Gilman SE, Rende R, Boergers J *et al.* Parental smoking and adolescent smoking initiation: an intergenerational perspective on tobacco control. *Pediatrics* 2009;123:e274–81.

48 Griesler PC, Kandel DB, Davies M. Ethnic differences in predictors of initiation and persistence of adolescent cigarette smoking in the National Longitudinal Survey of Youth. *Nicotine Tob Res* 2002;4:79–93.

49 Gritz ER, Prokhorov AV, Hudmon KS *et al.* Predictors of susceptibility to smoking and ever smoking: A longitudinal study in a triethnic sample of adolescents. *Nicotine Tob Res* 2003;5:493–506.

50 Hesketh T, Ding QJ, Tomkins A. Smoking among youths in China. *Am J Public Health* 2001;91:1653–5.

51 Hollis JF, Polen MR, Lichtenstein E, Whitlock EP. Tobacco use patterns and attitudes among teens being seen for routine primary care. *Am J Health Promot* 2003;17:231–9.

52 Johnson CC, Li D, Perry CL *et al.* Fifth through eighth grade longitudinal predictors of tobacco use among a racially diverse cohort: CATCH. *J Sch Health* 2002;72:58–64.

53 Johnson CC, Myers L, Webber LS, Boris NW. Profiles of the adolescent smoker: models of tobacco use among 9th grade high school students: Acadiana Coalition of Teens against Tobacco (ACTT). *Prev Med* 2004;39:551–8.

54 Kelishadi R, Mokhtari MR, Tavasoli AA *et al.* Determinants of tobacco use among youths in Isfahan, Iran. *Int J Public Health* 2007;52:173–9.

55 Komro KA, McCarty MC, Forster JL, Blaine TM, Chen V. Parental, family, and home characteristics associated with cigarette smoking among adolescents. *Am J Health Promot* 2003;17:291–9.

56 Malcon MC, Menezes AM, Maia Mde F, Chatkin M, Victora CG. Prevalence of and risk factors for cigarette smoking among adolescents in South America: a systematic literature review. *Rev Panam Salud Publica* 2003;13:222–8.

57 Menezes AMB, Goncalves H, Anselmi L, Hallal PC, Araujo CLP. Smoking in early adolescence: evidence from the 1993 Pelotas (Brazil) birth cohort study. *J Adolesc Health* 2006;39:669–77.

58 Milton B, Cook PA, Dugdill L *et al.* Why do primary school children smoke? A longitudinal analysis of predictors of smoking uptake during pre-adolescence. *Public Health* 2004;118:247–55.

59 Nichols TR, Birnbaum AS, Birnel S, Botvin GJ. Perceived smoking environment and smoking initiation among multi-ethnic urban girls. *J Adolesc Health* 2006;38:369–75.

60 Ogwell AE, Astrom AN, Haugejorden O. Socio-demographic factors of pupils who use tobacco in randomly-selected primary schools in Nairobi province, Kenya. *East Afr Med J* 2003;80:235–41.

61 Rozi S, Akhtar S, Ali S, Khan J. Prevalence and factors associated with current smoking among high school adolescents in Karachi, Pakistan. *Southeast Asian J Trop Med Public Health* 2005;36:498–504.

62 Siziya S, Rudatsikira E, Muula AS, Ntata PR. Predictors of cigarette smoking among adolescents in rural Zambia: results from a cross sectional study from Chongwe district. *Rural Remote Health* 2007a;7:728.

63 Vink JM, Willemsen G, Boomsma DI. The association of current smoking behavior with the smoking behavior of parents, siblings, friends and spouses. *Addiction* 2003;98: 923–31.

64 Wen X, Chen W, Muscat JE *et al.* Modifiable family and school environmental factors associated with smoking status among adolescents in Guangzhou, China. *Prev Med* 2007;45:189–97.

65 Withers NJ, Low JL, Holgate ST, Clough JB. Smoking habits in a cohort of UK adolescents. *Respir Med* 2000;94:391–6.

66 Yorulmaz F, Akturk Z, Dagdeviren N, Dalkilic A. Smoking among adolescents: relation to school success, socioeconomic status nutrition and self-esteem. *Swiss Med Wkly* 2002;132:449–54.

67 Zhang L, Wang WF, Zhou G. A cross-sectional study of smoking risk factors in junior high school students in Henan, China. *Southeast Asian J Trop Med Public Health* 2005;36:1580–4.

68 Office for National Statistics. Mortality statistics – deaths registered in 2008. Newport: Office for Public Sector Information, 2009. www.statistics.gov.uk/statbase/product.asp?vlnk=15096

7 The costs of passive smoking in children

7.1 Background

The financial burden of disease imposed on the NHS by smoking is considerable. In the 1990s, two estimates of the annual cost to the NHS of treating disease caused by smoking in the UK arrived at figures indicating a range of between £1.4 and 1.7 billion,[1,2] or about 4.9% of all NHS expenditure. By 2006, largely as a result of increased healthcare costs, direct costs to the NHS had been independently estimated to have risen to between £2.7[1] and £5.2 billion,[1] the latter figure representing 5.5% of all NHS expenditure. The percentage of total healthcare costs accounted for by smoking varies across developed countries, from 3.3% in Germany[1] to almost 12% in the USA.[1] Costs across the USA also vary significantly between States, with approximately 16% of California's healthcare budget attributable to treating disease arising from smoking.[6] The wider societal costs of smoking are far-reaching, with estimated workplace costs arising from smoking-related absenteeism, smoking breaks and fires, of approximately £450 million for Scotland alone.[1] Scaling these costs up to the UK population yields an estimate of around £5 billion.

To date, however, none of these cost estimates have included the costs arising from disease caused by passive smoking in children. The potential wider financial and economic impacts of passive smoking are considerable, but difficult to measure fully. No attempt is made in this chapter to calculate the impact of children's ill health on parental anxiety and wellbeing, or the impact on children's schooling and educational achievements. Such impacts are likely to reduce future earnings, and may have additional health and wellbeing effects for the children concerned. The costing undertaken for this report is limited to estimates of the passive smoking-related healthcare costs of children aged up to 16. In addition, an estimate is made of two of the lifetime impacts which may occur from the increased smoking uptake of children exposed to smoking in the home. The costs are expressed as present value sums – the cost in today's terms, after a discount rate of 3.5% had been applied to future costs.

In this chapter, we thus provide conservative estimates, both of the costs of treating this burden of disease, and of those arising from smoking uptake due to exposure to family smoking, using the estimates derived in chapters 5 and 6. All of these costs are direct and for the most part, relatively immediate consequences of passive smoking, and are thus almost completely avoidable. The methods and estimates used are now explained in detail.

7.2 Costs in primary care

The costs of primary care consultations for childhood disease caused by passive smoking are calculated by applying the cost of a GP consultation (taken for UK national estimates)[1] to the number of consultations attributable to passive smoking estimated in Table 5.2. A unit cost of £30 per consultation is used, which includes the full cost of GP consultations, taking into account practice overheads and staffing costs. The costs of primary care contacts arising from disease caused by passive smoking estimated by this approach are shown in Table 7.1, and come to a total of approximately £9.1 million. The major components of these costs are the treatment of middle ear infections (53% of total cost) and asthma and wheezing (39% of total cost).

Table 7.1 Cost at 2007 prices of primary care consultations for diseases in children caused by passive smoking in the home.

Disease	Age range in years	UK consultations attributable to smoking	Cost of consultations
Lower respiratory infections	≤2	26,000	£780,000
Middle ear infections	0–16	160,200	£4,806,000
Wheeze	≤2	10,300	£309,000
Asthma	3–4	7,600	£228,000
Asthma	5–16	99,000	£2,970,000
Meningitis	0–16	800	£24,000
Total		303,900	£9,117,000

However, such primary care contacts generate other NHS expenditure. The cost of providing the drugs and medical devices for asthma prescribed as part of primary care interventions represents a significant expenditure for the NHS. In 2000, the National Institute for Health and Clinical Excellence (NICE) estimated the total drugs budget for the treatment of asthma in England and Wales to be £8 million,[2] which, using the hospital and community health service (HCHS) inflation index, translates into £10.25 million at 2006/7 prices.[8] NICE guidance also estimates that 9% of males and 6% of females under the age of 5 (a total of 238,770 children) are prescribed drugs for the treatment of asthma.[9] We can thus estimate a cost of around £43 for each child under 5 presenting with asthma or wheezing. Assuming that this approximate unit cost also applies to those aged between 5 and 16, then the 15,400 new cases of asthma presenting in primary care each year (Table 5.2) will generate a medication cost of £0.7 million per annum.

Another way of calculating these costs is to estimate the total cost per child from diagnosis. For medications prescribed throughout childhood to the age of 16, the total cost is £538 per child (discounted at 3.5%). Using the age-banded incidence data presented in Table 5.2, and assuming for simplicity that new cases are diagnosed at an average of 3 years (1,700 cases) or 10 years of age (13,700 cases), we estimate a total cost of £4 million (discounted at 3.5%) for the provision of asthma drugs from age of diagnosis to 16 years of age.

The total primary care cost estimate per annum, which does not include equivalent treatment costs for other diseases caused by passive smoking, thus comes to approximately £9.8 million. A small proportion of the drugs budget will be accounted for in the reference costs which we use below to estimate the cost of inpatient treatment for asthma. We have therefore deducted the estimated cost of drugs consumed by these children receiving a hospital admission, to derive a revised total cost of primary care visits and asthma drugs of approximately £9.7 million per year.

7.3 Hospital costs

Costs for hospital admissions are available as a weighted average of elective and non-elective inpatient admissions taken from NHS Reference Costs.[3] These are the costs derived from estimates of the resources needed to provide the specific packages of care, called healthcare resource groups, in the English NHS. Costs for admissions for the diseases listed in Table 5.3, in the 2006/7 financial year, are given in Table 7.2, with a weighted estimates unit cost combining the different healthcare resource group components which make up each diagnostic code. Table 7.3 shows the total inpatient unit costs arising from the numbers of

Table 7.2 Costs of inpatient admissions for childhood disease, 2006/07.

HRG4 code		Weighted average of elective and non-elective inpatient	Weighted average per diagnosis
DZ22A	Unspecified acute lower respiratory infection with major complications	£2,185	
DZ22B	Unspecified acute lower respiratory infection with complications	£1,175	£1,350
DZ22C	Unspecified acute lower respiratory infection without complications	£739	
CZ09U	Intermediate ear procedures 18 years and under	£1,794	£1,794
A25[a]	Nervous system infections	£2,347	£2,347
PA12Z	Asthma or wheezing	£1,071	£1,071

Source: Department of Health.[8]
HRG = Health Resource Groups.
[a] HRG3.5

Table 7.3 Cost of hospital admissions in children aged 0–14 in England in 2005/06, at 2006/07 prices, from specified diseases attributable to passive smoke exposure.

	Age group	Admissions attributable to smoking	Cost of admissions
Lower respiratory infections	≤2	3,361	£4,537,350
Middle ear infections	0–14	2,517	£4,515,498
Wheeze	≤2	938	£1,004,598
Asthma	3–4	236	£252,756
	5–14	1,211	£1,296,981
Meningitis	0–14	231	£542,157
Total		8,494	£12,149,340

admissions attributable to smoking, by diagnosis, from Table 5.3. Multiplying the unit costs by the numbers of cases attributable to passive smoking, an estimate is made of £12.1 million per annum in hospital admissions in England, or £13.6 million for the whole of the UK, of which approximately 74% arises from the treatment of middle ear and lower respiratory infections.

7.4 Costs of uptake of smoking

7.4.1 Healthcare costs

In Chapter 6, we estimated that around 23,000 children and young people take up smoking in England and Wales as a result of exposure to smoking by family members in the home. In 2006, applying age-specific smoking rates to the UK population, there were an estimated 5,629,332 male smokers and 5,119,071 female smokers. Table 7.4 shows the costs of treating smoking-related disease as estimated by Allender *et al*[4] for the UK, by disease area. Dividing these costs by the total of 10,748,403 smokers in the UK and summing them across disease areas generates a total of £496 per smoker. Assuming that half of these smokers continue to smoke for most of their lives,[4] then multiplying the per smoker cost by the estimated 11,500 sustained smokers that result from exposure to smoking in the home, yields a conservative estimate of £5.7 million per annum in annual excess treatment costs. Equivalent costs based on the Callum estimates, derived for smokers in England,[3] are £292 per smoker, or £3.6 million per annum in excess treatment costs. However, it should be noted that these are simple point estimates, and that the great majority of these costs will be incurred well into the future. For the sustained smokers, the total excess healthcare treatment costs over the following 60 years are respectively an estimated £77 million, or £48 million when discounted at 3.5%, assuming an uptake of smoking by age 16.

7.4.2 Workplace costs

Lifetime productivity costs in the workplace are also calculated from literature-based estimates by multiplying a cost per employee per annum by the potential

Table 7.4 Cost of smoking attributable disease (adapted from Allender *et al*).[4]

Total smoking attributable costs UK	2006/07 (million)	Cost per smoker
Trachea/bronchus/lung cancer	£276.30	£25.70
Other cancers	£370.90	£34.51
Cardiovascular disease	£2,588.20	£240.80
COPD	£1,440.90	£134.06
Other cancers	£650.10	£60.49
Total		**£495.56**

COPD = Chronic obstructive pulmonary disease.

years worked over a lifetime, and discounting future costs at 3.5%, following the guidance of NICE.[5] A simple estimate of the workplace costs can also be constructed for these 23,000 smokers. Parrott *et al*'s 1998 estimate of a cost of £450 million imposed on workplaces by smokers in Scotland was based on a working population of 1,948,000. Inflating this cost to 2006/7 prices gives a total of £653 million, and, dividing by the working population, a cost of £335 per smoker per annum is derived. In August 2009, approximately 73% of people of working age in the UK were employed. This translates to around 16,800 smokers being employed, who would therefore impose an estimated £5.6 million per annum on the economy as a result of smoking-related absence from work and smoking breaks, based on the costs calculated for Scotland as outlined above. Over a 40-year working career, these costs escalate to £225 million before discounting is applied, or £72 million discounted over the period of the working career, at 3.5% per annum. If we assume that half of these smokers have quit by the age of 40, the total discounted productivity cost is approximately £63 million.

7.5 Summary

- The effects of passive smoking in the home on children have a far-reaching economic impact over and above the more often reported effects on child health.
- A conservative estimate is made of £9.7 million per annum in UK primary care visits and asthma treatment costs, and £12.1 million per annum in hospital admissions in England, or approximately £13.6 million for the UK.
- The discounted cost of providing asthma drugs for children who develop asthma each year as a result of passive smoking up until the age of 16 in the UK is approximately £4 million.
- The future treatment costs of smokers who take up smoking as a consequence of exposure to parental smoking could be as high as £5.7 million per annum, or £48 million over 60 years, when discounted at 3.5% per annum.
- These smokers may also impose an annual cost of £5.6 million in terms of lost productivity due to smoking-related absence and smoking breaks in the workplace, which translates to £72 million over their working careers when discounted at 3.5% per annum.
- These significant economic costs are all avoidable.
- Interventions to reduce passive smoking thus have the potential to make cost savings to the NHS and in the workplace, as well as improving the health of children.

References

1. Buck D, Godfrey C, Parrott S, Raw M. *Cost effectiveness of smoking cessation interventions.* London: Health Education Authority, 1997.
2. Parrott S, Godfrey C, Raw M, West R, McNeill A. Guidance for commissioners on the cost effectiveness of smoking cessation interventions. *Thorax* 1998;53(suppl 5):S2–S37.
3. Callum C. *Cost of smoking to the NHS in England, 2006.* London: Action on Smoking and Health, 2008.
4. Allender S, Balakrishnan R, Scarborough P, Webster P, Rayner M. The burden of smoking-related ill health in the UK. *Tob Control* 2009;18:262–7.
5. Neubauer S, Welte R, Beiche A *et al.* Mortality, morbidity and costs attributable to smoking in Germany: update and a 10-year comparison. *Tob Control* 2006;15:464–71.
6. Miller LS, Zhang X, Rice DP, Max W. State estimates of total medical expenditures attributable to cigarette smoking, 1993. *Public Health Rep* 1998;113:447–58.
7. Parrott S, Godfrey C, Raw M. Costs of employee smoking in the workplace in Scotland. *Tob Control* 2000;9:187–92.
8. Curtis LA (ed). *Unit costs of health and social care 2007.* Canterbury: Personal Social Services Research Unit, University of Kent, 2007. www.pssru.ac.uk/uc/uc2007contents.htm
9. National Institute for Clinical Excellence. *Guide to the methods of technology appraisal.* London: NICE, 2008.
10. Department of Health. *NHS costing manual and reference costs collection guidance (2006/07).* London: DH, 2008.
11. Royal College of Physicians. *Nicotine addiction in Britain.* Report of the Tobacco Advisory Group. London: RCP, 2000.

8 Public opinion on smoke-free policy

8.1 Introduction

Successful implementation of all legislation depends to some degree on the extent to which it is supported by the public, and this is especially true of laws that apply to private or individual behaviour. Before smoke-free legislation was implemented in each of the UK jurisdictions, and in Ireland and elsewhere, concerns were expressed that the public would not support the law, and that widespread compliance would be difficult to achieve. However, in the event, public opinion in the UK has been predominantly supportive of measures to restrict smoking in public and in workplaces. Furthermore, as has been the case elsewhere, that support has increased progressively in the periods before and after legislation.[1–4] A combination of public support with effective policing and, where necessary, prosecution of high-profile breaches of the legislation in the early days after implementation, has resulted in very high and sustained compliance with smoke-free legislation across the UK.

However, although legislation has proved to be a highly effective means of preventing passive smoke exposure in public and workplaces, it does not currently extend into the family home or other private spaces where most exposure of children to passive smoke occurs. Although legislating to prohibit smoking in these private places is possible, policing and enforcing such legislation effectively would be very difficult, if not impossible. Widespread reduction of the prevalence of smoking in the home will therefore only occur as a result of households making their homes smoke-free. This is unlikely to occur without equally widespread public understanding of, and support for, the need to protect children and other household members from passive smoke, particularly among smokers themselves. In this chapter, we examine public opinion on a range of aspects of existing smoke-free policy, and attempt to gauge support for further measures to prevent passive smoke exposure in UK homes. The data presented are from a number of sources, particularly a series of opinion surveys commissioned at various times by Action on Smoking and Health (ASH) and partners, to track public opinion on multiple occasions before and since smoke-free legislation. Sample sizes for these surveys varied, but involved a nationally representative sample of, at a minimum, 1,100 adults for surveys in England, and 3,300 for studies across Great Britain. The most recent poll, carried out by YouGov in March 2009, was an online survey of 13,000 adults in a sample weighted to be representative of adults in Great Britain aged 18 and over.

8.2 Support for smoke-free legislation

Smoke-free public places are popular. Before and after the smoke-free legislation in England, nearly 80% of the population, and over 90% of non-smokers, supported legislation banning smoking in most public places and workplaces (Fig 8.1). The

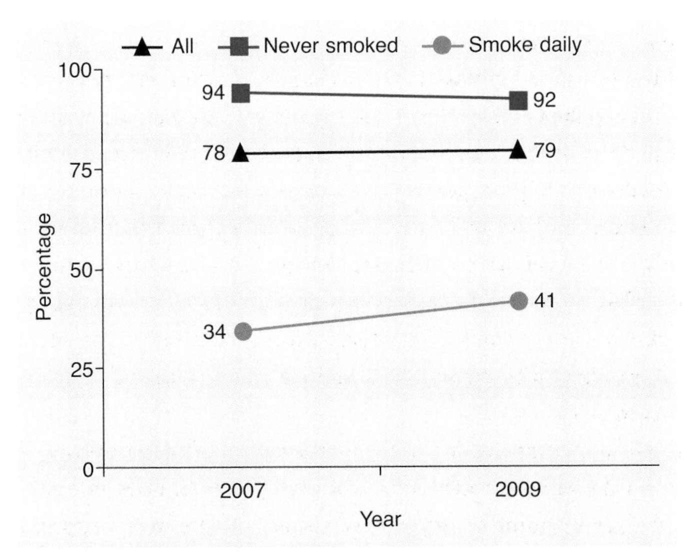

Fig 8.1 Support for smoke-free legislation applying to public and workplaces in England, 2007 and 2009.

improved quality of indoor air was recognised quickly: one month after the English legislation came into force, 74% of respondents reported pubs and restaurants to be more pleasant. This was accompanied by a widespread belief that the law banning smoking in the workplace was good for the health of workers (Fig 8.2), health in general, and respondents' own health.

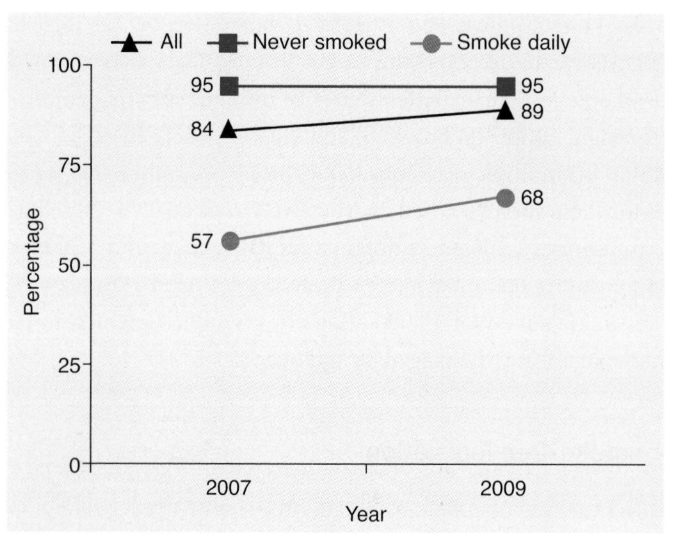

Fig 8.2 Percentage of adults in England agreeing that the law banning smoking in the workplace is good for the health of most workers.

In England, support for smoke-free public places among adults rose substantially while the legislation was being considered by parliament. By December 2005, 2 months before the crucial parliamentary vote, two-thirds of adults already supported legislation to make pubs and bars smoke-free. By April 2007, 3 months before the legislation came into force, support had risen to 72%, and 2 years later had risen so that almost four out of five (79%) adults supported the new law (Fig 8.3). In Scotland, similar legislation was introduced a year earlier, and by March 2009 support for the legislation reached 82%, slightly ahead of England.

8.3 Perceived exposure to passive smoke

The proportion of adult non-smokers in England reporting any exposure to passive smoke at home, at work, or both has remained relatively constant, at about 25%, over the period during which the legislation was introduced. However, within a few weeks of the legislation (August 2007), 41% of non-smokers reported being exposed a great deal less, and a further 17% a little less, than

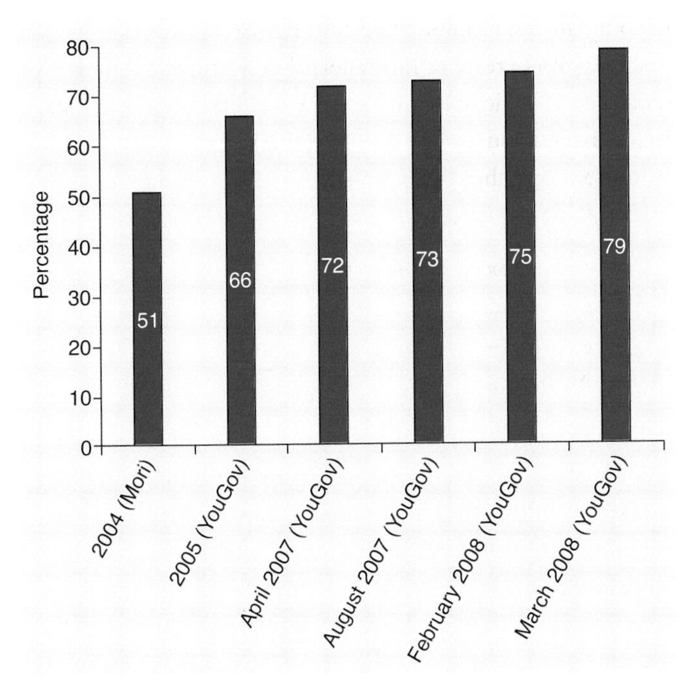

Fig 8.3 Percentage of adults in England who would support a law to make all pubs and bars smoke-free in public opinion surveys between 2004 and 2008. Mori = Ipsos Mori survey; YouGov = YouGov survey.

before legislation. By 2008, 73% of those who reported being exposed to passive smoke said that their overall exposure was less than before the legislation. These data provide evidence against the hypothesis that smoke-free legislation would displace the problem of passive smoke into the home, since only 6% of those non-smokers reporting passive smoke exposure in the home reported being more exposed after the legislation.

Perceived improvements in quality of indoor air in pubs, bars and restaurants were much more immediate. Within a month of legislation, 74% of English adults agreed that 'pubs, bars and restaurants are more pleasant places since they went smoke-free'. By February 2008, those agreeing with the statement outnumbered those who disagreed by a factor of ten (79% agreed, 8% disagreed).

8.4 Perceived health benefits of smoke-free places

There is a strong and growing view among the British public that smoke-free legislation is good for employees' health. In August 2007, 84% of English adults thought that smoke-free legislation was good for most workers' health. This rose to 89% in 2009, when only 3% disagreed with this statement. Furthermore, 83% of adults now believe that banning smoking in the workplace has been a benefit to the health of the public, and 79% agree that it has been good for their own health, including 59% who strongly agree. Only 2% strongly disagree. This is underpinned by a growing understanding of the harm that passive smoking causes. For example, in August 2007, 71% believed that passive smoking contributed to the onset of asthma in childhood, compared to 76% in February 2008, while the belief that passive smoking contributed to adult onset asthma rose from 65% to 71%.

8.5 Attitudes among smokers

After smoke-free legislation in New Zealand, one of the most notable shifts in public opinion was among smokers who came increasingly to support the right of bar workers to work in a smoke-free environment.[3] Much of the increase in support for smoke-free legislation in England has come from smokers. Support among daily smokers rose from 34% in April 2007 to 41% by 2009, and non-daily smokers' support increased from 59% in 2007 to 69% in 2009. There was also a rapid rise, between August 2007 and February 2009, among this group in the belief that banning smoking in the workplace was good for the health of most workers (rising from 57% to 68%), the general public (from 45% to 55%) and themselves (39% to 46%).

8.6 Perceived harms of passive smoke

As the general public perception of the benefits of smoke-free places has increased, so too has the perception of the harm caused by passive smoke exposure, particularly to children. In 2005, in a tracking survey of Department of Health Tobacco Education Campaigns, 28% of respondents reported that passive smoking was a risk to children's health. In 2009, in the YouGov survey, 88% of English adults reported that passive smoke exposure had an impact on child health (including 54% who believed it had a big impact) and 85% believed it had an impact on adult health (including 45% who believed it had a big impact) (Fig 8.4).

In YouGov surveys in 2007, 2008 and 2009, respondents were asked specifically about the impact passive smoke had on heart attacks and sudden infant death syndrome. In both cases, there has been an increasing perception of the harm from passive smoking. By 2009, 56% of adults in England believed that passive smoking increased the risk of sudden infant death (Fig 8.5), while 14% believed it had little or no impact. However, whilst it is encouraging that, in 2009, parents of children under the age of 18 were most likely to perceive a role for passive smoke on the risk

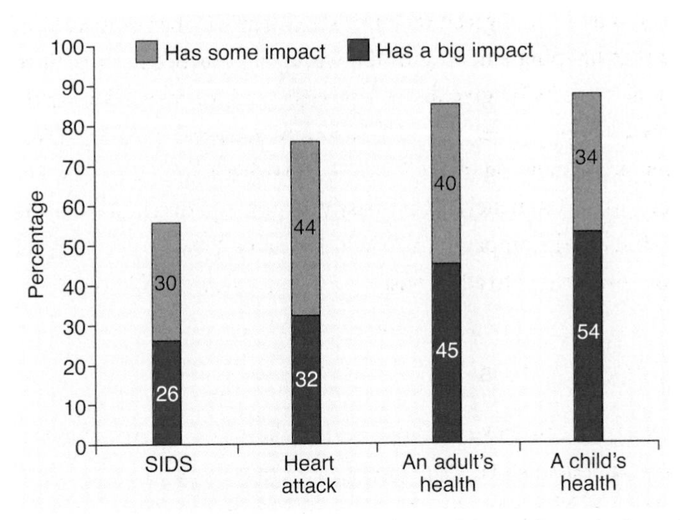

Fig 8.4 Percentage of adults in England perceiving an impact of passive smoke on general and specific health.

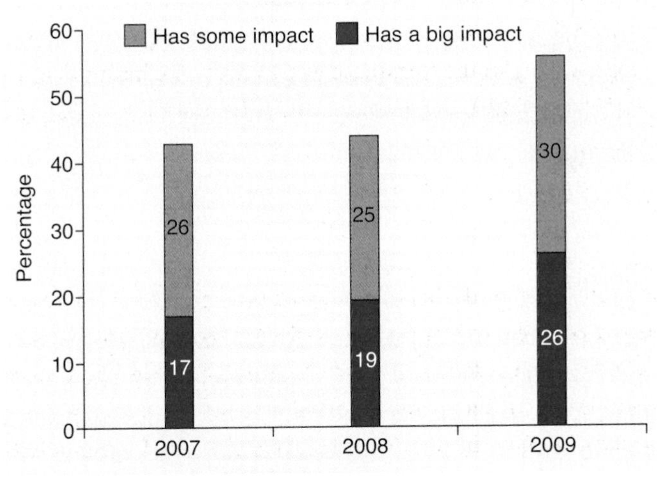

Fig 8.5 Percentage of adults in England perceiving an impact of passive smoking on the risk of sudden infant death syndrome.

of sudden infant death (70% believed there was an impact, including 39% who believed there was a big impact), it is a cause for concern that daily smokers were the least likely to report perceiving this effect (35%).

The effect of passive smoking on the risk of heart attacks was even more widely perceived. By 2009, 76% of adults in England believed that passive smoke contributes to the risk of a heart attack, an increase of 10% since 2007 (Fig 8.6). The group most aware of the risk appears to be non-smokers who are exposed to

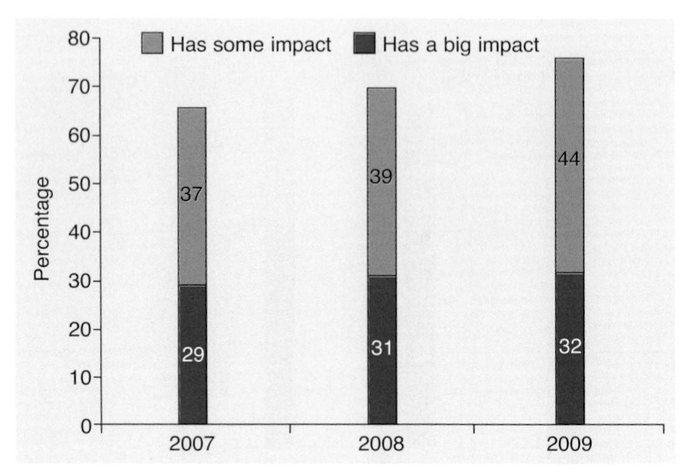

Fig 8.6 Percentage of adults in England perceiving an impact of passive smoking on the risk of heart attacks.

passive smoke both at home and at work, 42% of whom believe passive smoking has a big impact. Again, however, daily smokers seem least aware of the risk, with only 13% believing that there is a big impact. Smoking status is strongly associated with the perception of a smoker's risk to others. In the case of heart attacks, the perception that there is a high impact on the risk of a heart attack rises from 13% in daily smokers to 23% in occasional smokers, 34% in ex-smokers, and 40% in never-smokers.

8.7 New social norms

This changing perception of risk is changing the rules by which people live their lives. The Smoking Related Behaviour and Attitudes Survey[5] added a new question in 2006 about the extent to which smoking was allowed inside respondents' homes. The question was repeated in 2007, and again in 2008, when around two-thirds (67%) said that smoking was not allowed at all in their home, an increase of 6 percentage points since 2006 (Fig 8.7). One-fifth (21%) said that it was allowed in some rooms or at some times, and only 12% said it was allowed everywhere. The trend towards smoke-free homes continued into 2008, and data from the 2009 YouGov survey suggest a further increase, with 78% of adults in England not allowing smoking indoors and 47% prohibiting smoking in outside areas such as gardens or balconies. Only 8% allowed smoking everywhere. Among parents with children under the age of 18 in 2009, 83% reported that they required their homes to be smoke-free and only 5% permitted smoking throughout the home. Rules governing smoking in the home were strongly associated with smok-

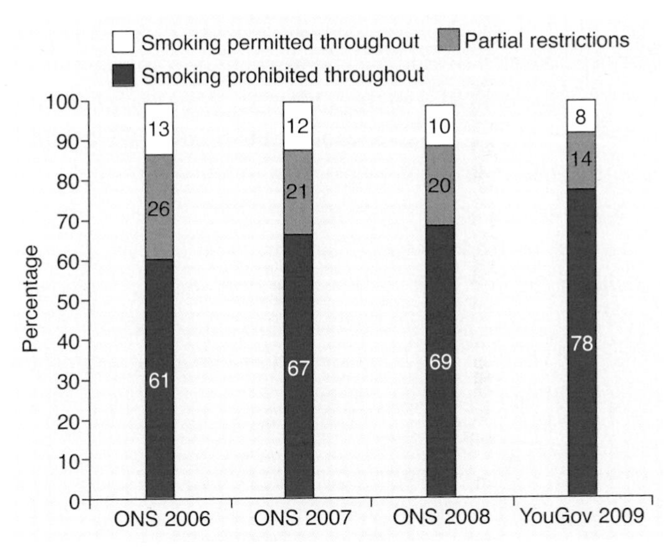

Fig 8.7 Percentage of adults in Great Britain reporting that their homes are smoke-free. Subtotals rounded to nearest 1%.

ing status, though 41% of all daily smokers, and 70% of all non-daily smokers, reported that smoking was prohibited inside their home.

These findings provide further evidence to that presented in Chapter 2, that the number of smoke-free households is increasing in the UK, and that the smoke-free legislation may have encouraged this. However, the specific impact of smoke-free legislation is hard to establish, since in England the proportion of homes allowing smoking indoors was falling as fast before legislation as in Ireland after legislation, and a study in Scotland[6] found few smokers who said that smoke-free legislation influenced their smoking in the home, and none who said it influenced how they restricted smoking in their homes. The Scottish study found that a sense of being 'a hospitable person' and 'a caring parent or grandparent' were more important determinants of policy on smoking in the home. However, many smokers who were ambivalent about the harm from passive smoking smoke were, nonetheless, reluctant to expose their children and grandchildren, partly out of fear of the children becoming smokers.

8.8 Opinions on smoking outdoors and in vehicles

Laws to protect people from passive smoking are based on well-established and robust evidence of direct physical harm,[1] but the evidence that harm arises from typical levels of exposure arising from smoking outdoors is less powerful.[7] The main arguments for outdoor smoking prohibition are to prevent drift of smoking into adjacent buildings, to avoid (for example) visitors to a building having to walk through a crowd of smokers to enter a building, and to avoid the demonstration of adult smoking role models to children. However, the need to protect children is widely recognised by smokers and non-smokers, and is sufficient enough to attract majority public support in many jurisdictions for the prohibition of smoking in outdoor areas where there are children.[8] Data from the 2009 YouGov survey in England reinforce this, with particularly strong support from non-smokers and from parents with a child aged under 18. Even among daily smokers, only 46% agree or strongly agree that smoking should be permitted in all outdoor spaces regardless of the presence of children (Fig 8.8), and of all adults, 76% support the prohibition of smoking in children's outdoor play areas.

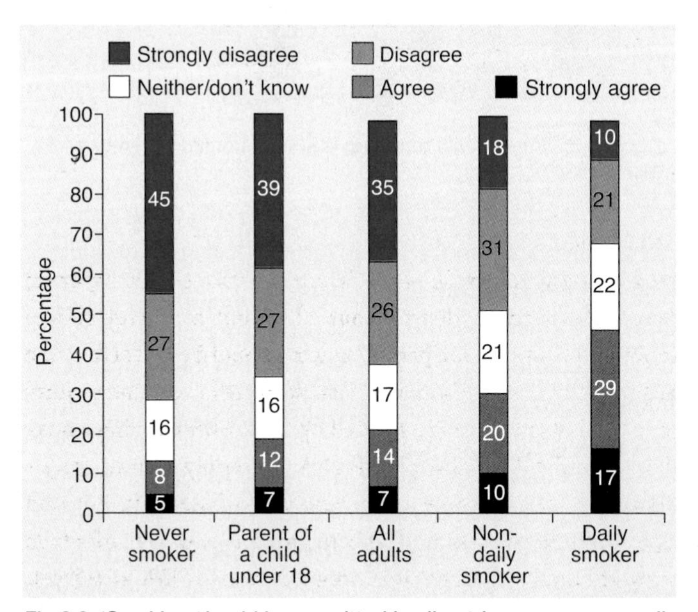

Fig 8.8 'Smoking should be permitted in all outdoor spaces regardless of the presence of children': opinions among adults in England. Subtotals rounded to nearest 1%.

Even before the legislation came into force in England, there was evidence that most adults felt the proposed legislation did not go far enough. A Populus survey for the BBC Daily Politics Show in 2007 found that 91% of adults felt there should be a ban on smoking in front of children, a view held most strongly by those in manual occupational groups, and 62% felt there should be a ban on smoking while driving a car. Indeed, there was already substantial support (45%) for banning smoking in some outdoor spaces. On smoking in cars, the 2009 YouGov survey demonstrates majority support among adults for prohibition, though most smokers would oppose this (Fig 8.9).

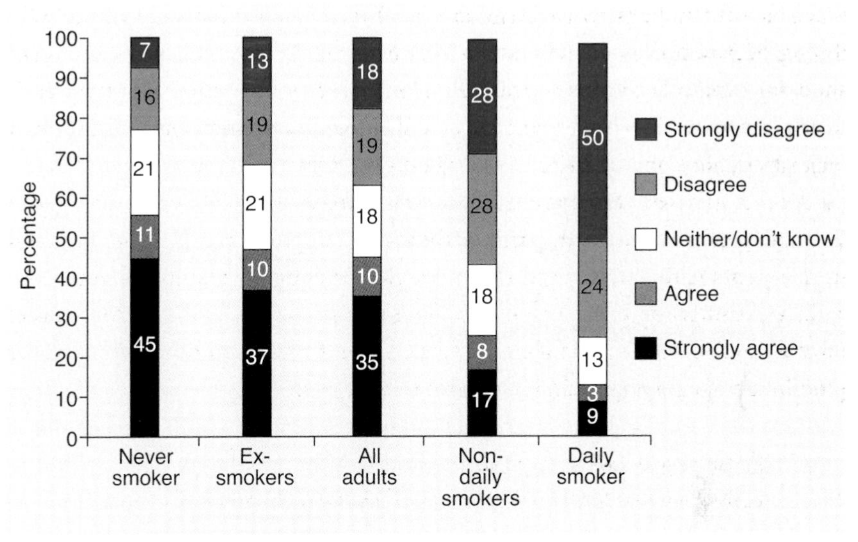

Fig 8.9 'Smoking should be banned in all cars': opinions among adults in England. Subtotals rounded to nearest 1%.

Although smoking by performers during a live performance has a partial exemption in England, 52% of respondents to our 2009 YouGov survey believe that all on-stage smoking during indoor performances should be banned, while only 24% disagree. In England, the Football Association resolved uncertainty about which parts of a football stadium are covered by the law by banning smoking throughout all stadia. Although this policy does not apply to non-league grounds or other sports, in the 2009 YouGov survey, 57% of adults in England agreed that smoking should be banned at all sports grounds and 49% of adults believed that smoking should be banned at outdoor concerts (30% disagree). The exemption for smoking in prisons attracts little public support, with 59% supporting an outright ban on smoking in the enclosed areas of prisons, and only 15% disagreeing.

An international literature review of 15 studies of public attitudes to laws for smoke-free private vehicles found high levels of support, including among smokers.[9] Support for a ban on smoking in cars exemplifies the widespread desire to protect non-smokers, especially children, and the gap between the attitudes of smokers and non-smokers. Voluntary restrictions on smoking in private cars are widespread: 70% of respondents in the 2009 YouGov survey reported that smoking was completely prohibited in the vehicle they usually travelled in, and only 8% said that people could smoke in their vehicle at any time. Despite this, cars are a significant setting for passive smoke exposure, with 26% of adult non-smokers often or sometimes exposed there. This is especially true of younger adults (37% of 18- to 24-year-olds), and of adults from lower socio-economic groups (31% of those in socio-economic groups C2DE). Proposals for restrictions attract considerable support: 76% (including 54% of daily smokers) support a ban on smoking in cars carrying children under the age of 18. Fifty-six per cent support a ban on smoking in cars carrying any passenger, and this rises with age from 45% of 18- to-24-year-olds to 63% of adults over 55.

8.9 Where the smoke still lingers

Of the 10,895 respondents in England to the 2009 YouGov survey, 78% were non-smokers. Of these, 11% were exposed to passive smoke in the home, 11% at work, and 3% both at work and in the home. Although the numbers with dual exposure were too few for further detailed analysis, the groups exposed only at work and those exposed only in the home were different in many ways. Both groups were younger and more likely to be from lower socio-economic groups than those not exposed. However, those exposed at work tended to be male, were less likely to live with a smoker, and expressed consistently negative attitudes towards passive smoke exposure. They were particularly supportive of smoke-free legislation (87%), and had a higher than average perception of the harm from passive smoke to adults and children. Perhaps reflecting their own experience and strong beliefs about the harm from smoking, this group believed more strongly than others that the government is not doing enough to limit the harm from smoking. In contrast, those exposed in the home were more likely to be ex-smokers themselves, tended to be sympathetic to smokers, and were generally more sceptical about the benefits of smoke-free legislation.

Although the question was not asked directly in this survey, exposure to smoke at work may be associated with exposure in vehicles which are supposed to be smoke-free. Non-smokers passively exposed to smoke at work were more likely than other non-smokers also to be exposed to smoke in vehicles. There was a mismatch between these non-smokers reporting that smoking is prohibited in the vehicle that they use most often (79%) and their report that they are exposed to smoke in vehicles (45%). It may be, therefore, that work vehicles are a common site for workplace passive exposure to smoke. Unfortunately, the survey does not tell specifically whether the vehicle in question was a work vehicle (covered by England's smoke-free law) or not, and this warrants further investigation.

Of those only exposed to smoke at work, 90% lived in homes where smoking indoors is prohibited. Interestingly, this is also true of almost half (47%) of adults exposed to passive smoke in the home, so it would seem that this group is either exposed to smoke that enters their home from outside, or that the rules prohibiting smoking in their homes are frequently breached.

8.10 Children's opinions on smoke-free policy

In August 2009, Populus surveyed 1,009 children in England aged 8 to 13 about their experience of and attitudes towards smoking and passive smoke. Awareness of the harm from passive smoking was high, and rose from 83% of 8-year-olds to 90% of 13-year-olds believing that people smoking around them damages their health. Awareness of the risk of exposure in cars was especially high, with 92% believing that parents smoking around children in the car is damaging to a child's health.

Children were most aware of the risk of lung cancer (76%), chest infections (56%) and asthma (53%). By contrast, they regarded the benefits of being brought up in a smoke-free environment as being better health for the whole family (84%), a more pleasant living environment (71%) and more money to spend on family activities (69%).

Of those whose mother or father smoked, 51% reported that their parent or parents smoked in the home, and 35% that they smoke in the car while the child is a passenger. Of children whose parents smoke in the car, 73% wished that they didn't, and 76% said that they were worried that their parents smoking in the car would damage their (the child's) health.

8.11 Summary

- Public support for smoke-free legislation is high and has increased substantially, among both smokers and non-smokers, since smoke-free legislation was introduced.
- Most of those exposed to passive smoke at work report that they are exposed less since the legislation was introduced, but a quarter of the population still report exposure either in the home or at work.
- A large majority of the population believe that passive smoking is harmful, and that banning smoking in public places has been good for the public health.
- A majority of people now prohibit smoking in their homes and vehicles.
- The majority of people believe that smoke-free legislation should extend further, to prohibit smoking in front of children, in cars, and in some other public areas including those where smokers congregate outside buildings.

- One in eight non-smokers, predominantly younger males of lower socio-economic status, still experience passive smoke exposure at work, albeit at much lower levels than before legislation. Much of this exposure may be occurring in work vehicles. This group in particular believes that the government is not doing enough to limit the harm from smoking.
- Over 80% of children are aware that passive smoking is harmful.
- Half of children with a parent who smokes report passive exposure in the home, and one-third report exposure in cars.

References

1 Royal College of Physicians. *Going smoke-free: The medical case for clean air in the home, at work and in public places.* Report of a working party. London: RCP, 2005.

2 Fong GT, Hyland A, Bordland R *et al.* Reductions in tobacco smoke pollution and increases in support for smoke-free public places following the implementation of comprehensive smoke-free workplace legislation in the Republic of Ireland. *Tob Control* 2006;15 (suppl III):iii51–8.

3 Edwards R, Thomson G, Wilson N *et al.* After the smoke has cleared: Evaluation of the impact of a new national smoke-free law in New Zealand. *Tob Control* 2008;17:e2.

4 Borland R, Yong HH, Siapush M *et al.* Support for and reported compliance with smoke-free restaurants and bars by smokers in four countries: Findings from the International Tobacco Control Four Country Survey. *Tob Control* 2006;15:iii34–41.

5 Office for National Statistics. *Smoking-related behaviour and attitudes, 2007.* London: ONS, 2008.

6 Philips R, Amos A, Richie D *et al.* Smoking in the home after the smoke-free legislation in Scotland: qualitative study. *BMJ* 2007;335:553–7.

7 Chapman S. Should smoking in outside public places be banned: No. *BMJ* 2008;337: a2804. www.bmj.com/cgi/content/full/337/dec11_3/a2804

8 Thompson G, Wilson N, Edwards R. Should smoking in outside public places be banned: Yes. *BMJ* 2008;337:a2806. www.bmj.com/cgi/content/full/337/dec11_3/a2806

9 Thomson G, Wilson N. Public attitudes to laws for smokefree private vehicles: A brief review. *Tob Control* 2009;18:245–61.

9 Ethics: children and smoking

9.1 Introduction

The central ethical focus of public health policy on tobacco smoking is the prevention of harm, particularly for the vulnerable. Smoking is harmful in its direct effects on the health of smokers, ex-smokers and future smokers, and its high level of addictiveness greatly enhances its ability to cause harm. Passive smoking also harms non-smokers.

Some libertarian advocates argue that competent adults may voluntarily assume the risks of smoking when they smoke, provided that they are adequately informed. This approach has obvious limits. First, it does not take full account of the addictive nature of smoking and tobacco consumption, the high levels of regret smokers express about starting smoking, and the frequent desire to quit among smokers. Second, it assumes that the decision to smoke is made freely and competently, by adults. It overlooks the way in which smoking is usually initiated and addiction established in childhood, as a teenager or sometimes even younger, when decision-making competence is incomplete and children's understanding of the degree and implications of the hazards from smoking are poor. Third, a policy of tolerance toward smoking on the basis that the smoker is making an informed choice often does not apply to the non-smoker exposed passively to smoke. The person thus exposed may not be given much choice in the matter (or any choice in the case of infants and young children), may consent but without knowing the full facts about the risks, or may actively object but lack control over the situation. Moreover, although most adults understand the hazards posed by passive smoking and smoking behaviour, and in particular those to babies and children, a significant proportion do not. For this reason, state regulation in the form of smoke-free legislation, regulations and by-laws is important, and has had considerable success in the UK and worldwide. Limitation of smokers' liberty to smoke in order to prevent non-consensual harm to others has widespread public support, even among smokers. The ethical and moral arguments for smoke-free legislation were set out in the Royal College of Physicians' report, *Going smoke-free*, in 2005.[1]

9.2 Protecting children from smoking

Given that the focus of public health policy is on prevention of harm, particularly where the people harmed have not consented or cannot consent to that harm, an obvious concern must be with the protection of children. Children develop their competence and ability to exercise their consent only gradually as they mature to adulthood, and the health risks from active and passive smoking and their implications may be poorly understood. In addition, the health effects of active and passive smoking on children are serious, the susceptibility of children to addiction and harm from both active and passive smoking may be greater, and children may also be psychologically impressionable and socially vulnerable. All of these reasons provide a robust foundation for tight regulation of minors' exposure and access to tobacco products, and protection of children from passive smoke exposure, and these considerations have been expressed in public policy for many years. Sale of tobacco products to children aged under 16 has been banned in the UK since the 1908 Children Act, and even before the general ban on advertising tobacco products, a consensus held that advertising tobacco products to children, or in ways children might find interesting or attractive, was unacceptable. However, perhaps the strongest influence on children taking up smoking is more or less entirely unregulated: the smoking behaviours of adults and peers around them. As noted in Chapter 6, children are significantly more likely to become smokers themselves if their parents or siblings smoke, and the same is likely to be true, to some extent, where other significant role models in children's lives smoke.[2] Policies designed to reduce smoking by role models in general, and specifically to prevent smoking in places or situations where children accompany or are in the presence of role models, would have a significant effect on this kind of 'advertising'.

Policies designed to limit exposure of adults to passive smoke protect children who are in the same contexts (for example, workplaces and other public buildings), and also reduce exposure of children to smoking behaviour among adults and peers. Concerns were expressed before the implementation of smoke-free legislation in the UK and elsewhere, that smoke-free policies may have an adverse impact on children by displacing smoking from public places (which may have rather few children, such as pubs and factories) to private areas, such as homes, where children are both more likely to be found and are less likely to be able to avoid smoke. However, this does not appear to be a significant problem in practice (see Chapters 2 and 8). On the contrary, the evidence suggests that smoke-free policies in private settings increase, and passive smoke exposure decreases, after the introduction of smoke-free legislation.

We have three reasons to focus on protecting children:

(1) to protect children from the harms arising from passive smoking

(2) to discourage children from experimenting with smoking, and hence becoming habitual smokers, by preventing exposure to smoking behaviour and role models

(3) to prevent unintended consequences of public places and other smoke-free policies, such as displacement of passive smoke exposure from public places to the home.

Many of the measures designed to protect children from others' smoke, or to prevent or discourage smoking by children, also have a discouraging effect on adult smokers themselves. This is not a primary goal of children's tobacco policy, although it may be welcome. It is important to keep these objectives clear, and when evaluating the merits of a policy, to assess it in the light of the relevant objective. It is also important to note that these are ethical justifications for intervention. In practice, the first two points are much more significant than the third, as there is little evidence for displacement of smoking from public to private places.

9.3 Preventing smoking among children

Traditional approaches here are well established and present no particular ethical challenges. Methods include prohibiting sale of tobacco products to under-18s; prohibiting advertising and other promotion of tobacco products; regulating tobacco packaging; prohibiting or regulating display of tobacco products in shops; increasing the price of tobacco products; prohibiting tobacco vending machines; prohibiting sales of single cigarettes or packets of small numbers of cigarettes; smoke-free policies in public places; health promotion campaigns; and all other standard aspects of tobacco control policy.[3] While many of these strategies are not specific to children, they all limit access by children to tobacco products, and restrictions on promotion and advertising help to prevent tobacco products from appearing glamorous and attractive. This is particularly the case when control of tobacco product packaging, point-of-sale, and advertising takes place against a backdrop of health education messages about the health-related dangers of smoking to children and adults. Adult smokers and retailers may question whether these measures are proportionate. It is clear that they are. They pose no significant limitation on adults' abilities to purchase tobacco products, or on retailers' ability to sell them. They may limit retailers' ability to *promote* sales of tobacco products, and they clearly limit manufacturers' ability to market their products, to attempt to differentiate them from each other, and to compete through differentiation and marketing at point-of-sale. But while liberty of consumption has some ethical significance, liberty to promote does not. Much more importantly, controlling point-of-sale marketing and access constrains children's ability to access products which it is unlawful to sell them. It also limits their exposure to positive images associated with tobacco products. Children are susceptible to such images. They may know about the harms of smoking, but positive images and attitudes may dominate their thinking about tobacco, given that children are more likely to discount future health problems against present gratification; more likely to dismiss the likelihood of becoming addicted; more likely to underestimate the difficulty of overcoming addiction; and are somewhat more likely to distrust 'authority' and authoritative advice such as health education messages, and to be attracted to behaviours and role models seen as anti-authority or 'cool'. Thus, a dual strategy of promoting positive messages about not smoking, and limiting exposure to positive messages about smoking, is required.

More recently, we have seen attempts to use the criminal law to punish people who supply cigarettes to underage smokers. A notable example was the reported case of a man jailed for 18 months in the UK in October 2009, for 'causing unnecessary suffering or injury to health' when he gave a 3-year-old child a cigarette to smoke, and then persuaded a 14-year-old to film her doing so with a mobile phone.[4] The offence for which he was charged was not clear from media reporting, but is likely to be that contained in the 1933 Children and Young People's Act of cruelty to children by causing the child to be assaulted, ill-treated, neglected, abandoned or exposed, in a manner likely to cause the child unnecessary suffering or injury to health. This legislation also allows police officers and park keepers in uniform to seize and destroy tobacco products from any person 'under the age of 16 years' who is found smoking in a public place. The Act has been modified in these provisions, most recently by the Children and Young Persons (Protection from Tobacco) Act 1991, but these sections of the 1933 Act remain in force. Whilst it is common for local government officials and Her Majesty's Revenue and Customs to take enforcement actions against retailers and smugglers, this case illustrates a strategy in which smoking prevention is taken out of the public arena and into private life. Whatever the legal and criminal justice merits of this approach to controlling the behaviour of individuals, it raises a question of how far the criminal law may reach into the home to protect children. We return to this issue below.

Aside from banning the sale and supply of cigarettes to children by retailers, and minimising positive messages to children about smoking by control of packaging and banning of tobacco advertising, what more can be done to discourage children from taking up smoking? A fundamental principle of English law (and international human rights law) relating to children is that the welfare of the child must be paramount.[5] Related to this is the importance of recognising that a child's right to develop into a competent and autonomous adult, such that children's rights to consent and decide – where they are competent to do so – must be respected.[6,7]

The welfare of the child principle here would imply that there is no value in criminalising children's own smoking. No legal or ethical argument suggests this as appropriate, although confiscation of tobacco products from under-16s is permitted by legislation, as noted above. Historically, many parents and some authorities (such as schools) have treated smoking by children as deserving punishment. Although pragmatically this may be sensible in an institutional context concerned with children's discipline and moral development, it would not be justifiable as general public policy. If children's smoking is understood as imperfectly grounded in consent, because children lack the necessary capacity and maturity to understand what smoking involves, this would make focusing on the child's own behaviour (rather than those of the adults around him or her) quite unfair. Pragmatically, it would also be counterproductive. It suggests that an approach to children's smoking should – like any other area of children's health behaviour or discipline – be nuanced, and that there may be quite considerable legitimate variation in how different parents, caregivers and children's services professionals approach it. This variation can be both with respect to the individual child and their personality and circumstances, and with respect to parenting styles, local authority policies, and the evolving evidence base about what is effective in changing and influencing children's behaviour.

Recognition of the importance of children's developing autonomy over the course of their childhood means that care must be taken to ensure that the information they receive about smoking is (as the Advertising Standards Agency slogan phrased it) 'legal, decent, honest, and truthful'. It should not mislead children with suggestions of glamour or rebellion fallaciously associated with smoking.

Corrective advertising and health education to overcome residual background misinformation by the industry can be justified both on the grounds of accuracy and of correcting misinformation. But is it possible, in focusing on discouraging children from smoking, to go to the opposite extreme and cause harm, by trading on fear, stigma, or other emotional content? The point is both ethical and pragmatic: terrorising children into not smoking is not respectful of their ability to learn and understand for themselves, and may not be successful in the long term if that terror proves to be based on exaggerated or selective information. However, this concern is exaggerated. Smoking is actually dangerous, to oneself and others, and a degree of anxiety about its effects on oneself and others is justified and rational. Strong messages about this are therefore reasonable and important. Although there is a possibility of merely terrorising children (by using information which is terrifying, but false, or exaggerated, or out of context), in reality health education messages to children are valid both in terms of their truthfulness and in conveying the harmfulness of smoking. The idea that anti-smoking messages are moralistic or terrorising is misleading. In contrast, industry's marketing of tobacco products takes no such care to be balanced, accurate, or informative about the hazards (or the benefits they wish to emphasise).

Since formal tobacco advertising is now prohibited in the UK, exposure of children to indirect forms of advertising, which normalise or glamourise smoking by displaying smoking role models or other positive smoking imagery in film or other media, is probably the major medium of promotion of tobacco products to children. Heavy-handed attempts to deglamourise smoking by modifying such images, for example by removing traces of cigarette smoking, come at the risk of ridiculousness and historical inaccuracy. However, there is a line between historical accuracy of representation (smoking was more common in the past) and exaggeration of its past importance or reinforcement of the equation between stylishness, smoking, and glamour. The US television programme *Mad Men*[8] is a case in point, illustrating just how difficult it is to disentangle media images of smoking and its significance. On the one hand, the characters are generally miserable and drink to excess and smoke; on the other hand they are chic, well-dressed, and drink to excess and smoke. Audiences draw their own conclusions. Children's interpretations may differ widely from those of their parents, and it is far from clear what the appropriate public health response should be to this sort of representation.

Another form of indirect communication to children about smoking is the smoking habits of real people with whom children come into contact, particularly family members and other adults involved in their social lives and their care. Given that this role-modelling effect is important in influencing children's uptake of smoking (see Chapter 6), a regulatory focus on restricting where smoking is allowed on the grounds of direct health effects needs to be supplemented by guidance to important adult role models (teachers, play leaders, sports coaches, youth leaders and so on) to restrict their own smoking behaviour in the vicinity of or anywhere where they are visible to children. It may be possible to go further than guidance in two ways. One way would be to make it a requirement of contracts for paid carers, teachers and so on, that they do not smoke while on duty and in care of children. This would not apply easily, if at all, to unpaid carers or parents acting as informal assistants. A stronger version of this approach would be to criminalise smoking in a public place while in care of children. This would have the virtue of generality, and have no obvious loopholes, but it would possibly be difficult to define what being 'in care of children' meant. The other strategy would be to focus attention on places where children gather, even where these are not 'public' places, rather than focusing on who is smoking and what their responsibilities are. We could make certain places smoke-free even if children are not present, on the basis that they are places where children generally congregate or pass through. This might include entrances and exits to buildings, patios outside hospitality venues, sports venues, parks, beaches, open air shopping centres, and perhaps private cars. We return to this idea below.

9.4 Controlling smoking within the home

If protecting children from passive smoking were a paramount objective of public policy, then on the face of it, prohibiting smoking in the home and around children is an obvious and simple solution. This is because the home is the place where children spend the most time, are least protected from passive smoking, and – for children who live with smokers – it is the place where most exposure occurs. In practice, however, compliance with laws restricting smoking in the home would be limited, and the laws themselves would either be unenforceable, or might be enforced in discriminatory or haphazard ways. Aside from a strongly and widely held view that an English person's home is his or her castle, Article 8 of the European Convention on Human Rights guarantees a right to private and family life, which can only be interfered with where there is a necessity in a democratic society to do so.[9] Granted, one ground of interference is 'for the protection of health' and another is 'for the protection of the rights and freedoms of others'. But necessity is the key here: the interference must be legitimate and proportionate to the aim pursued, and it must use the means 'least restrictive' of the liberties and rights of the citizen. Child protection is a good example of where there is a legitimate public interest in breaching the security of the home in order to interfere with private life quite legitimately. But child protection principles, although they place the welfare of the child as paramount, reflect the need for children to be able to live securely in their families, without undue interference, and recognising that formal court orders (up to and including removal from the family home or detention of one or both parents or caregivers) may be counterproductive.

Nevertheless, there are contexts in which smoking regulation does reach within the home, an example being where the 'home' is actually under public authority control or supervision (as in a children's home, prison, psychiatric facility, or registered childminder's home used as a place of work). Although there are some limited exceptions, there is nevertheless a presumption that these are public places first, and homes second. This is controversial, and the legality and reasonableness of regulations governing long-stay psychiatric facilities have been tested in England since the 2006 Health Act.[10] The courts have upheld the regulations so far. Some further contexts might be considered a grey area: for instance, children's parties. In the light of the recent change of policy by the Office for Standards in Education, Children's Services and Skills (Ofsted), such that informal shared childcare arrangements between families without payment do not require registration or inspection,[11] it is clear that public policy is uncertain as to how far it wants to cross the threshold of the home. Moreover, from the points of view of effectiveness, practicality and proportionate intervention, it is arguable that cultural change and peer pressure would be preferable to legal enforcement of a rule banning smoking in the presence of children, even under the special circumstances of a private party, never mind ordinary daily life.

There are specific circumstances in which society does cross the threshold of the home, for example, when health professionals visit children in the home. Pre-conception advice, assisted conception, antenatal care, community midwifery services and health visiting all stress the importance of smoking cessation to parents and others, promote smoke-free homes, and provide advice and support to achieve these. Here, the emphasis is on advice and support to the mother, and to some extent the father or co-parent, given in a context in which broader advice and support is given to promote maternal and child health. Although legal action has been taken in some US states against women for drug use during pregnancy, this approach has been widely criticised. In the UK, the emphasis is on education and support for behaviour change, rather than on compulsion, and not at all on punishment.

The emphasis in this approach is on advice, persuasion and support for families, rather than on the use of formal methods of compulsion, or on placing the children under the care and supervision of the courts either in the home or through removing the child from the home. The Children Act 1989 s.31(2) requires the courts to consider first whether the child is suffering significant harm, and second whether that harm is attributable to the care being given by the parent not being what it would be reasonable to expect a parent to give. Under s.1(5), the court must be satisfied that making an order concerning the child's care must be better for the child than obtaining no such order. It is, and is likely to remain, unusual and controversial to use formal legal means either to compel parents not to smoke near their children, or inside their own homes and private vehicles in the interests of their children, or to remove children to a 'place of safety' away from smoke exposure. This is because the welfare of children must be considered in the round, and generally this is best served by keeping the child within a stable home and family environment, and formal legal actions may transgress the rights of the parents to a private family life. There may, however, be a case for defining a threshold of smoke exposure over which the harm to children is so significant that it is not outweighed by other considerations of parental care and family life, as we have seen by analogy in some recent cases involving child protection powers being used to protect children from overeating.[12,13] Similar 'threshold' arguments may apply in some other legal contexts, such as divorce and residence hearings.

9.5 Special cases: looked-after children, foster carers and potential adoptive parents

Much more important in terms of formal restrictions on smoking and parenting is the policy relating to adoption and fostering by would-be adoptive or foster parents who smoke. Here, the focus is not on removing a child from a family to protect him or her from smoke, until such time as the smoking behaviour of concern changes, or on using the possibility of removal of the child as part of a negotiation with the child's carers. Instead, it is on deciding whether a particular home is a suitable place for a child to be placed for fostering or adoption. Although this affects a small number of children, it has a more general significance. Approaches developed in the care of 'looked-after' children might be a template for policy approaches to protecting all children in their homes generally.

The British Association for Adoption and Fostering (BAAF) prepared a practice note in 2006 on 'Reducing the risks of environmental tobacco smoke for looked after children and their carers', which has been adopted by local authorities very widely across the UK as the basis of their policy on placement of children with foster carers and adoptive families.[14] Similarly, the Fostering Network adopted a policy paper in 2007 on this topic.[15] The emphasis in both papers is on presenting the evidence for harm caused by passive smoking in the home to children (and non-smoking partners), and on the wider policy context relating to smoke-free public places and to children's health promotion. They also argue, as does this report, that moderating smoking behaviour short of stopping smoking inside the home altogether is ineffective. Finally, they relate the health risks of smoking to more general safety considerations about keeping a home safe from fire risks.

A simple ban on fostering or adopting children by smokers has been adopted in some places.[16] However, a less definitive position is taken by most local authorities and agencies responsible for looked-after children. These have a duty to consider the welfare of children under their care as paramount, and must take note of the shortage of foster care and adoptive parents, and the difficulties experienced by children and teenagers while in children's homes and once they leave these homes. In addition, the wishes and preferences of children themselves are a factor when placing children with foster carers or adoptive parents.

A balanced policy in this area considers the best interests of children not in absolute terms, but comparatively, in light of the available alternatives. There are two obvious circumstances in which smoking behaviour on the part of a foster carer or would-be adoptive parent would be decisive. First, where the child is young or at particular risk of respiratory or other recognised health problems caused by passive smoke exposure, there is a clear and strong reason not to expose that child to smoke. The BAAF and the Fostering Network both advise that children under 5 years of age should not be placed with carers who smoke, and that children with significant underlying health problems should not be placed with carers who are ex-smokers until at least 12 months after smoking cessation (because of the risk of relapse on the part of the ex-smoker before 12 months). This policy is clearly grounded in the need to minimise a specific risk of significant and proximate harm to the child. Second, the smoking behaviour of a would-be foster carer or adoptive parent might act as a tie-breaker, where there are two or more alternative placement possibilities for the child and no other factor determines which placement would be best for the child.

Once a child has been placed with foster or adoptive parents, the emphasis of both policy documents is on supporting parental cessation of smoking, minimising the impact of smoking practices on the health and environmental safety of the child, and on health promotion for the child. In the health promotion context, the key concerns raised by the BAAF and Fostering Network are that children would get positive messages about smoking from their positive relationship with their smoker foster carer or adoptive parent and, more concretely, that smoking might play a role in the disciplining of the child. For example, in some homes, tobacco may be used as a reward or incentive for good behaviour. In addition, what should a foster carer do about a teenager who smokes while in their care, and how might smoking by the foster parent affect this process? While there is a clear understanding that teenagers should not be smoking, and that parental complicity in that would be highly problematic, there is also a need to recognise that the children in question often have complex needs and behaviours which require a mixture of clear boundaries and subtle parenting.

There are four relationships to be considered in the context of foster care and adoption: the relationship between the child and their birth family (which is presumably disrupted in a significant way); that between the child and the public body with a duty of care; that between the child and the foster carer or potential adoptive parents; and that between the public body and the foster carer or potential adoptive parents. This last relationship is not a contractual one. Although the public body has considerable negotiating power up to the point of adoption, once a child has been adopted, ordinary child protection rules apply and the local authority has no power to enforce any agreement reached with the parent before adoption (on smoking cessation, for example). Where the relationship between child and carer is one of fostering, there is much wider scope for local authority management of that relationship, and one possibility would be for fostering to be considered a *public* relationship. If we consider that the foster carer is looking after a child on behalf of a public body, which discharges its duty of care to the child through that foster placement, it is not implausible to say that the home of the foster carer is analogous to a public place, and to extend the prohibition of smoking which already applies to home-based child-minding (and some other homes which are workplaces) to foster carers' homes.

The principal problems here are of enforcement of smoke-free policies in foster homes, and the wider issue of further limiting the supply of existing and potential foster carers for vulnerable children. Discouraging otherwise caring and law-abiding people from fostering, where there is already a shortage of foster carers, is clearly not in the best interests of children. This explains the strategy largely taken by councils and by the BAAF of discouraging smoking but stopping short of prohibiting it among foster carers. Enforcement would be controlled by principle of the welfare of the child: a social worker would be slow to seek to remove a child from a foster carer's home, where in all other respects a placement was working well, if the carer was in breach of a smoking regulation. However, a general cultural shift away from the acceptability of smoking, and a recognition among foster carers and would-be adoptive parents that they have a special obligation to protect the health and welfare of the vulnerable children in their care, means that the same shift that we saw in smoking in public places (from being the norm, to being unacceptable, through voluntary regulation, to legally-backed prohibition) may come to apply to the quasi-public space of the foster home.

This discussion of children who are 'looked after' by the state, or on behalf of the state, considers a small minority of children and homes. What it illustrates is of more general importance. First, it shows ways in which the law and the state reach into the home of some children who are considered to be at risk for various reasons. It shows how limited and delicate specific decisions about the state response to parental smoking need to be, even when there is a presumption that the state will act. Second, it highlights the evident inconsistency between what the state can do when a child is 'looked after' and what it can do otherwise. Parental smoking is bad for any child, but public authorities can currently intervene only case-by-case, and when there is some other significant ground for intervention. Yet once the authorities have intervened, smoking behaviour of potential carers can become a determining factor in what happens next in the child's life, with long-term consequences. Having thus established these principles, similar consequences may flow from residence and contact decisions in divorce, where one parent's smoking might be involved as a relevant factor in making orders or in negotiations between the parents. The crucial point is that the law should try to be consistent for all children, with the welfare of the child paramount, and with (actual or potential) parent or carer smoking being seen as a factor in the child's welfare.

9.6 Children in their home

Once we concentrate on the home under ordinary circumstances, where there is no question of it being a public place or place of work, or of the children being under formal care or supervision arrangements administered by the courts or local authorities, then the case for a legislative approach to preventing smoking in the home becomes more difficult. It is clear that children have a right to health, both in the sense that all human beings have such a right, and in terms of their special rights under the UN Convention on the Rights of the Child. However, this right must be understood in light of the whole range of rights and welfare considerations they have, and the often adverse impact formal intervention may have, except in cases of obvious harm and abuse.[17] We wish to protect children from smoke and from incentives to take up smoking, but this needs to be proportionate, effective, and reasonable in the context of the overall welfare of the child. Some authors have made an analogy between exposing children to smoke and child abuse.[18] However, except in rare cases of intentional harm, this seems an inappropriate analogy. Few parents, with knowledge of the harm that passive smoking does to their children, would voluntarily expose their children to it. Most parents who smoke do seek to avoid exposing their children to do so, however ineffectively, and few parents who smoke are happy for their children to smoke, even when they are of legal age. The child abuse analogy provides a very strong message to parents to think about the harm their smoking causes, in various ways, and this should be evaluated as any other health promotion message is, for its veracity and effectiveness, and its counter-effects.

In one context, there is clear reason to think that enforceable public powers might be necessary. This is in connection with infants in the first few months of life, when the risk of sudden infant death is real and serious. Involvement of health visitors in the family home may give them reason to be concerned that a baby is at risk because of parental smoking habits, and it would be possible to involve local child protection teams if there were persistent smoking in the home, and no attempts at persuasion to change smoking behaviour (even to move it outside) succeeded. In such a case, application to the court for an order under the Children Act might be considered. Similar steps could be taken even to protect an older child, if there is an underlying health condition, such as asthma, such that smoking presents a real, immediate and serious threat to his or her health. These powers already exist, and are used on health grounds from time to time, though there is great caution in so using them because of the stigma attaching to parents and children when child protection issues are raised.

A purely health-oriented approach may not exhaust the ethical options. Everyone agrees that parents have ethical, as well as legal, duties to their children. Indeed, for many people, the relationship between parent and child is that with the greatest sense of moral duty. Keeping this in mind, there is room for mounting ethical arguments addressed directly to parents. This is much more attractive than looking directly to the law to enforce protections of children, in that it need be neither paternalistic nor invasive and intrusive, and addresses the parent directly as a moral person who cares for his or her child first and foremost. Although there are clear limits on states moralising to their citizens, and on doctors giving moral advice – or appearing judgemental – to their patients, as citizens there is every reason to insist that parents have responsibilities for their children's health and education, and that avoiding exposing them to passive smoking, and discouraging them from smoking, are an important part of those responsibilities.[19]

9.7 Children outside the home

As outlined in Chapter 1, many of the places in which children were exposed to passive smoking are now smoke-free, such as public buildings, offices, enclosed places of public entertainment, and so on. Many more places are subject to local authority regulations over and above national regulations.[20] An important step for public policy would be to recognise that where direct harm prevention may not require prohibition of smoking in (for example) open spaces where children gather, such as parks and play areas, the necessity of limiting children's exposure to the idea that smoking is acceptable or normal, safe, or even characteristic of being adult remains important, on the assumption that this can influence the likelihood of children starting to smoke.

A policy of prohibiting smoking in publicly visible places, particularly those frequented by children, and within the vicinity of schools, nurseries, and other areas where children gather in the open air, could have important public health benefits. This could also include areas where smokers tend to congregate, such as the entrances and exits to buildings and patios outside hospitality venues, which children have to pass by or through. Such restrictions could be argued as being proportionate in their limitation of the liberties of adult smokers when compared with children's health and educational needs. A comprehensive policy in this area might go as far as applying licensing conditions on tobacco retailers, so that tobacco could not be lawfully sold within a defined vicinity of a school or nursery. A balanced policy which, incorporating concern both for limitation of direct harm caused by passive smoking and for promoting positive role modelling and health educational messages to children, considers that the burden of proof should lie with those who would like to smoke or sell tobacco near a school or in a play area, rather than with those who would like not to have their children exposed to passive smoking.[2,21] The issue of the contractual or criminal liability of formal or informal carers of children in such places was discussed above, but an advantage of a zonal approach is that it applies to anyone in such a defined zone, not just those responsible for children.

Aside from fixed places, the other important place where children are exposed to smoking is in vehicles. Public carriage vehicles such as taxis, trains, trams, buses, and aeroplanes are already subject to smoking bans, but no such prohibition currently applies to private cars. Road safety legislation prohibits behaviours which pose a risk to other road users (such as driving while intoxicated, using a mobile phone while driving, or behaving in a way which amounts to recklessness while driving). Trying to light a cigarette or looking for a cigarette packet while driving clearly could pose such a risk, but the approach of the police and the courts is most likely to be to punish offences that have caused an accident, rather than acting preventatively, by treating smoking behaviours as offences in themselves, unless there is primary legislation to make smoking in a car into an offence. From a child health point of view, while the risk of being in a smoking-induced accident is serious and important, on a day-to-day basis, the much more common smoking-related hazard is being exposed to smoke while riding in the car of a smoker. Even where the smoker is not smoking while the child is in the vehicle, the child is still exposed to any tobacco smoke lingering in the atmosphere or deposited inside the vehicle. Levels of exposure in private vehicles when someone is smoking are high, and hence have significant potential for harm, not just to children but also to adults, particularly those with pre-existing cardiovascular disease. Legislation on behaviour in vehicles is also practically workable. Thus, there is a strong case for legal prohibition of smoking in private vehicles, and for more general measures that encourage adult smokers simply to avoid smoking around children, and in places frequented by children, even where there are no children currently present.

9.8 Summary

- Passive smoking is an involuntary exposure that is harmful to children. All adults therefore have a duty to avoid exposing children to tobacco smoke.
- Exposure of children to smoking role models increases the likelihood that they will sustain substantial future harm as a result of experimenting with, and becoming addicted to, smoking. All adults therefore also have a duty to prevent exposing children to smoking behaviour.
- Governments also have a duty to ensure that people are aware of these obligations, and to do all in their power to prevent exposure.
- Current legislation prevents exposure of children to tobacco smoke in public buildings, but exposure to smoke and to smoking role models elsewhere, particularly in the home, remains common.
- Extending current smoke-free legislation to include all public places frequented by children, whether or not enclosed as currently defined in law, would prevent much of this exposure. The legislation could also be extended to cover private vehicles.
- There is also a duty on governments to ensure that children are not exposed to smoking role models in film, television programmes, internet content, music videos, computer games, and other media.
- Proportionate measures to minimise the risk of passive smoking in the home are already in place for children cared for by the state.
- Legislation to prohibit smoking in the family home and many other private places would be difficult to design, implement and enforce.
- The objective of preventing children's exposure to smoke, and to smoking role models, also needs to be balanced against the other needs of the child.

- There is therefore a duty on governments to ensure that parents, carers and adults in general are aware of the wider risks of smoking in sight of children as well as of exposing children to smoke in the home, and to develop and promote strategies to help minimise exposure.

References

1 Royal College of Physicians. *Going smoke-free: the medical case for clean air in the home, at work and in public places.* Report of a working party. London: RCP, 2005.
2 Thomson G, Wilson N, Edwards R, Woodward A. Should smoking in outside public spaces be banned? Yes. *BMJ* 2008;337:a2806.
3 World Health Organization. *Tobacco control legislation: an introductory guide*, 2nd edn. Geneva: WHO, 2004.
4 BBC News. *Man jailed for letting girl smoke.* http://news.bbc.co.uk/1/hi/england/tyne/8308946.stm
5 Bainham A. *Children: the modern law*, 3rd edn. London: Family Law Publications, 2005.
6 Fortin J. *Children's rights and the developing law*, 3rd edn. Cambridge: CUP, 2009.
7 Archard D. *Children: rights and childhood.* London: Routledge, 2004.
8 www.amctv.com/originals/madmen
9 Council of Europe: Convention for the protection of human rights and fundamental freedoms, 1950. www.conventions.coe.int/treaty/en/treaties/html/005.htm
10 Coggan J. Public health, responsibility and English law: Are there such things as no smoke without ire, or needless clean needles? *Med Law Rev* 2009; 17:127–39
11 BBC News. *Rethink on 'illegal' childcaring.* http://news.bbc.co.uk/1/hi/education/8279274.stm
12 www.telegraph.co.uk/news/uknews/1554579/take-obese-children-from-parents-say-doctors.html
13 Royal College of Paediatrics and Child Health. *Child protection companion.* London: RCPCH, 2006.
14 British Association for Adoption and Fostering. *Reducing the risks of environmental tobacco smoke for looked after children and their carers: practice note 51.* London: BAAF, 2006.
15 The Fostering Network. *Foster carers and smoking: policy paper.* London: The Fostering Network, 2007. www.fostering.net/sites/www.fostering.net/files/public/resources/policy-and-position-statements/smoking_policy_june07.pdf
16 Perth and Kinross Council. www.pkc.gov.uk/NR/rdonlyres/48EFB35F-CA77-4D3C-9688-3D4EF51A5F46/0/SmokingandFosterCarePolicy.pdf
17 UN Convention on the Rights of the Child, in particular article 24 on the 'right of the child to the enjoyment of the highest attainable standard of health' and its subsections.
18 Johansson AK, Hermansson G, Ludvigsson J. When does exposure of children to tobacco smoke become child abuse? *Lancet* 2003;361:1828.
19 Brennan S, White A. Responsibility and children's rights: The case for restricting parental smoking. In: Brennan S, Noggle R (eds), *Taking responsibility for children.* Ontario: Wilfred Laurier Press, 2007:97–111.
20 LACORS. *Implementation of smokefree legislation in England.* www.cieh.org/library/Knowledge/Public_health/Smoking_in_the_workplace/LACORS_guide%20_MAR07.pdf
21 Chapman S. *Public health advocacy and tobacco control: making smoking history.* Oxford: Blackwell Scientific, 2007.

10 Strategies to reduce passive smoking in children

10.1 Introduction

Whilst policies prohibiting smoking in public places and workplaces have received global attention, policies aimed specifically at reducing passive smoke exposure in children in the home have received relatively little consideration. In Chapter 2 we demonstrated that exposure of children to passive smoke is determined primarily by whether the child's parents or carers smoke, whether the child's home is smoke-free, and by the socio-economic status of the household. The data in Table 2.3 also demonstrate that almost all children whose parents (or single parent) are non-smokers live in smoke-free homes. Thus the prevention of passive smoke exposure in children depends firstly on preventing parental or carer smoking, and secondly on encouraging those who continue to smoke to make their homes, and other private places used by their children, smoke-free. Importantly, these actions will also result in reduced smoking uptake among children, due to the reduced role modelling of smoking as a normal adult behaviour.[1]

The prevalence of adult smoking in the UK has fallen substantially over the past three decades, from 40% in 1978 to 21% in 2007, [2] and although still relatively high in younger adults (31% and 26% in the 20–24 and 25–34 age groups respectively), the number of children whose parents smoke is now considerably lower than 30 years ago. The proportion of children whose parents allow smoking in the home has also fallen substantially (Table 2.3). Both of these trends have contributed to a progressive reduction in passive smoke exposure in children. In this chapter, we discuss how these two approaches to prevention are interrelated, and can be promoted.

10.2 Reducing the number of parents and carers who smoke

Reducing the prevalence of smoking among parents and carers is the most effective means of preventing passive smoking in children. The implementation of a wide and increasingly effective range of tobacco control policies, including tax increases, advertising bans, mass media campaigns, health warnings, cessation services and smoke-free legislation, has contributed to a substantial reduction in the prevalence of smoking in all UK adults over the past half century. However, whilst this trend has encompassed all demographic groups, the rate of decline has been considerably less marked in adults of parental age (Fig 10.1).[64] The percentage of ever-smokers who have quit smoking has also increased over time, but less in younger than in older adults (Fig 10.2). Although these trends appear to be of similar magnitude in manual and non-manual occupational groups (Figs 10.1 and 10.2), the higher prevalence of smoking and lower quit rates in manual groups in general mean that adults in this group are especially likely to have taken up smoking, and to have remained smokers.

It is generally held that tobacco control policies such as health publicity campaigns have had the greatest impact on smokers in higher socio-economic groups, although price policies, if not undermined by tobacco smuggling, are thought to affect particularly deprived groups more.[3] However, a recent systematic review found little evidence of differential effects from a range of tobacco control policies in different socio-economic groups, including mixed evidence on the effects of price in relation to income.[4] There was also little evidence that tobacco control policies had a differential effect by age,[4] though a further systematic review of the

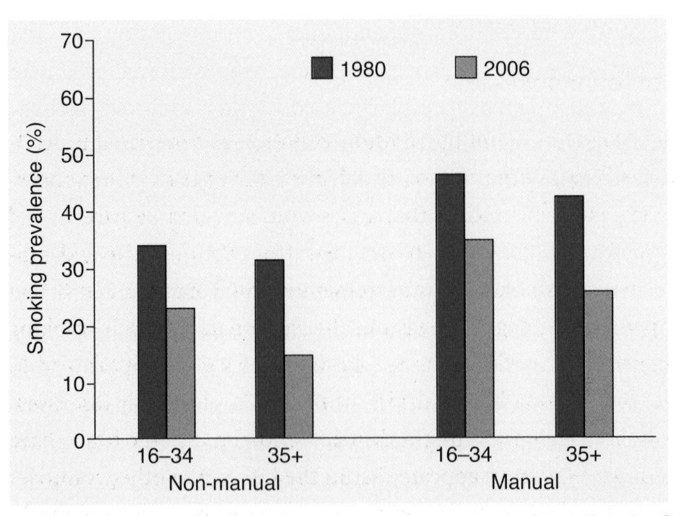

Fig 10.1 **Cigarette smoking by age and deprivation in Great Britain.** Source: General Household Survey 1980 and 2006.

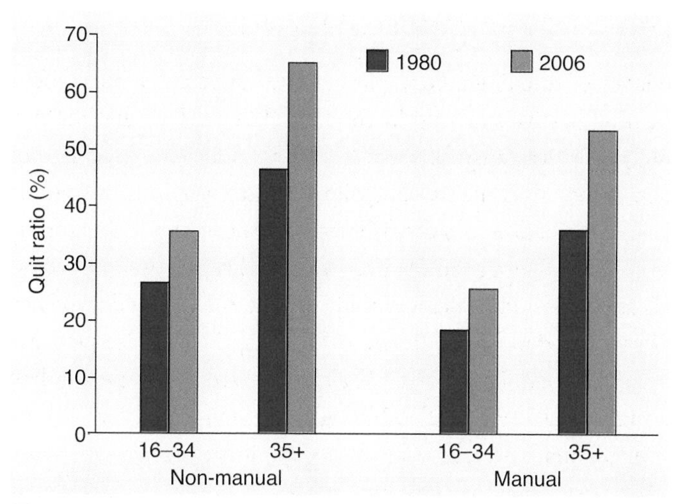

Fig 10.2 Proportion of ever-smokers who have quit smoking, by age and deprivation in Great Britain. Source: General Household Survey 1980 and 2006.

effects of price on smoking in young people (aged 25 years or less) found evidence of an effect on both smoking uptake and cessation.[6]

These observations suggest that while it remains imperative to the continued reduction of smoking prevalence that existing conventional tobacco control measures continue to be implemented and developed, boosting the rate of decline in young adult groups may require further refinement and targeting. Further options for this, and for reducing uptake of smoking in young adults, are discussed in Chapter 11.

10.3 Making homes smoke-free

If the ideal solution of parental (and other adult) cessation as a means of protecting children from passive smoking cannot be achieved, then the next best option is to minimise the exposure to children that arises from smoking by parents and other household members in the home. It is evident from the objective and subjective measures of passive smoke exposure presented in Chapters 2 and 8 that this is already happening to a degree. Measures that have reduced adult smoking prevalence, and particularly perhaps the smoke-free legislation, appear also to have had an impact on smoking behaviour in the home. As previously discussed, concerns that smoke-free legislation might displace smoking into the home have proved to be unfounded. Rather, it appears that in the UK and in other countries that have introduced smoke-free legislation, reductions in passive smoking in children have occurred.[7,8] Newly published data indicate that, in England at least, smoke-free legislation has had a positive effect on this trend,[9] and such an effect is plausible. Parents who are continually reminded of the need to smoke outdoors to protect the health of others in the workplace and other public places are perhaps more likely to adopt the same strategies to protect children and other family members in the home.

A review of population-level tobacco control policies and their impact on the prevalence of smoke-free homes in four countries, including the UK, emphasised that comprehensive tobacco control programmes aimed at reducing the overall prevalence of smoking may indeed be the most effective means of increasing the prevalence of smoke-free homes.[10] However, given that exposure remains substantial, particularly in relatively low socio-economic status households, other approaches to reducing exposure are required.

Encouraging parents and carers, and particularly those who still smoke or allow others to smoke in their home, to implement smoke-free policies in the home is therefore an important complement to general population strategies aimed at reducing smoking prevalence. For smoke-free policies in the home to be effective in reducing levels of exposure in children, it is essential that they are comprehensive and robustly implemented. Less restrictive measures, such as opening windows whilst smoking, or limiting smoking to a single room, have little impact on ambient tobacco smoke levels in homes,[11] whereas strict no-smoking policies in the home have been associated with significantly lower levels of passive smoke exposure in children.[12,13] A further benefit of smoke-free policies in the home is that parents who implement them also appear to be more likely to quit smoking themselves,[14] and it is likely that stricter policies are more effective in this respect.[15] As is also evident from the data in Chapter 6, smoke-free policies in the home are also likely to reduce the risk of uptake among children and adolescents.[16,17]

A number of intervention strategies, including health promotion and mass media campaigns, individual or household-focused social–behavioural therapy, and educational and clinical programmes intended to encourage parents to make their homes smoke-free, have all been studied. In a recent systematic review of 36 intervention studies for reducing passive smoke exposure in children, Priest *et al*[18] concluded that there is currently insufficient evidence to recommend any particular approach, although intensive counselling interventions with carers did show some consistency of effect. This conclusion was similar to that of an earlier systematic review, of 18 interventions, by the same authors[19] and summarised in an earlier RCP report.[20] The quality of the studies was mixed, however, and this remains the case with the more recent evidence. For their outcomes, eight studies included an objective measurement of children's exposure, one measured smoke particles in the ambient air, nine validated cessation in parents who smoked, and six included some combination of these three different measurements. Only two of these studies were from the UK, one testing an intensive counselling intervention delivered in the home,[21] and one testing postnatal support for disadvantaged inner city mothers.[22] Neither of these studies found evidence that the intervention was effective. Although smoke-free home initiatives are being developed in the UK, to date they have been inadequately evaluated. A further recent review of interventions to promote smoking cessation in pregnancy and childbirth by NICE[24] used slightly different inclusion criteria and assessed 17 studies, nine of which were included in the recent Priest *et al* review. The NICE review concluded that there was limited evidence that any of the interventions assessed were effective, and expressed concerns about the quality of the evidence available. We now review the evidence in relation to all of the major strategic approaches explored to date.

10.3.1 Mass media campaigns

Gilpin *et al*[25] demonstrated that adults in California whose homes were smoke-free tended to be more aware of the harmfulness of passive smoking. However, a more recent US study indicated that beliefs about the harms of passive smoking smoke were not independently related to rules prohibiting smoking in the home, whereas beliefs about harms from 'third-hand' smoke (residual tobacco smoke contamination that lingers after a cigarette has been extinguished) were independently associated with home smoking bans.[26] As awareness of the specific harms caused by passive smoking is still low among smokers (see Chapter 8), measures to increase knowledge about the effects of passive smoking are likely to be helpful in promoting smoke-free homes. Improving the depth and quality of knowledge about the adverse effects of passive smoking is likely to be particularly important, as carer smoking behaviour around children is influenced, among other factors, by the degree of their knowledge and on the emotional value of that information to them.[25,27,28]

There are a number of ways in which awareness of the harmful effects of passive smoking could be increased, the most notable being the use of mass media campaigns and health warnings on packs. Health warnings have been demonstrated to be a prominent source of health information to smokers,[29] and are therefore likely to be an effective means of communicating the risks of passive smoking. However, the impact of health warnings on smoking behaviour in the home has not been evaluated.

Mass media campaigns are also highly effective approaches to building knowledge. In 2003, the Department of Health launched a high profile mass media campaign, 'Smoking near children', which emphasised the impact of passive smoke on children and babies, backed up by educational materials. In an evaluation, the proportion of respondents reporting that second-hand smoke was a risk to children's health increased from 28% before to 50% after the campaign. The Department of Health ran further similar campaigns on passive smoking aimed at increasing awareness of the specific effects of passive smoking on adults. 'Second hand smoke affects adults' in 2005 and 'Wedding' in 2007, aimed to raise awareness of the dangers to the health of non-smokers, and in particular to highlight the fact that 85% of cigarette smoke in ambient air is invisible. Awareness of specific effects of passive smoking increased after the 2005 campaign. For example, 79% of respondents to a British Market Research Bureau (BMRB) survey were aware that passive smoking could cause heart disease in non-smokers after the campaign, compared to 67% before.[30] An evaluation of the 2007 campaign indicated that over half of the respondents were moved to think about the impact of their smoking on friends and family, and a similar proportion said that they were less likely to smoke around non-smokers. The majority of adults (92%) accepted that passive smoking carries a risk for non-smokers (an increase from 84% in 2003), although this proportion was slightly lower among smokers (84%).[31] A Cancer Research UK campaign, 'Smoke is poison', initiated in December 2006, aimed to increase public awareness of the poisonous chemicals in tobacco smoke. This campaign was evaluated in 2007 via the BMRB Omnibus survey of 1,600 adults, which demonstrated that, while the campaign had raised awareness of the poisons in cigarette smoke, there was little evidence that it had influenced attitudes towards passive smoking. In particular, 16- to 24-year-olds were less likely to be convinced of the dangers of passive smoking and less likely to feel the need to quit.[32]

Since 2008, there have been five Department of Health mass media campaigns that have specifically focused on children in a bid to encourage parents to stop smoking, including the 'Wanna be like you' (June–August 2008), 'Reasons' (October–November 2008), 'Scared' (October–November 2008), 'Worried' (February–March 2009), and 'Smoke-free generation/real kids' (September–November 2009) campaigns. Further details of each of these campaigns can be found on the smoke-free resources website.[33] Research on the impact of these campaigns is not yet available.

10.3.2 Community setting interventions

Four of the studies included in the updated systematic review cited above[18] evaluated the impact of interventions targeted at communities or populations. One study in the USA evaluated the impact of a telephone smoking cessation counselling service that targeted smoking mothers through an advertising campaign.[34] Another, which included biological validation, used a community-based intervention to train lay health advisors in working with families to lower smoke exposure in the home.[35] Two studies evaluated interventions in schools: a cardiovascular health promotion programme which included an intervention to reduce ETS exposure in children in the USA,[36] and a study in China[37] which involved a tobacco prevention curriculum intended to encourage students to help their fathers to quit smoking. Of these, only the latter[37] appeared to be effective, resulting in a reduction in fathers' self-reported smoking rates in the intervention group.

10.3.3 Individual parent and carer interventions

Sixteen studies in the updated review[18] involved interventions for parents attending routine immunisation or other health visits for healthy children; 13 targeted parents whose children were ill with respiratory or other problems. A further two studies recruited children visiting paediatric clinics where the purpose of the visit was unclear or included both settings.

Although several of these studies reported significant intervention effects, only three included validated outcomes and are described here. Emmons *et al*[38] found a significant reduction in air nicotine measurements in the kitchen and one other room in the house 6 months after an intervention involving a 30–45 minute motivational interview at the carer's home by a trained health educator, and four brief (approximately 10-minute) follow-up telephone calls. A study in China[39] found that a 20–30 minute counselling session with information based on individual's needs, and provision of nicotine replacement therapy if requested, had an effect on parental quitting after 6 months. The third study, carried out in a hospital outpatient clinic in Japan,[40] reported a reduction in urinary cotinine levels in children, though the precise nature of the parental intervention used was not well described, simply that parents agreed to stop smoking.

In a paper published since the Priest *et al*[18] and NICE[24] reviews, Hovell and colleagues[41] tested a combined intervention to reduce children's passive smoke exposure and help parents to quit smoking, compared with usual care. Mothers who exposed their children to more than 10 cigarettes per week were randomised into intervention and control groups. The intervention involved 14 counselling sessions (10 in person and four via telephone) over a period of 6 months. The counselling intervention targeted passive smoke exposure for the family's youngest child, and involved an individually tailored cessation component for each participant. The results showed a significantly greater decrease in reported second-hand smoke exposure and mothers' smoking in the intervention group compared to the group who received usual care. However, whilst self-reported home smoking and children's urinary cotinine decreased in both the intervention and usual care groups, there was no significant difference in these outcomes between intervention and control groups.

10.3.4 Barriers to success

Qualitative research provides insights into the barriers to, and reasons for, restricting smoking in the home, particularly among disadvantaged parents.[42–44] In these families, awareness of the risks of passive smoking in children did not result in measures to make homes smoke-free. For example, in a cross-sectional survey of UK families, Blackburn *et al*[27] reported that 86% of parents knew the potential adverse health effects of passive smoking on their children, yet over 80% of these families continued to smoke in their home. Early work, carried out before widespread public health promotion of the dangers of passive smoke, suggested that smoking was used by mothers as a means to 'cope' with caring in circumstances of poverty and hardship.[45] A more recent study[43,44] explored the reasons why mothers continue to smoke in the home, even knowing the risks of passive smoke exposure following public health promotion. The authors concluded that mothers continue to have to deal with the tension between 'coping' and 'caring'. They found that some mothers construct alternative explanations for their children's ill health, and few continue their efforts to protect babies from passive smoke into infancy. Overall, their ability to initiate and maintain a smoke-free environment for their children competes with their caring responsibilities, and they are further restricted from smoking outside the home by the physical environment in which they live. However, an Australian study suggested that a lack of outdoor space may be less of an issue[42] than the desire to smoke in comfort, the difficulty of asking family and friends who may be helping with childcare not to smoke, the difficulty of supervising children, and the expense of cessation products.

10.3.5 Legislation

Another option, already discussed in earlier chapters, would be to implement legislation to mandate smoke-free homes. This would be a controversial strategy, which would be likely to encounter substantial opposition, as it would be perceived to represent undue interference in people's private lives[46] (see Chapter 9). As discussed in

Chapters 8 and 9, such an option, outside the special case of children in state care, would require widespread public support to succeed, and even then would be extremely difficult to enforce. To our knowledge, no jurisdiction has yet introduced such legislation, or has plans to do so.

One residential setting where regulations may be more likely to be effective and to be supported, however, is multiple occupancy housing. In this environment, tobacco smoke can, and does, enter non-smokers' homes through shared areas such as ventilation systems, open windows, hallways, or stairwells.[47] It is possible that contractual conditions could be brought to bear on all residents in multiple occupancy buildings to prohibit smoking in any home on the basis that drift of smoke to others' homes cannot be prevented with certainty.

10.4 Passive smoking in cars and other vehicles

Cars and other vehicles are another source of high levels of smoke exposure for children and adults,[48–50] and are associated with adverse health effects, including an increased risk of respiratory and allergic symptoms,[51,52] and in one study of 10- to 12-year-old never-smokers, an increased risk of reporting at least one symptom of nicotine dependence.[53]

Several studies have examined the prevalence of smoking in cars with children present, and collected data on car smoking restrictions.[54–60] Unpublished data from the 2007/8 survey wave from the International Tobacco Control (ITC) Policy Evaluation Study showed that 71% of UK smokers reported never smoking in the car with non-smokers (as did 71% in Australia, 66% in Canada and 56% in the USA); males and young smokers were generally more likely to smoke in cars carrying non-smokers (Hitchman, personal communication). Similar findings were reported in a study of smokers in the EU,[61] although only 15% of UK smokers in this study reported smoking in cars in the presence of children. Unpublished data from the ITC study also suggest that those who smoke in cars tend to be regular and heavier smokers, with weaker intentions to quit. They tend not to believe that cigarette smoke is dangerous and could cause lung cancer in non-smokers, and they are less likely to support laws prohibiting smoking in cars with children (Hitchman, personal communication). Whilst carers are, in general, aware of the negative health effects of passive smoke exposure, there is limited evidence of specific knowledge about the dangers associated with exposure from smoking in cars.[62] For example, in a nationally representative telephone survey in the US, 95% of respondents recognised the dangers of passive smoking in general, but only 77% recognised that passive smoking in cars was a specific danger.[63]

These findings suggest that improved educational interventions and media campaigns are needed to highlight that all passive smoking carries some degree of risk, and to target smoking families with information on the health benefits of initiating and maintaining smoke-free cars. Messages can be similar to those given out in other passive smoking campaigns, including the impact of the smoke on children's health and future propensity of children to smoke, as well as the impact on accidents. Media campaigns advocating no smoking in cars have been carried out in New Zealand,[64] but we are not aware of any assessment of their effectiveness.

Legislation is another approach to preventing passive smoking in cars and other private vehicles, and the data reported in Chapter 8 indicate that 77% of adults in England would support a total ban on smoking in motor vehicles carrying children under the age of 18 years. Similar majorities in support of smoke-free car legislation have also been observed in Australia and North America.[62] A range of jurisdictions have now introduced legislation prohibiting smoking in cars, including several States in Australia, Canada, and the USA. For example, in South Australia and Tasmania, smoking by the driver or passengers is prohibited in cars carrying children under the age of 16 years, whether the car is moving or stationary, whilst in Mauritius, smoking is now prohibited in all private vehicles carrying passengers.

Potential regulatory options for the UK include: prohibition in private vehicles carrying children; prohibition if any passenger is present (so that enforcement is not inhibited by the difficulty of determining the age of vehicle occupants); or prohibition of all smoking in any private vehicle. The last of these is probably the simplest and most easily enforceable option, and has the advantage that it would also help to address the problem of persistent breaches of smoke-free legislation in vehicles that are also workplaces, and improve road safety.

10.5 Use of medicinal substitution to support smoke-free settings

The research outlined above highlights the need for innovative interventions that help to reduce the barriers to initiating and maintaining smoke-free homes and cars. One option that has not been extensively studied is the use of nicotine replacement therapies (NRT) as a harm reduction option to support temporary abstinence from smoking in these settings. This could include the use of NRT either as a substitute for smoking when in the home, or as a first step in a structured programme to reduce the number of cigarettes smoked within the home, with quitting as the ultimate goal. The recent extension of the UK licence for use of some forms of NRT for temporary abstinence from smoking, and/or cutting down cigarette consumption, offers this new opportunity to use an effective treatment to promote smoke-free homes and reduce children's exposure to passive smoke. Research work piloting NRT use in homes where carers smoke is under way.

10.6 Summary

- The predominant source of passive smoke exposure in children is smoking in the home by parents.
- The best way to prevent passive smoking in the home is therefore to reduce the prevalence of smoking among parents and would-be parents, and hence typically younger adults.
- The prevalence of smoking in younger adults is falling less quickly than in older adults.
- Tobacco control initiatives at population and individual level therefore need to be adapted and improved to target this age group more effectively. Real price increases and mass media campaigns are likely to be particularly effective in this respect.
- The next best way to prevent passive smoking in the home is to encourage parents to make their homes completely smoke-free.
- Mass media campaigns and health warnings are probably the most effective method of increasing awareness of the hazards of passive smoking, and the need to make homes completely smoke-free.
- Behavioural interventions for parents who smoke may also be helpful in promoting smoke-free homes.
- Smoking in private vehicles is a significant source of passive smoke exposure in children and adults.
- Mass media campaigns on the risks of passive smoking in cars and other vehicles, backed by legislation prohibiting smoking in all vehicles, is probably the most effective means of preventing exposure of children and adults in vehicles.
- The use of NRT to support temporary abstinence in the home and in cars has potential that needs to be explored.
- All of the above interventions need to be pursued and evaluated, to reduce passive smoking in children as quickly as possible.

References

1 International Agency for Research on Cancer. Home smoking restrictions: effects on exposure to SHS and smoking behaviour. In: *Handbook of cancer prevention, tobacco control: evaluating the effectiveness of smoke-free policies.* Lyon: WHO IARC, 2009.

2 Office for National Statistics. Results from the General Household Survey: GHS 2007 data. www.statistics.gov.uk/downloads/theme_compendia/GHS07/GeneralHouseholdSurvey 2007.pdf

3 Townsend J, Roderick P, Cooper J. Cigarette smoking by socio-economic group, sex, and age: effects of price, income, and health publicity. *BMJ* 1994;309(6959):923–7.

4 Thomas S *et al.* Population tobacco control interventions and their effects on social inequalities in smoking: systematic review. *Tob Control* 2008;17(4):230–7.

5 General Household Survey. Economic and Social Data Service. www.esds.ac.uk/finding Data/ghs.asp

6 Godfrey C, Rice N, Slack R, Sowden A, Worthy G. Systematic review of the effects of price on the smoking behaviour of young people – final report. Centre for Health Economics, the Centre for Reviews and Dissemination and the Department of Health Sciences (University of York) as part of the Public Health Research Consortium. 2008.

7 Akhtar PC, Currie DB, Currie CE, Haw SJ. Changes in child exposure to environmental tobacco smoke (CHETS) study after implementation of smoke-free legislation in Scotland: national cross sectional survey. *BMJ* 2007;335(7619):545.

8 Fong GT *et al.* Reductions in tobacco smoke pollution and increases in support for smoke-free public places following the implementation of comprehensive smoke-free workplace legislation in the Republic of Ireland: findings from the ITC Ireland/UK Survey. *Tob Control* 2006;15 (suppl 3):iii51–8.

9 Jarvis MJ *et al.* Smoke-free homes in England: prevalence, trends and validation by cotinine in children. *Tob Control* 2009;18(6):491–5.

10 Thomson G, Wilson N, Howden-Chapman P. Population level policy options for increasing the prevalence of smokefree homes. *J Epidemiol Community Health* 2006;60(4): 298–304.

11 Ashley MJ, Ferrence R. Reducing children's exposure to environmental tobacco smoke in homes: issues and strategies. *Tob Control* 1998;7(1):61–5.

12 Johansson A, Hermansson G, Ludvigsson J. How should parents protect their children from environmental tobacco-smoke exposure in the home? *Pediatrics* 2004;113(4):e291–5.

13 Wakefield M *et al.* Restrictions on smoking at home and urinary cotinine levels among children with asthma. *Am J Prev Med* 2000;19(3):188–92.

14 Mills AL *et al.* The effect of smoke-free homes on adult smoking behavior: a review. *Nicotine Tob Res* 2009;11(10):1131–41.

15 Farkas AJ *et al.* The effects of household and workplace smoking restrictions on quitting behaviours. *Tob Control* 1999;8(3):261–5.

16 Farkas AJ *et al.* Association between household and workplace smoking restrictions and adolescent smoking. *JAMA* 2000;284(6):717–22.

17 Muilenburg Legge J *et al.* The home smoking environment: influence on behaviors and attitudes in a racially diverse adolescent population. *Health Educ Behav* 2009;36(4): 777–93.

18 Priest N *et al.* Family and carer smoking control programmes for reducing children's exposure to environmental tobacco smoke. *Cochrane Database Syst Rev* 2008(4): CD001746.

19 Roseby R *et al.* Family and carer smoking control programmes for reducing children's exposure to environmental tobacco smoke. *Cochrane Database Syst Rev* 2003(3): CD001746.

20 Royal College of Physicians. *Going smoke-free: The medical case for clean air in the home, at work and in public places.* Report of the Tobacco Advisory Group. London: RCP, 2005.

21 Irvine L *et al.* Advising parents of asthmatic children on passive smoking: randomised controlled trial. *BMJ* 1999;318(7196):1456–9.

22 Wiggins M *et al.* Postnatal support for mothers living in disadvantaged inner city areas: a randomised controlled trial. *J Epidemiol Community Health* 2005;59(4):288–95.

23 Al-Alawy K *et al.* Smoke-free homes: outcomes of a local service development. *Community Pract* 2008;81(12):30–3.

24 Baxter S *et al.* Systematic review of how to stop smoking in pregnancy and following childbirth. NICE Guidance (currently under review). London: NICE, 2009.

25 Gilpin EA *et al.* Home smoking restrictions: which smokers have them and how they are associated with smoking behavior. *Nicotine Tob Res* 1999;1(2):153–62.

26 Winickoff JP *et al.* Beliefs about the health effects of "thirdhand" smoke and home smoking bans. *Pediatrics* 2009;123(1):e74–9.

27 Blackburn C *et al.* Effect of strategies to reduce exposure of infants to environmental tobacco smoke in the home: cross sectional survey. *BMJ* 2003;327(7409):257.

28 Thomson G, Wilson N, Howden-Chapman P. Attitudes to, and knowledge of, secondhand smoke in New Zealand homes and cars. *NZ Med J* 2005;118(1213):U1407.

29 Hammond D *et al.* Effectiveness of cigarette warning labels in informing smokers about the risks of smoking: findings from the International Tobacco Control (ITC) Four Country Survey. *Tob Control* 2006;15(suppl 3):iii19–25.

30 Malam S, Sohal T, Buckley K. *Second hand smoke adults campaign evaluation.* BMRB for COI/DH. 2005.

31 Malam S, Buckley K. Second Hand Smoke 'Wedding' – pre and post campaign tracking, BMRB for COI/DH. 2007.

32 Department of Health. CRUK 'Smoke is Poison' Campaign Evaluation. COI Research Management Summary on Behalf of the Department of Health. 2007 www.dh.gov.uk/prod_consum_dh/groups/dh_digitalassets/@dh/@en/documents/digitalasset/dh_084428.pdf

33 Department of Health. Smoke free resource centre. http://smokefree.nhs.uk/resources/campaigns

34 Davis SW *et al.* The impact of tailored self-help smoking cessation guides on young mothers. *Health Educ Q* 1992;19(4):495–504.

35 Conway TL *et al.* Intervention to reduce environmental tobacco smoke exposure in Latino children: null effects on hair biomarkers and parent reports. *Tob Control* 2004;13(1):90–2.

36 Elder JP *et al.* Tobacco use measurement, prediction, and intervention in elementary schools in four states: the CATCH Study. *Prev Med* 1996;25(4):486–94.

37 Zhang D, Qiu X. School-based tobacco-use prevention – People's Republic of China, May 1989–January 1990. *MMWR Morb Mortal Wkly Rep* 1993;42(19):370–1.

38 Emmons KM *et al.* A randomized trial to reduce passive smoke exposure in low-income households with young children. *Pediatrics* 2001.108(1):18–24.

39 Abdullah AS *et al.* Smoking cessation intervention in parents of young children: a randomised controlled trial. *Addiction* 2005.100(11):1731–40.

40 Kimata H. Cessation of passive smoking reduces allergic responses and plasma neurotrophin. *Eur J Clin Invest* 2004.34(2):165–6.

41 Hovell MF *et al.* Counseling to reduce children's secondhand smoke exposure and help parents quit smoking: a controlled trial. *Nicotine Tob Res* 2009;11(12):1383–94.

42 Hill L, Farquharson K, Borland R. Blowing smoke: strategies smokers use to protect non-smokers from environmental tobacco smoke in the home. *Health Promot J Austr* 2003;14(3):196–201.

43 Robinson J, Kirkcaldy AJ. 'You think that I'm smoking and they're not': why mothers still smoke in the home. *Soc Sci Med* 2007;65(4):641–52.

44 Robinson J, Kirkcaldy AJ, Disadvantaged mothers, young children and smoking in the home: mothers' use of space within their homes. *Health Place* 2007;13(4):894–903.

45 Graham H. *Women, Health and the family*. Brighton: Wheatsheaf Books, 1984.

46 Department of Health. *Consultation on the future of tobacco control*. London: DH, 2008.

47 Kraev TA *et al.* Indoor concentrations of nicotine in low-income, multi-unit housing: associations with smoking behaviours and housing characteristics. *Tob Control* 2009; 18(6):438–44.

48 Edwards R, Wilson N, Pierse N. Highly hazardous air quality associated with smoking in cars: New Zealand pilot study. *NZ Med J* 2006.119(1244):U2294.

49 Jones MR *et al.* Secondhand tobacco smoke concentrations in motor vehicles: a pilot study. *Tob Control* 2009;18(5):399–404.

50 Sendzik T *et al.* An experimental investigation of tobacco smoke pollution in cars. *Nicotine Tob Res* 2009;1(6):627–34.

51 Kabir Z *et al.* Second-hand smoke exposure in cars and respiratory health effects in children. *Eur Respir J* 2009;34(3):629–33.

52 Sly PD *et al.* Exposure to environmental tobacco smoke in cars increases the risk of persistent wheeze in adolescents. *Med J Aust* 2007;186(6):322.

53 Belanger M *et al.* Nicotine dependence symptoms among young never-smokers exposed to secondhand tobacco smoke. *Addict Behav* 2008;33(12):1557–63.

54 Binns HJ *et al.* Influences on parents' decisions for home and automobile smoking bans in households with smokers. *Patient Educ Couns* 2009;74(2):272–6.

55 Dunn J *et al.* Community knowledge, attitudes and behaviours about environmental tobacco smoke in homes and cars. *Health Promot J Austr* 2008;19(2):113–17.

56 Gonzales M *et al.* Prevalence and predictors of home and automobile smoking bans and child environmental tobacco smoke exposure: a cross-sectional study of U.S.- and Mexico-born Hispanic women with young children. *BMC Public Health* 2006;6:265.

57 Kegler MC, Malcoe LH. Smoking restrictions in the home and car among rural Native American and white families with young children. *Prev Med* 2002;35(4):334–42.

58 King G *et al.* Personal space smoking restrictions among African Americans. *Am J Prev Med* 2005;28(1):33–40.

59 Norman GJ *et al.* Smoking bans in the home and car: Do those who really need them have them? *Prev Med* 1999;29(6 Pt 1)581–9.

60 Rees VW, Connolly GN. Measuring air quality to protect children from secondhand smoke in cars. *Am J Prev Med* 2006;31(5)363–8.

61 European Commission. Attitudes of Europeans towards tobacco. Eurobarometer: Special Report, 272c. 2007 http://ec.europa.eu/public_opinion/archives/ebs/ebs_272c_en.pdf

62 Thomson G, Wilson N, Public attitudes to laws for smoke-free private vehicles: a brief review. *Tob Control* 2009;18(4):256–61.

63 McMillen RC *et al.* US adult attitudes and practices regarding smoking restrictions and child exposure to environmental tobacco smoke: changes in the social climate from 2000–2001. *Pediatrics* 2003;112(1 Pt 1):e55–60.

64 Martin J *et al.* Observed smoking in cars: a method and differences by socio-economic area. *Tob Control* 2006;15(5):409–11.

11 Overview and conclusions

11.1 The UK smoke-free legislation

Smoke-free legislation in the UK has been a success. Making enclosed public places smoke-free has proved highly popular, achieved widespread compliance, improved indoor air quality, and reduced passive smoke exposure. Most businesses, including those in the hospitality trade, have adapted successfully to the legislation. The health benefits, particularly in terms of reductions in acute cardiovascular disease, have proved substantial. With a few exceptions, of which the tobacco industry is one, smoke-free legislation has been good for just about everyone.

When smoke-free legislation was introduced in England, a commitment was made by the secretary of state for health in England to a review it in 2010. That review will be an opportunity to learn from the experience of implementation and to resolve the legislative gaps, loopholes and inconsistencies that persist. Some of the areas that merit attention in that review are listed in Chapter 1, and include the location and design of covered but unenclosed smoking areas; smoking in sports arenas and concert venues; smoking around the entrances to buildings; and smoking in hotels, hostels, prisons, other multiple occupancy housing, and other areas where avoidable involuntary exposure to smoke still occurs. These and other inconsistencies in the coverage of the legislation between UK jurisdictions, summarised in Table 1.1, could all be resolved by relatively simple revisions of the relevant regulations.

Smoking in vehicles is an area in which the legislation has been less successful, and where grounds for further protection of vehicle users are strong, given the high levels of exposure in vehicles containing smokers. Currently, vehicles that meet the definition of workplaces are required to be smoke-free, but the data in Chapter 8 indicate that compliance with this requirement may still be less than complete, and that employees, particularly younger people in lower socio-economic groups, continue to be exposed. Enforcement of the smoke-free regulations in work vehicles by external agencies is difficult, not least because it is not always clear whether a vehicle is a workplace or not. These difficulties could easily be resolved by extending smoke-free legislation to all vehicles. External policing would then be practically feasible.

There is also scope to extend the legislation to include other outside areas where smoking is still commonplace and some degree of passive smoke exposure still occurs, such as beaches, children's playgrounds, parks and other public areas. Extensions of smoke-free legislation into areas such as these has been pursued in other countries (see Table 11.1 for examples), and demonstrate that, with public support, smoke-free policies can be applied much more widely than is currently the case in the UK. The 2006 Health Act provides for regulations to designate additional places smoke-free which are not necessarily enclosed or substantially enclosed, but where there is significant risk that people present would be exposed to significant quantities of smoke. We suggest that this provision should be used to extend substantially the range of smoke-free outdoor public areas to prevent any passive exposure to smoke that might occur, but also, and perhaps more importantly, to prevent exposure of children and young people to smoking behaviour.

11.2 Health effects of passive smoking in children

The UK smoke-free legislation was not drafted or intended directly to protect children. However, the trends in cotinine levels described in Chapter 2 indicate that smoke-free legislation, in common with other successful tobacco control policy in the UK over recent years, has almost certainly contributed to a sustained secular decline in levels of passive exposure of children to tobacco smoke. They also demonstrate that children, particularly those who live with smokers, and those in relatively disadvantaged households, continue to experience substantial levels of exposure. Most of that exposure occurs in the home. Exposure is highest in children whose mothers smoke.

Our reviews and meta-analyses in Chapters 3 and 4 confirm that passive exposure of children to tobacco smoke, both before and after birth, has a substantial impact on the risks of a range of fetal and childhood health problems. The results

Table 11.1 Examples of smoke-free laws in other jurisdictions which go further than UK legislation.

	Outside areas					Enclosed areas	
Jurisdiction	Buffer zones (entrances and exits)	Restaurant patio bans or restrictions	Pubs and bars patios bans or restrictions	Children's playgrounds, parks, other outside areas	Beaches	Private vehicles with children	Prisons
Australia (number of territories)	3	5	2	2	2	5	No legislation
Kenya[a]	Yes	Yes	Yes	Yes	Yes	No	Yes
Canada (number of provinces)[b]	9, of which 5 are partial	4	4	3	0	7	All federal prisons, and 13 provinces/territories, of which 1 is smoke-free indoors only
Mauritius	No	No	No	No	No	All private vehicles carrying passengers	No
USA (number of states)[b]	17	4, of which 3 are partial	3	26	2	9	All federal prisons; 16 States, of which 6 are smoke-free indoors only

[a] The Kenyan smoke-free legislation allows for smoking rooms, but these must be ventilated directly outside, separate and enclosed and sealed, and cleaned and maintained only when smoking is not occurring in the area. It also requires there to be no smoking in residential houses and other premises where children are cared for.
[b] In Canada and the USA, many individual local authorities/municipalities have enacted legislation, but for simplicity we have only included legislation at State or Commonwealth level in the USA, and Territory or Province level in Canada.
This table has been compiled from a request for information from the tobacco control network through Globalink (www.globalink.org), and so is only partial in nature. However, it demonstrates the variety of jurisdictions where legislation going further than that in place in the UK have already been put in place, both for enclosed and outside areas, as at December 2009.
Sources of information: Australia: Quit Victoria and the VicHealth Centre for Tobacco Control; Canada: Non-Smokers' Rights Association and Canadian Cancer Society; Kenya: Institute for Legislative Affairs; USA: American Nonsmokers' Rights Foundation.

demonstrate modest impacts of maternal passive smoking on birth weight, and possibly on fetal and perinatal mortality, and the risk of congenital abnormalities. They also demonstrate important effects of family and household smoking on the risk of sudden infant death, lower respiratory infection, middle ear disease, wheeze, asthma, and meningitis in the child. As is consistent with the data on exposure levels, maternal smoking typically has the strongest effects. Whilst the magnitude of the results of our meta-analyses may have been biased by confounding and other factors, our subgroup analyses of adjusted studies suggest that these influences have not appreciably biased the effect estimates. We are aware that passive smoking has been implicated in a wide range of health, developmental and behavioural effects in children, including some rare cancers such as hepatoblastoma and leukaemia, and that the list of outcomes studied in this report is far from comprehensive. We have also not included harm arising from domestic fires. However, the figures we provide do include the more common, or in the case of sudden infant death, serious outcomes.

The burden of disease caused by passive smoking in children in the UK, as outlined in Chapter 5, is substantial. Passive smoking results in over 165,000 new episodes of disease, 300,000 primary care contacts, 9,500 hospital admissions, at least 200 cases of bacterial meningitis, and about 40 sudden infant deaths each year. Most of this additional burden of disease falls on the more disadvantaged children in our society. All of it is avoidable.

11.3 Passive smoking and smoking uptake in children

It has been recognised for some time that children who grow up in contact with smokers, in their family, friends, peer groups and role models, are more likely to become smokers themselves. The systematic review and meta-analysis in this report provides estimates of the practical significance of that effect, demonstrating that children who grow up with a parent or other household member who smokes are about twice as likely to become smokers themselves. Although also strongest for maternal smoking and hence potentially due to prenatal as well as postnatal exposure, the effect of smoking by any family member is of broadly similar magnitude, and thus suggests that the effect is predominantly due to exposure to smoking behaviour. We estimate that about 23,000 children in England and Wales (and therefore probably about 25,000 in the UK) start smoking by the age of 16 as a result of exposure to smoking by family members. Whilst this total may have been inflated by the effects of other causal factors confounded with exposure to smoking behaviour, it also excludes uptake of smoking after age 16, and the effect of exposure to other smoking role models outside the home.

Taking up smoking has massive consequences for the future health and economic status of the individual. Once addicted, most smokers continue to smoke for many years,[1] and half of those who continue to smoke die prematurely from a disease caused by their smoking.[2] The cost of maintaining regular smoking, which is currently over £2,000 per year when buying 20 cigarettes each day at typical UK retail prices, is substantial, and exacerbates poverty. These impacts are an important additional component of the harm caused by passive smoking in children. Like the other health impacts of passive smoking, these consequences of smoking uptake are avoidable through measures to prevent exposure of children to smoking, but in this case to smokers' behaviour rather than the smoke itself.

11.4 The costs of passive smoking

The costs to the NHS of treating disease caused by passive smoking in UK children are substantial. Each year, primary care contacts account for around £10 million, and hospital admissions around £13.6 million in costs in the UK. The future cost of treating disease caused by the uptake of smoking by about 23,000 children annually amounts to around £5.7 million per year, and of lost productivity £5.6 million per year. These costs are also all potentially avoidable.

11.5 Ethics

Passive smoking is an involuntary exposure that is directly harmful to children's health, and increases the risk that the child will become a smoker. Therefore, as far as is reasonably possible, this exposure should be prevented. The responsibility to do so falls on individual smokers, who have a duty to avoid smoking in the home or where children see them smoke, and on governments, who have a duty to implement policies, including legislation where necessary, to protect children from this exposure. The existing smoke-free legislation protects children in enclosed public places but does not prevent exposure to smoke, or to smoking behavioural models, in the home, in vehicles, in unenclosed public places, and the many other places where children spend time. Proportionate measures to minimise this exposure are justified.

11.6 Preventing the harm caused by passive smoking in children

All of the harms caused by passive smoking, including the direct health effects and effects on smoking uptake summarised above, are preventable by protecting children from exposure not just to cigarette smoke, but from exposure to smokers.

There are two broad approaches to this objective. The first, and by far the most effective, is to reduce the number of people, particularly parents, family members and other carers, who smoke. The second is to maximise the number of homes, and places that children visit, in which smoking does not occur.

As explained in Chapter 10, tobacco control policies in the UK have helped to reduce exposure of children to smoking by both of these means. The overall prevalence of smoking in young adults, and indeed in all adults, is falling. Since this means that fewer parents, grandparents, relatives, family friends and other family contacts are smokers, this in turn means that children are increasingly less likely to encounter smoking in their everyday lives. However, the data in Chapter 10 also demonstrate that the prevalence of smoking is highest, and falling least quickly, in the young adult age groups that include most parents, and are particularly high in the relatively disadvantaged. The proportion of households that allow smoking in the home is also falling, but over 20% of children, or over 2 million of those aged 16 and under in the UK in 2009, still live in a household in which they are exposed to smoke. This is a massive problem. It is therefore important to consider strategies to reduce the prevalence of smoking in adults, and the proportion of smokers who smoke indoors, as quickly as possible.

11.6.1 Strategies to reduce the prevalence of smoking in adults

Reducing the prevalence of smoking in adults requires measures to reduce the number of people who take up smoking, and increase the proportion of smokers who quit. Since preventing uptake inevitably takes some years to affect prevalence, even in young adults, promoting cessation is likely to deliver more immediate reductions in exposure. However, these two approaches are in fact very closely interrelated. Policies that encourage smokers to quit smoking also tend to inhibit smoking uptake, and since smoking uptake is driven in part by adult role-modelling, helping adult smokers to quit will also reduce the numbers of children and young people who take up smoking.

Conventional approaches to preventing smoking include advertising bans, smoke-free policies, price rises, health promotion campaigns and health warnings, and cessation services.[3] Implementation of these measures, judged in relation to objective markers, is now well advanced in the UK.[4] However, it is also important that policies continue to be developed, improved and innovated to retain initiative and impact with smokers and the general public. It is also important to consider that the individual components of tobacco control policy typically have modest effects. It is their collective impact in the context of a comprehensive range of policies that becomes substantial.

A detailed discussion of individual policy initiatives and their relative effectiveness is beyond the scope of this report, but a range of potential policy initiatives recommended by the RCP in 2008,[5] and of particular relevance to passive smoking, is summarised in Box 11.1. All of these have the potential to reduce the prevalence of smoking in young adults in the short- or medium-term future, but, as outlined in Chapter 10, price and mass media campaigns are probably of

Box 11.1 Policies to reduce the uptake and prevalence of smoking in the UK.[5]

Increase the retail price of tobacco; reduce availability of smuggled and counterfeit tobacco

- Increase retail price of all smoked tobacco products by at least 10%, year-on-year
- Use tax to remove the current price differential between manufactured and hand-rolled cigarettes
- Apply Class A drug penalties for persons convicted of involvement in illicit tobacco trade
- Monitor availability and use of smuggled and counterfeit tobacco
- Set challenging targets to reduce market share of smuggled and counterfeit tobacco products
- Cooperate fully with international initiatives to combat illicit trade in tobacco

Reduce the retail availability of smoked tobacco

- License all existing retail tobacco outlets; set and progressively increase an annual retail license fee
- Add a proportional levy on sales to discourage large volume retailers
- Progressively reduce, year-on-year, the number of licensed retailers
- Prohibit sale of tobacco within a defined distance from schools
- Prohibit internet purchase of smoked tobacco
- Restrict the number of hours each day in which tobacco products can be sold
- Prosecute and revoke the retail licence of anyone who sells tobacco illegally or purchases tobacco for a child
- Prohibit sale of smoked tobacco products from vending machines

Prevent promotion of smoking and tobacco brand imagery

- Prohibit all point-of-sale displays of tobacco
- Prohibit advertising and promotion of tobacco accessories such as cigarette papers
- Require all new films that endorse, glamourise or otherwise condone smoking to be 18-certified
- Prohibit screening of TV programmes that endorse, glamourise or otherwise condone smoking before the 9 pm watershed
- Require plain generic packaging for all tobacco products

continued over

Box 11.1 Policies to reduce the uptake and prevalence of smoking in the UK[5] – *continued.*

Protect children

- Prohibit sale of smoked tobacco products in premises to which children are admitted
- Require proof of age for purchase in all who appear to be under 25 years of age
- Apply Class A drug penalties to individuals who breach laws on under-age sale
- Promote strategies, including use of medicinal nicotine for temporary abstinence, to protect children from passive smoke exposure in the home

Inform the public

- Deliver sustained, varied, imaginative and effective mass media campaigns
- Replace tar and nicotine data on cigarette packs with more effective communications on harm
- Increase size and improve content of pictorial health warnings on tobacco packaging

Support cessation

- Continue to provide and develop evidence-based cessation services to support all quit attempts
- Provide nicotine or other cessation pharmacotherapy free of charge through the NHS
- Encourage development of new service models to support cessation
- Ensure that healthcare providers build smoking cessation interventions for all smokers into routine service provision

Harm reduction

- Increase availability, affordability and effectiveness of medicinal nicotine as a substitute for smoking
- Require medicinal nicotine to be displayed prominently for sale wherever tobacco is on sale
- Reform advertising and promotion rules to encourage marketing of medicinal nicotine for cessation and temporary or sustained substitution for smoking
- Use media campaigns and pack warnings to communicate potential health risks and benefits of nicotine substitution in absolute terms and relative to smoking
- Establish Nicotine Regulatory Authority, or similar body, to promote harm reduction and to monitor and regulate the nicotine market

particular potential relevance to young adult smokers. The price of cigarettes in the UK, although high in relation to other countries,[4] has changed little in real terms over recent years,[6] and remains undermined by illicit supplies. Regular price increases well above the rate of inflation, underpinned by much more comprehensive approaches to preventing smuggling and illicit supply of tobacco products, are therefore policy priorities. Investment in mass media campaigns needs to be increased to include targeted campaigns conveying the harms of passive smoking and the importance of smoke-free homes to young adult smokers. Since the relationship between parent and child entails a moral duty on the part of the parent, there is a strong case to use mass media campaigns to address parental smoking in part through ethical arguments addressed directly to parents, supported by communication of the health impacts of passive smoking on their children's health and future risk of smoking uptake, and effective means of quitting smoking. Critics of UK tobacco control policy have argued that mass media campaigns have not received sufficient priority.[7] This is an area in which targeted investment may be particularly appropriate. However, attention to other policy areas is also important, including prevention of point-of-sale display, use of generic standardised packaging to prevent use of the cigarette pack itself as a medium of promotion, wider extension of smoke-free legislation to other areas outside the home, and improved provision of cessation services for those who try to quit smoking. The potential for the use of alternative sources of nicotine as a means of cessation by long-term substitution[8] also needs to be explored. Cessation interventions in pregnant women, and methods of relapse prevention after the birth of the child, when many mothers start to smoke again, need further research.

11.6.2 Strategies to prevent uptake of smoking

Uptake of smoking among young people in the UK has fallen in recent years,[9] probably because the smoke-free legislation and the falling prevalence of smoking among adults has reduced the perception among young people that smoking is a common, normal, or desirable adult behaviour. Driving down the prevalence of smoking in adults, and particularly young adults, is likely to remain the key to reducing uptake of smoking in children and young people. It will also be important to employ other strategies to protect young people from exposure to persisting forms of tobacco promotion, and to minimise the accessibility of tobacco products.

Although the UK tobacco advertising and promotion ban greatly reduced tobacco marketing, two key channels of promotion remain. The first is tobacco advertising displays at the point-of-sale. Since the tobacco advertising ban, point-of-sale displays have grown in prominence and size, and a recent survey in two cities in England showed that the vast majority of tobacco displays and gantries were provided and maintained by the tobacco industry.[10] Tobacco pack displays are typically placed in the most prominent position behind the main counter in shops, close to sweets or other products attractive to children, with health warnings on packs often obscured.[11] Given that it has been established that tobacco promotion causes children to initiate tobacco use and continue smoking,[12,13] point-of-sale displays should be prohibited as legislated for in the Health Act

2009. Point-of-sale displays have also been shown to stimulate impulse purchases of cigarettes and may reduce quitting.[14–16] As cues to smoke that are prominently sited in most retail outlets, they undermine investment in the NHS Stop Smoking Services and other tobacco control measures. In July 2009, Ireland removed point-of-sale tobacco displays, with very high compliance rates,[17] and unpublished data suggest that support for this measure has remained high, while the proportion of 14- to 16-year-olds believing that more than 20% of teenagers their age smoke, has fallen significantly from 63% before to 45% after the ban.

The second key channel of tobacco marketing which has grown in importance with the introduction of tobacco promotion restrictions is the pack itself.[18] Although use of terms such as 'light' and 'mild' on cigarette packs is now prohibited, research has demonstrated that the tobacco industry currently uses a number of techniques which mislead consumers, including children, into believing that some cigarettes are less harmful than others.[19] The only way to eliminate such misperceptions entirely is to introduce standardised, generic plain packaging. Generic packaging would remove any liveries from packs, mandating that packs are the same colour, design, size and shape, with only government warnings and information being shown and the name of the pack being displayed in a consistent font and colour. Such packaging increases the salience of health warnings, reduces misperceptions about the relative harms of different packs, and reduces the appeal and attractiveness of packs to children.[19–21]

In October 2007, the legal age of purchase of tobacco throughout the UK increased from 16 to 18 years. Despite this, the latest in a series of annual surveys carried out in 2008 indicated that 44% of 11- to 15-year-old smokers reported usually buying their cigarettes from shops, with a similar proportion buying from others, and 28% buying from people who were not friends or relatives.[9] Although in 2008 there was a sharp increase in the proportion of current smokers finding it difficult to buy cigarettes from any shop, 43% of those who tried to buy cigarettes from a shop reported that they were always able to do so. In addition, one in ten 11- to 15-year-olds reported buying tobacco from vending machines, even though it is illegal for under-18s to make such purchases. Prohibiting sale of cigarettes from vending machines is the simplest way to eliminate this source of supply, and the Health Act 2009 again includes legislation to achieve this. Further strategies to reduce the number and accessibility of retail outlets selling tobacco are also needed. Options include licensing to reduce the number of retailers (particularly in locations frequented by children, such as close to schools), prohibition of tobacco retailing in premises that admit children, prohibition of financial incentives to retailers to stock tobacco products, prohibition of internet sale, and application of more punitive penalties to retailers who sell to children, for proxy purchasing, or those who supply illicit or counterfeit tobacco. These, and more general policy proposals for more effective tobacco control policy, are summarised in detail elsewhere.[5]

Other areas of potential development include: the implementation of strong smoke-free policies in schools and school grounds,[22–27] as is now recommended by the Department for Children Schools and Families, and required to gain National Healthy Schools Status;[28] promotion of school cultures that discourage smoking;[29,30] and the use of peer-led interventions.[31] Helping children and young people who are becoming established smokers to quit smoking is clearly also important, but it is still not clear how cessation services should be configured for young people.

11.6.3 Strategies to make homes smoke-free

The evidence summarised in Chapter 10 indicates that intensifying the above more general population preventive measures will, in addition to reducing smoking prevalence, increase the proportion of smokers who make their homes smoke-free. Since legislation is probably not an effective or ethically justifiable approach to reducing smoking in the home, creative approaches based on persuasion, choice and parental responsibility[32] are more attractive. Mass media campaigns promoting the importance of smoke-free homes, supported by behavioural interventions for individual families, are likely to represent the most suitable approach. The potential for use of harm reduction strategies based on short- or long-term substitution with alternative forms of nicotine needs to be explored in this context.[8]

11.7 Smoke-free vehicles

Smoking in vehicles is an important and persistent source of high levels of exposure to tobacco smoke for both children and adults. The simplest means of preventing this exposure is to prohibit smoking in vehicles, with support from media campaigns to publicise the law change and explain the reasons for doing so.

11.8 Smoking in other public places

Children are potentially exposed to passive smoking wherever people smoke, and to the smoking behavioural model wherever they see people smoking. The extension of smoke-free regulations to include areas frequented by children, as outlined in section 11.1 above, would prevent both of these exposures.[33,34]

11.9 Public opinion on extensions to smoke-free legislation

Public support for smoke-free legislation in the UK, and awareness that passive smoking is a hazard to health, are high. A large majority of people think that smoke-free legislation has been good for public health, and increasing numbers of people are taking measures to make their homes and private vehicles smoke-free. A majority of children are also aware that passive smoking is harmful to them. There is strong public support for more extensive smoke-free legislation, prohibiting smoking in front of children, in cars, and in other public areas.

11.10 Summary

- Passive smoking is a significant cause of death and disability in children as well as adults, and of smoking uptake among children and young people.
- About 2 million children currently live in a household where they are exposed to cigarette smoke; more are exposed outside the home.
- Governments and individuals have a duty to protect children from exposure to smoke and to smoking.
- Smoke-free legislation has been successful but should be extended much more widely, to include public places frequented by children and young people.
- Smoking in cars and other vehicles should also be prohibited.
- The most effective means of protecting children from passive smoking is to reduce the prevalence of smoking in adults, and particularly young adults.
- This will require sustained increases in the real price of tobacco, further investment in mass media campaigns targeting smoking in younger adults, more effective health warnings, prohibition of point of sale display, mandatory generic standardised packaging, provision of tailored cessation services, and a range of other policies.
- Specific measures to prevent uptake of smoking, by reducing the number and accessibility of tobacco retailers, imposing strict penalties on those who sell to children, and promoting peer-led and other school-based interventions, are also required.
- It is also important to promote smoke-free homes, through mass media campaigns, behavioural interventions and to explore new approaches such as short-term nicotine substitution.
- There is public support for wider smoke-free policy, and a strong ethical justification for these measures.

- Further investment in these and other comprehensive conventional tobacco control strategies will yield significant future financial savings and health benefits to society through prevention of passive smoking in children.

References

1 Royal College of Physicians. *Nicotine addiction in Britain.* Report of the Tobacco Advisory Group. London: RCP, 2000.

2 Doll R, Peto R, Boreham J, Sutherland I. Mortality in relation to smoking: 50 years' observations on male British doctors. *BMJ* 2004;328:1519–33.

3 World Health Organization. WHO framework convention on tobacco control. Geneva: WHO, 2003.

4 Joossens L, Raw M. *Progress in tobacco control in 30 European countries, 2005 to 2007.* Berne: Swiss Cancer League, 2007.

5 Royal College of Physicians. *Ending tobacco smoking in Britain: Radical strategies for prevention and harm reduction in nicotine addiction.* London: RCP, 2008.

6 Action on Smoking and Health. *Beyond smoking kills: protecting children, reducing inequalities.* London: ASH, 2008.

7 Chapman S. The inverse impact law of smoking cessation. *Lancet* 2009;373:701–3.

8 Royal College of Physicians. *Harm reduction in nicotine addiction.* Report of the Tobacco Advisory Group. London: RCP, 2007.

9 The Health and Social Care Information Centre. *Drug use, smoking and drinking among young people in England in 2008.* London: NHS IC, 2009.

10 Rooke C, Cheeseman H, Dockrell M, Millward D, Sandford A. Tobacco point of sale (POS) displays in England: a snapshot survey of current practices. *Tob Control.* In press 2010.

11 MacGregor J. *Tobacco advertising at point of sale.* Report to ASH. MacGregor Consulting Ltd 2008. www.ash.org.uk/files/documents/ASH_693.pdf

12 DiFranza JR, Wellman RJ, Sargent JD, *et al.* Tobacco promotion and the initiation of tobacco use: assessing the evidence for causality. *Pediatrics* 2006;117:e1237–48.

13 Lovato C, Linn G, Stead LF, Best A. Impact of tobacco advertising and promotion on increasing adolescent smoking behaviours. *Cochrane Database Syst Rev* CD003439, 2003.

14 Wakefield M, Germain D, Henriksen L. The effect of retail cigarette pack displays on impulse purchase. *Addiction* 2008;103:322–8.

15 Germain D, McCarthy M, Wakefield M. Smoker sensitivity to retail tobacco displays and quitting: a cohort study. *Addiction* 2010;105(1):159–63.

16 Carter OB, Mills BW, Donovan RJ. The effect of retail cigarette pack displays on unplanned purchases: results from immediate postpurchase interviews. *Tob Control* 2009; 18:218–21.

17 Office of Tobacco Control. *National Tobacco Retail Audit – 2009 monitoring report.* Naas: Office of Tobacco Control, 2009. www.otc.ie/uploads/Monitoring-Report-2009.pdf

18 Freeman B, Chapman S, Rimmer M. The case for the plain packaging of tobacco products. *Addiction* 2008;103:580–90.

19 Hammond D, Dockrell M, Arnott D, Lee A, McNeill A. Cigarette pack design and perceptions of risk among UK adults and youth. *Eur J Public Health* 2009; 19:631–7.

20 Germain D, Wakefield MA, Durkin SJ. Adolescents' perceptions of cigarette brand image: Does plain packaging make a difference. *J Adolesc Health.* In press 2009.

21 Environics Research Group. Consumer research on the size of health warning messages – quantitative study of Canadian youth – Final Report. Toronto: Environics Research Group, 2008. www.smoke-free.ca/warnings/WarningsResearch/environics-size-youth-english.pdf

22 Moore L, Roberts C, Tudor-Smith C. School smoking policies and smoking prevalence among adolescents: multilevel analysis of cross-sectional data from Wales. *Tob Control* 2001;10:117–23.

23 Aveyard P, Markham WA, Cheng KK. A methodological and substantive review of the evidence that schools cause pupils to smoke. *Soc Sci Med* 2004; 58:2253–65.

24 Wakefield MA, Chaloupka FJ, Kaufman NJ *et al.* Effect of restrictions on smoking at home, at school, and in public places on teenage smoking: cross sectional study. *BMJ* 2000;321:333–7.

25 Hamilton G, Cross D, Lower T, Resnicow K, Williams P. School policy: what helps to reduce teenage smoking? *Nicotine Tob Res* 2003;5:507–13.

26 Kumar R, O'Malley PM, Johnston LD. School tobacco control policies related to students' smoking and attitudes toward smoking: national survey results, 1999-2000. *Health Educ Behav* 2005;32:780–94.

27 Barnett TA, Gauvin L, Lambert M *et al.* The influence of school smoking policies on student tobacco use. *Arch Pediatr Adolesc Med* 2007;161:842–8.

28 Department for Education and Skills, Department of Health. *National healthy schools status: a guide for schools.* London: DH Publications, 2005.

29 Aveyard P, Markham WA, Lancashire E *et al.* The influence of school culture on smoking among pupils. *Soc Sci Med* 2004;58:1767–80.

30 Markham WA, Aveyard P, Bisset SL *et al.* Value-added education and smoking uptake in schools: a cohort study. *Addiction* 2008;103:155–61.

31 Campbell R, Starkey F, Holliday J *et al.* An informal school-based peer-led intervention for smoking prevention in adolescence (ASSIST): a cluster randomised trial. *Lancet* 2008;371:1595–1602.

32 Brennan S, White A. Responsibility and children's rights: The case for restricting parental smoking. In: Brennan S, Noggle R (eds). *Taking responsibility for children.* Waterloo, ON: Wilfred Laurier Press, 2007:97–111.

33 Thomson G, Wilson N, Edwards R. At the frontier of tobacco control: a brief review of public attitudes toward smoke-free outdoor places. *Nicotine Tob Res* 2009;11:584–90.

34 Thomson G, Wilson N, Edwards R, Woodward A. Should smoking in outside public places be banned? Yes. *BMJ* 2008;337:a2806.

12 Key conclusions and recommendations

Smoke-free legislation in the UK

- Smoke-free legislation in the UK has been highly effective in reducing exposure to passive smoke at work and in public places.
- Smoke-free legislation has realised some substantial health benefits, and in particular a marked reduction in hospital admissions with coronary heart disease.
- There are some persisting inconsistencies and gaps in the legislation that could easily be resolved by changes or extensions to existing regulations.
- Experience elsewhere indicates that extension of smoke-free policies to a wider range of public places can be popular and successful.
- However, the legislation does not address exposure to passive smoke in the home and in other private places such as cars.
- New approaches are therefore needed to address this persistent and substantial source of passive smoke exposure.

Passive smoking in UK children

- Children are particularly vulnerable to passive smoke exposure, most of which occurs in the home.
- The most important determinants of passive smoke exposure in children are whether their parents or carers smoke, and whether smoking is allowed in the home.
- Relative to children whose parents are non-smokers, passive smoke exposure in children is typically around three times higher if the father smokes, over six times higher if the mother smokes, and nearly nine times higher if both parents smoke.
- Smoking by other carers is also a significant source of passive smoke exposure.

- Children who live in households where someone smokes on most days are exposed to about seven times more smoke than children who live in smoke-free homes.
- Children who live with non-smoking parents are much more likely to live in smoke-free homes than those whose parents are smokers.
- Children from socio-economically disadvantaged backgrounds are generally more heavily exposed to smoke than other children, probably because of heavier smoking inside the family home and in other places visited by children.
- The overall level of passive smoke exposure in children has fallen substantially over recent years.
- This is probably because the number of parents and carers who smoke, and the number of parents who allow smoking inside the family home, have both fallen over this period.
- The reductions in passive smoke exposure have occurred in all sectors of society, but a significant proportion of children are still exposed, and exposure is still greatest among lower socio-economic status households.

Effects of maternal active and passive smoking on fetal and reproductive health

- Active maternal smoking (and hence passive exposure of the fetus) causes up to about 5,000 miscarriages, 300 perinatal deaths, and 2,200 premature singleton births in the UK each year.
- Passive exposure of the fetus to active maternal smoking impairs fetal growth and development, increasing the risk of being small for gestational age and reducing birth weight by about 250 g, and probably increases the risk of congenital abnormalities of the heart, limbs, and face.
- Passive exposure of the fetus to active maternal smoking also causes around 19,000 babies to be born with low birth weight in the UK each year.
- Maternal passive smoking is likely to have similar adverse effects on fetal and reproductive health, but of smaller magnitude.
- Maternal passive smoking reduces birth weight by around 30–40 g, and may also have modest effects on the risk of prematurity and being small for gestational age.
- Maternal passive smoking may reduce fertility, increase fetal and perinatal mortality, and increase the risk of some congenital abnormalities

(particularly of the face and genitourinary system), though the available evidence is not yet conclusive.

- Maternal passive smoking is thus a cause of potentially significant health impacts to the fetus.
- These adverse effects are entirely avoidable.

Health effects of passive smoking in children

- Living in a household in which one or more people smoke more than doubles the risk of sudden infant death.
- Passive smoking increases the risk of lower respiratory infections in children. Smoking by the mother increases the risk by about 60%, and smoking by any household member by over 50%.
- Passive smoking increases the risk of wheezing at all ages. Again, the effect is strongest for smoking by the mother, with increases in risk of between 65 and 77% according to the age of the child.
- Passive smoking also increases the risk of asthma by about 50% in school-age children exposed to household smoking.
- Passive smoking increases the risk of middle ear disease. The risk is increased by around 35% for household smoking and around 46% for smoking by the mother.
- Passive smoking results in modest impairment of lung function in infants and children. The long term practical significance of this effect is not known.
- Passive smoking appears to more than double the risk of meningitis.
- Since most mothers who smoke through pregnancy also smoke after the child is born, it is difficult to determine the relative importance of maternal smoking before and after birth on these outcomes. However, the evidence suggests that postnatal smoking is the more important. But the higher odds ratios for postnatal maternal smoking, and the presence of effects from other household smokers, suggest that postnatal smoking is the more important.

How much disease in children is caused by passive smoking?

- Passive smoking causes around 40 sudden infant deaths in the UK each year.
- Passive smoking also causes over 20,000 cases of lower respiratory tract infection, 120,000 cases of middle ear disease, at least 22,000 new cases of wheeze and asthma, and 200 cases of bacterial meningitis in UK children each year.

- These cases of disease generate over 300,000 UK general practice consultations, and about 9,500 hospital admissions in the UK each year.
- It is likely that passive smoke exposure is a significant contributor to the socio-economic gradient of incidence of most of the childhood illnesses studied.
- This entire excess disease burden is avoidable.

Effect of parent and sibling smoking on smoking uptake

- Children growing up with parents or siblings who smoke are around 90% more likely to become smokers themselves.
- Similar, though less strong, influences on smoking behaviour are likely to result from exposure to smoking outside the home.
- At least 23,000 young people in England and Wales each year start smoking by the age of 15 as a result of exposure to smoking in the home.
- Since uptake of regular smoking has significant health implications for the child, including a 50% likelihood of premature death if smoking continues, this represents a major health hazard to children.
- Together, these influences are likely to perpetuate the association between smoking and social disadvantage.
- Maximising measures to reduce the prevalence of exposure of children to smokers is thus a high priority not only to avoid harm caused by passive smoke, but also from the increased risk of smoking uptake.

The costs of passive smoking in children

- Passive smoking in children costs at least £9.7 million each year in UK primary care visits and asthma treatment costs, and £13.6 million in UK hospital admissions.
- The cost of providing asthma drugs for children who develop asthma each year as a result of passive smoking up until the age 16 in the UK is approximately £4 million.
- The future treatment costs of smokers who take up smoking as a consequence of exposure to smoking by parents could be as high as £5.7 million each year, or £48 million over 60 years.
- These smokers may also impose an annual cost of £5.6 million in lost productivity due to smoking-related absence and smoking breaks in the workplace, which translates to an estimated £72 million over their working careers.

- These significant economic costs are all avoidable.
- Interventions to reduce passive smoking thus have potential to make cost savings to the NHS and in the workplace, as well as improving the health of children.

Public opinion on smoke-free policy

- Public support for smoke-free legislation is high and has increased substantially, among smokers as well as non-smokers, since smoke-free legislation was introduced.
- Most of those exposed to passive smoke at work report that they are exposed less since the legislation was introduced, but a quarter of the population still report exposure either in the home or at work.
- A large majority of the population believe that passive smoking is harmful, and that banning smoking in public places has been good for the public health.
- A majority of people now prohibit smoking in their homes and vehicles.
- Most people believe that smoke-free legislation should extend further, to prohibit smoking in front of children, in cars, and in some other public areas including those where smokers congregate outside buildings.
- One in eight non-smokers, predominantly younger males of lower socio-economic status, still experience passive smoke exposure at work, albeit at much lower levels than before legislation. Much of this exposure may be occurring in work vehicles. This group in particular believes the government is not doing enough to limit the harm from smoking.
- Over 80% of children are aware that passive smoking is harmful.
- Half of children with a parent who smokes report passive exposure in the home, and one-third report exposure in cars.

Ethics

- Passive smoking is an involuntary exposure that is harmful to children. All adults therefore have a duty to avoid exposing children to tobacco smoke.
- Exposure of children to smoking also increases the likelihood that they will sustain substantial future harm as a result of becoming smokers. All adults therefore have a duty to prevent exposing children to smoking behaviour.
- Governments also have a duty to ensure that people are aware of these obligations, and to do all in their power to prevent exposure.

- Smoke-free legislation should therefore include all public places frequented by children, whether or not enclosed as currently defined in law, and should include private vehicles.
- There is also a duty on governments to ensure that children are not exposed to smoking role models in film, television programmes, internet content, music videos, computer games, and other media.
- Proportionate measures to minimise the risk of passive smoking in the home are already in place for children cared for by the state.
- Legislation to prohibit smoking in the family home and many other private places would be difficult to design, implement and enforce.
- There is therefore a duty on governments to ensure that parents, carers and adults in general are aware of the wider risks of smoking in sight of children as well as of exposing children to smoke in the home, and to develop and promote strategies to help minimise exposure.

Strategies to reduce passive smoking in children

- The best way to reduce the number of children exposed to smoke in the home is to reduce the prevalence of smoking among parents and would-be parents, and hence typically younger adults.
- The prevalence of smoking in younger adults is falling less quickly than in older adults.
- Tobacco control initiatives at population and individual level therefore need to be adapted and improved to target this age group more effectively.
- A comprehensive tobacco control strategy, including real price increases and mass media campaigns, is likely to be most effective in this respect.
- The next best way to prevent passive smoking in the home is to encourage parents to make their homes completely smoke-free.
- Mass media campaigns and health warnings are probably the most effective method of increasing awareness of the hazards of smoking in the home, and encouraging and sustaining behaviour change.
- Mass media campaigns on the risks of passive smoking in cars and other vehicles, backed by legislation prohibiting smoking in all vehicles, is probably the most effective means of preventing exposure of children and adults in vehicles.
- The use of nicotine replacement therapy and behavioural interventions to support abstinence in the home and in cars needs further research and development.

- All of the above interventions need to be pursued and evaluated, to reduce passive smoking in children as quickly as possible.

Conclusions

- Passive smoking is a cause of significant morbidity and mortality in babies and children, and cost to the NHS, that is completely avoidable.
- About 2 million children currently live in a household where they are exposed to cigarette smoke, and many more are exposed outside the home.
- The most effective means of protecting children from passive smoking is to reduce the prevalence of smoking in adults, and particularly parents and other carers.
- Tobacco control initiatives at population and individual level therefore need to be adapted and improved to target younger adults more effectively.
- This will require a comprehensive strategy including sustained increases in the real price of tobacco; further reduction in smuggling and illicit trade; sustained investment in mass media campaigns targeting smoking in younger adults; more effective health warnings; prohibition of point-of-sale display; mandatory generic standardised packaging; provision of tailored cessation services; and a range of other policies.
- Specific measures to prevent uptake of smoking, by reducing the number and accessibility of tobacco retailers to children, imposing strict penalties on those who sell to children, and promoting peer-led and other school-based interventions, are also required.
- It is important to promote smoke-free homes through mass media campaigns amd behavioural interventions, and to explore new approaches such as substituting cigarettes with medicinal nicotine.
- Smoke-free legislation should be extended much more widely, to include public places frequented by children and young people, and to prohibit all smoking in cars and other vehicles.
- Governments and individuals have a duty to protect children from exposure to smoke and to smoking.
- There is public support for more comprehensive tobacco control policies, and a strong ethical justification for these measures.
- All of the above interventions need to be pursued and evaluated, to reduce passive smoking in children as quickly as possible.